NORTH PACIFIC OCEAN

HAWAIIAN ISLANDS

LINE

DATE

EQUATOR

KIRIBATI

SAMOA

COOK ISLANDS

FIJI

TONGA

TAHITI

INTERNATIONAL

SOUTH PACIFIC OCEAN

NEW ZEALAND

MILES

0   500   1000

A BEGINNER'S GUIDE TO
PARADISE

A BEGINNER'S GUIDE TO PARADISE

9 Steps to Giving Up Everything So You Too Can:

- ☑ Move to a South Pacific Island
- ☑ Wear a Loincloth
- ☑ Read a Hundred Books
- ☑ Build a Bungalow
- ☑ Diaper a Baby Monkey
- ☑ and Maybe, Just Maybe, Fall in Love!*

* Individual results may vary. Baby monkey not included.

ALEX SHESHUNOFF

NEW AMERICAN LIBRARY

NEW AMERICAN LIBRARY
Published by the Penguin Group
Penguin Group (USA) LLC, 375 Hudson Street,
New York, New York 10014

USA | Canada | UK | Ireland | Australia | New Zealand | India | South Africa | China
penguin.com
A Penguin Random House Company

First published by New American Library,
a division of Penguin Group (USA) LLC

First Printing, September 2015

REGISTERED TRADEMARK—MARCA REGISTRADA

LIBRARY OF CONGRESS CATALOGING-IN-PUBLICATION DATA
Sheshunoff, Alex.
A beginner's guide to Paradise/Alex Sheshunoff.
p. cm.
ISBN 978-0-451-47586-2 (hardback)
1. Yap (Micronesia)—Description and travel.   2. Sheshunoff, Alex—Travel—Micronesia
(Federated States)—Yap.   3. Sheshunoff, Alex—Homes and haunts—Micronesia
(Federated States)—Yap.   4. Young men—Micronesia (Federated States)—Yap—
Memoir.   5. Americans—Micronesia (Federated States)—Yap—Memoir.   6. Moving,
Household.   7. Life-change events.   8. Burn-out (Psychology)   9. Escape (Psychology)
10. Self-actualization (Psychology)   I. Title.
DU568.Y3S43   2015
996.6—dc23   2015008757

Printed in the United States of America
1 3 5 7 9 10 8 6 4 2

Designed by Nancy Resnick

To my dad

Contents

STEP 6: MEET SOMEONE

STEP 7: REGROUP

STEP 8: BUILD A HOUSE

STEP 9: LIVE PRETTY MUCH HAPPILY EVER AFTER

About This Guide

No one really wants to hear about your trip (unless you were the victim of a crime, in which case, they want to hear all about it). So from the start I should say that during the two years or so that I lived in the western Pacific, I was the victim of only one crime. It was minor but culturally revealing. I'll get to that in time, but first a little background.

Back in 2001, I was running a small Internet company in New York City and, confronting a sort of quarter-life crisis, I quit my job and bought a one-way ticket to Yap, a small island about five hundred miles south of Guam. My plan: read the one hundred books I was most embarrassed not to have read in college and, hopefully, find Paradise.

When people hear—usually by standing too close to me in a grocery store line—that I once moved to a small island with only three letters in its name, they all have the same questions: *How did it go? Was it a mistake? How did you afford it?*

The short answers to those questions are: 1) pretty well; 2) for the most part, it wasn't; and 3) by subletting my apartment and office in a good real estate market. But responding that way isn't much fun. Nor does it make me rich, rich, rich—the main reason people go into writing. So I decided to create this—a kind of how-to manual for escaping from it all.

My hope is that it might inspire you to do something similar or better—choosing an island with, say, only two letters in its name. Or you might decide that staying at home is the best choice all along, which is good too.

To make this more fun, I've broken the process of moving to a small island in the Pacific into these nine easy-to-follow steps:

Step 1: Make Some Big Choices
Step 2: Show Up
Step 3: Find the Right Island
Step 4: Stop Being So Picky and Just Pick a Damn Island
Step 5: Settle In
Step 6: Meet Someone
Step 7: Regroup
Step 8: Build a House
Step 9: Live Pretty Much Happily Ever After

Feel free to skip around. For example, already have an island picked out? Take a pass on the first four steps. Have a partner to do this with but don't have an island yet? Ignore Step 6. Most readers, however, will just start at the beginning, read a few chapters, and then do something more worthwhile. Like help people. Or make some toast.

Author's Note

Every so often, usually by strangers with a conspiratorial bent, I'm asked, "How much of this is true?" The answer: basically all of it. I kept a journal the entire time I was in the Pacific, and I've tried to be as accurate as possible with everything that gives the reader a grounded sense of time and place—island histories, politics, physical descriptions, place names, etc. Also, there are no composite characters here; there'd be no need to mush personalities together—as you'll see, the Pacific is home to plenty of loons. But I have taken liberties with . . .

Names: Most of the names have been changed, especially those belonging to people I really skewer. Bruce's name, however, is really Bruce's name. This will make sense later.

Dialogue: I've tried to convey dialogue faithfully, but anyone who has ever read a court transcript will understand why I've had to make some adjustments. As the writer H. H. Munro said on this subject, "A little inaccuracy sometimes saves tons of explanation."

Timing: There isn't much correlation between the number of pages devoted to a place and the amount of time I spent there. That's just the way life is sometimes.

OK, enough of that. Photographs, maps and superspecial bonus materials are available online at either www.abeginnersguidetopara dise.com or www.facebook.com/asheshunoff.

—A.S.

"What we find exotic abroad may be what we hunger for in vain at home."

—Alain de Botton, *The Art of Travel*

"An idealist is one who, on noticing that a rose smells better than a cabbage, concludes that it will also make a better soup."

—H. L. Mencken, *Sententiae*

A BEGINNER'S GUIDE TO
PARADISE

INTRODUCTION

SO THERE I WAS, IN THE MIDDLE OF
THE PACIFIC . . .

Ten days aboard the *Microspirit*, an aptly named freighter not so much threatened by rust as held together by it, convinced me that it was time to pick an island. Any island. So I picked Pig. Part travel agent calendar and part *Far Side* cartoon, the island of Pig, itself an outer island of Yap, already seemed from the pictures like a destination so familiar that I wondered why I'd even bother showing up—I figured I already knew what I was in for.

I'd come in search of capital P Paradise. Not a unique mission, but I needed to know if Paul Gauguin's Paradise still existed—the one with the flowering trees glistening with recent rain, the beautiful women carrying baskets of fruit, the smiling tigers. And if it did still exist, why didn't people just move there? Was it lack of ambition or too much ambition that kept them away? Or was life simply too hard—or too easy—in a place like Pig? I didn't know. But I had a hunch that an ideal life is not something you just back into. An ideal life would require some arrangements.

For me, those arrangements finished here, in a small cabin of the *Microspirit*, with me trying to tie on a *thu*. According to custom, I was supposed to wrap eight feet of blue cloth in such a way that it covered the right places without making me feel, well, ridiculous. I failed in both respects. Flamboyant hoops of extra material draped off my hips, yet I could feel cool air in increasingly funny places. Unsure what else to do, I crammed the extra bits inside an inner loop—sufficiently loosening the outer loop to send the cottony contraption sliding down to my ankles.

Then genius struck: *a safety pin.* In a humbling moment of desperation akin to looking for a misplaced wallet in the freezer, I scoured the floor under my metal bed: perhaps a safety pin had just fallen down there. I was in luck. Sort of. Along with a few ramen noodles, some dust, and a Pop-Tart wrapper, I found the safety pin's pot-selling, high-school dropout cousin: a paper clip. Not perfect, but with optimism and a little pluck, I managed to bend the paper clip in such a way that it nicely accessorized, if not actually fastened, my loincloth.

I next grabbed a Ziploc bag of Lucky Strikes and headed to the deck. My plan: present the cigarettes to the island's chiefs, take a look around, and—assuming it was the Paradise I pretty much expected it to be—ask if I could stay.

Given the *Microspirit*'s tight schedule, I'd have only an hour to make a good impression, ask for permission to stay, and rush back to the boat to get my bag of clothes and books. But I was too focused on my slipping *thu* to notice the absurdity of the plan. I'm pretty sure what my answer would have been had a guy from Yap showed up at my door in New York and said, "Do you mind if I stay here? I have this idea of Paradise, and it looks almost exactly like your apartment."

One problem: I wasn't quite onshore. To actually get the last quarter mile to Pig I had to board the *Microspirit*'s dinghy, a sort of *Nanospirit*, which rocked in the waves thirty-five feet below the deck. I hesitated for a long moment.

Getting into a small boat is always a tricky proposition. Getting into a small, rocking boat in the open ocean: even harder.

Doing so on a rope ladder in a *thu* seemed . . . unwise, at best. Even if I somehow made it down, I worried there would hardly be room: the *Nanospirit* was loaded to the rim with elderly, topless women, and a wooden coffin. Baskets of fish and clothes and toothpaste filled the remaining pockets of space.

But this was my Pacific coming-out party. I wanted to wow them.

Thu and carton of smokes in hand, I stepped toward the edge—but, seeing the boat so far below, hesitated again.

"Use the ladder," a man said behind me. His tone was helpful, not sarcastic, as though I'd been considering making a leap. I turned. It was my cabinmate, Chief Chuck from Chuuk. An enormous man, even by Pacific standards, Chief Chuck had a preference for snug white *thu*s.

"Watch," he said and, just as a wave raised the dinghy closer, Chief Chuck stepped in front of me and slid down the ladder, skipping every single rung. He landed on his side, rolled across half a dozen baskets, and came to a heavy stop against the side of the coffin. He gave a jaunty wave for me to follow.

With one hand holding both the cigarettes and my *thu*, I took a few steps down the ladder that now swung across the side of the ship. Then a few more steps.

With twenty-five feet still to go, I discovered why the inventor of the paper clip, Walter Hunt, later built America's first sewing machine: *paper clips bend*. My *thu* covered me in the same way that holding up a pair of jeans in front of a mirror covers you—it worked well enough, but not all angles were created equal.

While in the Pacific, I'd hoped to reduce the number of variables in my life to find out which were the most important—take away electricity and friends and see which I miss the most—but clothes were never supposed to be on the list. On my way down, I found myself fixating on the physicality of things: the handles on a woven basket, the sun reflecting off the dinghy's small outboard engine, the scar on a woman's ankle.

Then gravity took over. That, frothing fear, and the basic instinct not to dangle nearly naked in front of twenty elderly women. I slid down the ladder. Effectively naked, I tumbled into the dinghy, managing to hold on . . . only to my Lucky Strikes. Not exactly Fred Astaire, but Chief Chuck from Chuuk was hardly Ginger Rogers.

I had arrived. And I was pretty sure I'd wowed them.

STEP 1

MAKE SOME BIG CHOICES

CHAPTER 1

What You Can Expect to Learn in This Chapter:

► When do you know it's time to pull up stakes?

► Is it motivating—or depressing—to be ranked ninety-sixth in a small trade magazine's top 100 list?

F our months before landing on Pig, the all-caps subject line of an email pulsated in my inbox. It read: "HOSTILE WORK ENVI-RONMENT." The email was from Shannon, a computer programmer in her late thirties who worked just across the room.

While waiting for Shannon's email to load (yes, we once had to wait for such things), I glanced over to the office foosball table (yes, that too). The company I'd started with friends in college, a few years earlier—back in 1996—wasn't supposed to be like all the other dot-com cash-ins; instead, it would be a better use of a new medium. The plan was to use the Internet to help people connect to their government via a database of 140,000 officials. Using just their address, users could find their council members or their dogcatchers or whomever and send them an email or an online petition. Advertising, along with a service to pay parking tickets online, somehow would pay for the whole thing. We even had a late-nineties pun for a name: E-The People. Based on a description not much longer than the above, we raised money from venture capitalists. A California investor once sent us a check for $100,000—printed on the check were half a dozen very happy clowns.

Shannon's email finally came up on the screen. Her complaint was about the new programmer, Brian. Specifically, his screen saver. I was surprised. I'd thought all screen savers were pedestrian like mine—just the standard tropical island with a few palm trees. Brian's screen saver, however, was different. "It's a woman in a bathing suit," her email reported "and she's squatting on a soccer ball." Hmm, I thought, that's not good.

She continued. "I'm formally informing you that it's creating a hostile work environment. A Hostile Work Environment is a form of discrimination that violates Title VII of the Civil Rights Act of 1964 and other federal authority . . . p.s. I've hired a lawyer."

I took a deep breath and stood up to take a walk around the office. As I passed various desks, I thought how our open, uncubicled floor plan had felt so progressive, so fittingly democratic. But now that plan felt forced and naive, like the cheery yellow paint I'd so carefully chosen for the walls. And not unlike the idea that people really wanted to participate in their democracy, but only lacked the time and the tools.

I paused by the desk of a youngish salesperson named Kevin. He looked happy enough, if not especially busy. I'd hoped the business would make money while making the world a better place, but it wasn't really doing either. Most Americans were finding plenty to do other than write their congressmen. The few users we did have tended to be older and from rural areas. The kind of folks with time to write letters to politicians. And not the kind of folks high-tech advertisers were scrambling to reach.

Back at my desk, I closed the email. For five years, my reservoir of optimism had been slowly leaking. I'd found that starting a business was just another way of going into sales. Like any salesman, my job was to convince people to do things they didn't really want to do: investors to invest, citizens to participate, government officials to respond to letters, advertisers to choose our site from among a million others. And, apparently, convince programmers not to download screen savers with women squatting on soccer balls.

I looked at my to-do list. I had a brochure to write, a consultant report to review, and a Christmas party to organize—a party I didn't want to attend, much less plan. I noticed that beside my phone was a message saying one of our investors had called "just to check in." That can't be good, I thought.

Next to that message was the latest issue of the *Silicon Alley Reporter*, a lightly read trade magazine devoted to the technology industry in New York. Somehow, I'd been ranked ninety-sixth out of the hundred most important people working in the industry in the city. Though surprised to be on the list, I also found the ranking a wee bit depressing. In a way, better to not be included. At least then you could think you'd been overlooked or were the secret Oz-like power behind the power.

In theory, my life in New York had all the best ingredients: I was living in a nice apartment in Greenwich Village, I was dating a pretty Spanish woman, and I was running a little Internet company. It should have been great. But it wasn't. I wasn't destitute or bedridden or addicted to heroin. Just unhappy. Flipping through the magazine's pages—first looking at the four poor schmos behind me, then the ninety-five ahead of me—I realized I had two career choices: spend the rest of my life working my way up the magazine's list or cancel my subscription.

CHAPTER 2

What You Can Expect to Learn in This Chapter:

► When you go to the hospital with severe chest pain and a crew from the Discovery Channel asks you to sign a release to be on their show about New York City emergency rooms, should you?

► What if it's three a.m. and you aren't thinking clearly?

O n the way home that night, I passed a bearded man selling Christmas trees near the corner of Hudson and Leroy streets. My girlfriend, Lorena, and I could certainly use some holiday cheer.

We'd met at a wedding in Spain. She was a friend of the Spanish bride. I was friends with the American groom. That weekend, we'd danced for hours and hours. She was a lovely dancer. And I was smitten by her light blue eyes and long, curly black hair. We first kissed on the roof of a seventeenth-century castle. A few weeks later I returned to Spain. "We'll never know if this is going to work, if we don't live near each another," she said as we walked together one night in the walled city of Avalon. She was right. She visited New York not too much later, and said she'd love to live there. A month later she moved in.

But now, as the Christmas tree vendor pushed a six-foot blue spruce through a narrow metal tube, all of that seemed long ago. The tree came out the other end neatly wrapped in a tight-fitting plastic net. With one hand on the trunk, the other buried deep in thick branches, I hoisted the tree over my head and began the nine-block walk to our Greenwich Street studio.

A block later the tree slipped off my shoulder. Then it started to rain. If this were a movie, I thought, snow would be falling. Instead, it was raining. Not a pouring rain, but not a drizzle either. Just a steady, cold rain.

My arm was tired, so I tried carrying the tree under my arm. A few blocks later the tip must have drooped a bit because it got caught on something. I yanked. Still stuck. I looked back. The netting was snagged on the sharp stub of a former street sign. Other cities have trash on their sidewalks, but we have three-inch shanks of serrated metal sticking out of ours. I glanced at the boutique cupcake store across the street. Despite the rain, a line curled out the front. I wondered who waited in line to pay $4.50 for a cupcake. Well, I did. Or I had. I'd even convinced myself that overpaying for cupcakes and just about everything else in New York signaled my refined good taste and not, say, what a schmuck I was. I yanked harder on the stuck tree. It stayed stuck. As annoyed by the jerky materialism of New York as by my own jerky materialism, I yanked harder still. This time, I tore a seam in the netting, causing my new blue spruce to pop open like a giant, spiky umbrella.

When Lorena and I met, she was twenty-eight and still living with her parents in the family's flat in Madrid. Her father was a recently retired submarine captain. Given that Spain had only two submarines, that wasn't an easy job to get. Even with my crappy Spanish, I could tell he was charming. Her mother, however, not so much. I heard once that women who've had five children go slightly insane. Lorena was a twin, the sixth or seventh of an eventual eight kids. Almost all of the others lived within a four-block radius. Her moving all the way to New York was a scandal mitigated only by the fiction that we maintained separate bedrooms. Every time her mother came to visit, we'd plug in an alarm clock next to the couch to suggest that was where I slept. I said it was silly; she was thirty. She said it was important; she was Spanish.

The rain picked up. Seven blocks to go. I couldn't see anything with the branches scratching at my face. Screw this, I decided. I'll just drag it. And I did. I dragged that tree up Hudson, across Christopher Street, then across Charles Street, and down the sidewalk of Eleventh Street through oily puddles with floating cigarette butts, through the garbage juice of an all-you-can-eat deli, probably through dog barf and late-night pee, and up a flight of stairs to our apartment.

"Hi, honey." I smiled wanly. "I'm home"—she picked a ketchup-stained napkin out of the branches—"and I brought you this."

"No vas a traerlo aquí," she said in her Castilian accent. *You're not going to bring that in here.* The plastic sheathing trailed down a dozen steps.

"Umm, OK, but the people across the landing may want to leave someday."

"Fine," she said. I kissed her on the cheek and propped the tree against the wall. It fell moistly against the couch. I don't think she saw the coffee cup stuck in the lower branches.

"Colleen and Jason still haven't called back," she said from the bathroom, just a few steps away in our small apartment. "Don't you think that is rude? Or is it an American thing? We are supposed to go to dinner with them on Thursday. . . ."

"Hmm, I guess it is rude, but maybe they—"

"What? I can't hear you."

"Yes, I said, that it is rude but—"

"So rude," Lorena said. In Spain you *always* call people back.

I was too self-centered, too busy, too American to see just how independent she was for a woman who'd grown up in a pro-Franco, Catholic military family. Instead I focused on her lack of doubt and how few questions she asked of me, of herself. For her, New York, the Salamanca district of Madrid, the stone-walled compound and gnarled olive trees of her family's ancestral home in Mallorca, weren't places of wonder to be explored, but a set of rules to be navigated.

I told her about Shannon and the soccer ball.

"Lo has visto antes?" Had you seen it before?

"No, I hadn't seen it," I said, resenting the implication. Either I was negligent for not having noticed, or worse, I had noticed it and chosen to ignore it.

"If I don't like this dumb little business," I said, "and our employees, users, and advertisers don't either, then why am I bothering?"

"In Spain, you always call people back. Right away. Even if just to tell them . . ." she said, her voice trailing off. I'd hoped our cultural differences would lead to exciting, unknown possibilities. She'd make paella; I would barbecue: we would be happy. But for three years those cultural differences had only masked a deeper problem. After finally becoming fluent in each other's language, we discovered we didn't have all that much to say.

"So inappropriate," she said.

While waiting for Lorena to finish brushing her teeth, I realized I wasn't happy. Our relationship wasn't what I felt it could and should be. My rent was going up. The company was struggling. Employees were quitting or suing or both. And it didn't seem like increasing the length of my fourteen-hour workdays was going to help anything.

Two days later, I was lying in bed at about midnight, when I felt a searing pain in the left side of my chest. Sweat streamed down my forehead and pooled in the middle of my back. I was twenty-eight. A few weeks earlier I'd fainted in the shower and woken up on the bottom of the bathtub. This wasn't good. I told Lorena to call 911.

While lying in the ambulance, I thought, I can't believe I'm going to die for this company no one cares about. Screw this. If I live, I'm out of here. Not just out of New York, but out of everything else.

The pain in my chest was still intense as nurses attached an IV and all sorts of monitoring equipment. Multiple lines ticked across the heart monitor. One was flat. Sticky pads pulled at my chest hair. A plastic mask pumped oxygen. The nurses looked at the machines; only Lorena looked at me. Her face was pale, her blue eyes alert and concerned.

Slowly, my breathing began to return to normal and, though still dangerously high, my heart rate steadied.

"You had a panic attack," the doctor said nonchalantly while unclipping something. "We'll watch you for an hour. After that, you can leave whenever you want."

Lorena went to the waiting room as a nurse dimmed the lights and the late-night hospital routines began. A bearded man in jeans approached my bed. He held a clipboard.

"Hello. I'm with the Discovery Channel," he said. "We're filming a documentary about New York emergency rooms. Would you be OK signing this release?"

"What?"

"We won't necessarily use your material, but just in case we'll need a release."

"No, thanks," I said, confused.

I'd been screwing up my life, I thought, pissing away years on this failing company, this failing relationship, this fucking materialistic city and its dead-end ideas of success, this hope that enough hours at work could make me rich, my parents proud, and democracy stronger. Worse still, I'd embraced the time-sucking illusion that loyalty to bad choices would somehow make them better. And now I'd seen how it would end: in a hospital, clutching my chest and wondering about all the bad choices I'd made. Best case, I'd die on TV.

Lorena and I didn't speak for most of the taxi ride home. She looked out the window at the wet West Village streets, the closed florists, the open but empty pizza-by-the-slice places. I scratched at the plastic hospital bracelet wrapped tightly around my wrist. The stakes were too high for tweaking. I needed to toss the whole thing, baby, bathwater, and all.

All I could think to tell Lorena was that I needed to make some changes. She nodded, held my hand, and continued to look out the window. Her skin felt soft but cold.

I later got a bill in the mail. That trip to the hospital cost me $500. But it was a pretty good value—it made me realize I needed an escape.

I knew my problems were First World problems. At least I had a job. At least I had an apartment. But simply accepting my particular trajectory, or tweaking some things on the margin, felt dangerous. At twenty-eight, a flat relationship, a hypermaterialistic city, and a job in sales weren't turn-your-life-upside-down bad, but in thirty years they would be. And by that time, the cost of change, the cost of a lifetime of compromises, would be unbearable. In thirty years, I'd be Willy Loman from *Death of a Salesman* or Sinclair Lewis' Babbitt— depressed middle-aged men who begin to realize they'd wanted the wrong things. But by that time it'd be too late. Better, I figured, to make a break for it now.

CHAPTER 3

What You Can Expect to Learn in This Chapter:

- ▶ The Pacific has 25,995 islands. . . . How do you choose one?

- ▶ When making huge life decisions, how much should you rely on the casual Internet musings of strangers?

I don't have statistics to back it up, but my hunch is that the three most common escape-from-it-all fantasies are: 1) running a bed-and-breakfast in Vermont; 2) moving to a tiny island in the Pacific; and 3) opening a bar. I had little interest in quilting and homemade preserves, so the first one was out. And though profiting from other people's addictions is a better business model than online democracy, it doesn't exactly set the heart aflutter. So that left the island. A lazy man's fantasy—and not especially creative—but I'd stared at the same screen saver for five years, only to see it disappear with each move of the mouse. And my brief stint in the hospital reminded me I had a limited number of spins around the sun—better make the most of the ones I had left. In other words . . . it was time to make the screen saver real. Or at least try.

But which island? The following Monday afternoon, I sat down at my desk and looked at my computer. Any island I'd heard of I wouldn't want to go to, I realized, but how do you brainstorm a place you've never heard of? My screen saver, not surprisingly, didn't list a photo credit or a place-name. So I did the next most reasonable thing and turned to the Internet, or what I like to call "cyberspace." Turns out, the Pacific has a lot of islands—25,995, in fact—so I needed to narrow my search. I typed *nice Pacific island* into Google. The first recommended site was something called Concealed Weapon Talk. "God save us from the gun-grabbers!" it read.

> Will my supply of brass, bullets, bullet molds, primers, and powder suddenly become contraband? If so, does anyone know of a nice Pacific island I can move to? Preferably one with some good hunting and fishing opportunities.

Helpful. The next site began:

> The Pacific Islands Business Network (PIBN) is a project of the United States–Pacific Islands Nations Joint Commercial Commission (JCC) being carried out by Pacific Islands Development Program of the East-West Center in Honolulu.

Surprised they didn't go with the catchier USPINJCC. I obviously needed a new approach.

I typed in *Really nice pacific island*. A message on a travel site came up:

> There were some really nice Pacific islands, but my favorite was Yap. The weather was steamy but pleasant. Best of all, the people speak English (ever since it was a U.S. territory), they use stone money, and the women are topless—
> JungleBuff27

I knew next to nothing about Yap, but as my grandmother used to say, "If it's good enough for JungleBuff27, it's good enough for me."

The main difference between teen rebellion, postcollege wanderings, and midlife crises is the amount of money at your disposal. Teen rebellion is largely a budget affair expressed by cigarettes, bad haircuts, and worse decisions. Postcollege wanderings, however, are often financed by parents fearing a lapse into the bad-haircut years unless they provide sufficient funds. Midlife crises are the best-funded stage of rebellion, because, finally, the rebel himself can lavish the amount of money he feels befits the depth of his self-pity. Given my financial state, I figured I was facing more of a quarter-life crisis.

I knew there were plenty of better uses for my savings—a new sofa, say, or a donation to just about any charity—but after five years of fourteen-hour days, I felt I'd at least earned some tokens from life's Skee-Ball machine. Instead of the spider ring or bubble gum, I'd cash them in for a little time, time to be alone with my own thoughts and, possibly, create a better life for myself. I knew that many people had it much, much worse, but that didn't mean I shouldn't try to improve my own situation, only that I shouldn't whine or feel sorry for myself in the process.

I started typing my resignation letter. But I had a problem: If you're running a company and have no board of directors, to whom do you address your letter of resignation?

I walked by Shannon's desk. "Umm, Shannon, can I talk to you?"

"OK," she said, reaching extra slowly for her mouse to close a program on her computer.

"Where would you like to talk?" Because of our open offices, the only place for a private conversation was either the supply room or the Caribbean diner around the corner. I opened the supply room door for her.

"Shannon," I said against a backdrop of blank envelopes and extra toner, "I'm quitting."

"You can't quit."

"Why not?" I said.

"Because you started it," she said.

"No, you started it." We both twisted our faces a little. "Shannon," I said, "the company needs someone different. This isn't right for me."

"OK," she said, looking at a box of staples.

"Well, I guess that's it, then," I said.

"Whatever," she said. A reasonable reaction. Why should she care about what I needed any more than I cared about Brian's screen saver? We reached for the door at the same time.

As a society, we know how to respond to people who say they need a vacation. Those who are going on sabbatical, slightly less so. But indefinite idleness in a place called Yap? That was unsustainable at best, subversive at worst. At the least, it was weird. When I started telling people, from friends to my dentist, I found myself falling back on the same limp phrases—"take a break" or "recharge my batteries"—but those weren't good enough. As much as I wanted to chuck it all and move to Paradise, I felt I needed a *mission*, something responsible sounding. While walking home one evening, I began thinking about what I'd learned while running this Internet company: namely, don't start an Internet company. Useful, I supposed, but preferable to learn from the mistakes of others rather than my own. Passing a familiar deli that I'd never actually been inside of, I thought, What better way to do that than books? I could save lifetimes of bad decisions if I just read enough books. I liked the structure that reading one hundred great books would give my trip, a purpose to my potentially unpurposeful time in the Pacific. But which ones?

That night, while Lorena slept, I started a list of the books I felt most embarrassed not to have read: *Crime and Punishment, Moby-Dick, War and Peace,* etc. That came to about fifty. For the remainder I started emailing friends, even acquaintances, "If you could take just one book with you to a remote island, which would it be?" As each reply came in, my online shopping cart filled up with compelling (if rarely purchased-together) titles like the Old Testament and *Dave Barry Turns 40*. A few days later and still years before the e-book, I had about eighty volumes lined up on my kitchen table. I then bought ten books that sounded like they might provide some context for my sojourn (e.g., *The Catholic Church in Micronesia*; *Words of the Lagoon*). I decided I'd pick up the remaining ten along the way.

It was only after all of this that I realized I had a problem: How would I carry ninety books? I'd have to take a dozen or so and have the rest sent. But sent where? And by whom? It was time to call my mother.

CHAPTER 4

What You Can Expect to Learn in This Chapter:

➤ Among the qualities one looks for in a mother, where does efficiency rank?

➤ Is the American Egg Board a reliable source of health information when it comes to eggs?

Bullshit," she said over the phone.

"Well, Mom, that's the plan," I said.

"When are you coming back?"

"Not sure. Soon . . . soonish. I'm bringing a lot of books. Maybe you have one you could recommend?"

"Soonish? Books? What are you talking about?" That, apparently, was a rhetorical question. "And where is Yap? You know how danger-ous Africa is, right?"

"I guess Africa has some dangerous parts, but Yap isn't in Africa. It's to the left of Hawaii. Way left. Anyway, I think some time off will be good for me."

"Good for you? How is it good for you to wake up in someone's soup?"

"What?"

"You know, like that Rockefeller guy."

"Mom, that was in New Guinea and that was, like, fifty years ago. I really don't think I'm going to be eaten."

"He didn't either."

"Mom, no one ever thinks they're going to be eaten."

"Exactly," she said.

I took a deep breath before continuing, "I feel really good about this choice."

"You know I love you dearly, darling. I'm just worried. Do you want to, you know, talk to someone?"

"Mom, I just need to recharge my batteries, take a break, that kind of thing."

I assumed this was the end of the conversation until Jon Krakauer's *Into the Wild* arrived in the mail. I immediately called my mother. "I got the book you sent. The one about the guy who heads into the wilderness and dies."

"Good," she said. "I suggest you read it before you go."

Had you peeked into my childhood kitchen any late August of the 1970s, you wouldn't have been surprised that someday I'd buy a one-way ticket to Yap. With its stout cedar beams, dark wood flooring, and off-white stucco walls, that neo-Tudor kitchen belonged more to the old Westmount neighborhood of my mother's native Montreal than the suburbs of Austin, Texas. The refrigerator, the walls, the countertops, the cabinets, the table, and the dog underneath were all the same dark, musty brown. The only thing that wasn't brown was the charcoal black stove at the center of the room. It was ignited only once a year. The last Saturday in August.

That was the day my mother made a nine-month supply of scrambled-egg sandwiches for my brother's lunch. Being nine years older than me, he was on the front lines of what would become known as the Sandwich Wars.

"Mom, please, no more scrambled egg sandwiches," my brother would plead as he watched her quickly open a dozen bags of Wonder Bread lengthwise with a sharp knife, as a fishmonger might the last crate of salmon at the end of his shift. She wasn't the type to waste time with twisty ties.

"Egg sandwiches are good," she'd say.

"But not every day," he'd say.

"Then trade them for something," she'd say. That my mother would suggest such a thing to my brother revealed a fundamental misunderstanding of the market. Then, as now, I suppose, the social economy of elementary school revolved around trade, and trade required having something marketable at your disposal. Just as a Phoenician merchant might sail the Mediterranean for years and over time parlay olive oil, wine, and slaves into a villa, careful trading around the lunchroom could gradually raise one's social standing and overall position. Hence, an orange could be turned into two Fig Newtons, two Fig Newtons into an Oreo. An Oreo, plus a little talent, could land one a nonstarting position on the recess kickball team. But a defrosted scrambled egg sandwich? He was through before it began.

Her first step was to turn all six burners to high—she didn't so much want a cooking surface as a full slab of heat—warm up the skillets, then start tossing in tabs of butter. Butter that turned immediately into smoke. Then, as though in the final round of a country-fair competition, she'd grab an egg in each hand and, with a quick whip of her wrist, crack its calcium-carbonate shell, flinging the contents into the superheated skillet. She'd do this over and over until the heat and the force of her will transformed gallons of embryonic fluid into fluffy yellow clouds of fat and protein. She'd then pour in salt and stir. To save time, she never stirred that skillet more than once.

One year my brother came prepared. He showed her an advertisement ripped from a magazine. It had a picture of two fried eggs. The text read: "Two eggs a week is fine for your health."

"Well, if two a week is fine," she said, "two every day should be great."

"Mom," he pleaded, "the ad was paid for by the American Egg Board." He was wise that way. But she couldn't hear. She'd already flipped on the giant wind turbine above the stove.

As the eggs cooked, she'd begin whacking off crusts, not slice by slice, but in whole clumps squeezed firmly in the middle. Cutting off the crusts was her parsley on the side, her way of saying she cared. But to us, it spoke only to a deep appreciation of efficiency. And of the qualities one looks for in a mother, efficiency is rarely at the top of the list.

I grew up thinking working long hours was just something you did. Unlike most moms in central Texas in the 1970s, mine worked outside the house and didn't have time to make a new lunch every day. She ran a bank-consulting business she'd started with my father in 1971. They sold technical management books to banks and, later, hosted conferences on "High Performance Banking." The first year, they ran it out of the kitchen. By 1973, they'd expanded to the living room. Two years later into an actual office building.

Though behind the scenes my mom actually ran the back office, my dad's name was on the door. She was happy to hand over the marquee, as she wasn't especially interested in hanging out in hotel meeting rooms with small-town bankers. My dad, however, could relate well. He'd grown up in Magnolia, Arkansas, and had the Southern accent, folksy sense of humor, and languid storytelling to prove it. So he gave the speeches and went to the many early-morning breakfasts. So many, in fact, that starting in the midseventies, a few years after I was born, he was gone two hundred days a year, giving speeches about "High Performance Banking" at various state banking conventions. (The fact that he'd never worked in a bank didn't seem to matter much; the ideas were concise, and the jokes funny, especially by the standards of, say, the Indiana Bankers Association.) Unfortunately, the underlying math of the business required him to travel constantly. He twice tore his rotator cuff from carrying so many suitcases through so many airports; he once told me he spent so much time in Atlanta's Hartsfield International Airport that he thought he had a pretty good chance of dying there.

Starting in the late 1970s, the business evolved to include

computer-generated reports for bankers. Back then, however, computers were room-sized machines that read data from index cards punched with tiny holes. To save money, my mother rented the computers at night. With my dad on the road, she'd stay up till dawn loading cards into little racks. I picture her up to her ankles in fallen chads.

She brought that same intensity to most everything, including the preparation of a year's supply of lunch in a single afternoon. For the final step, she'd sweep the egg-filled skillets over the waiting formations of crustless bread and carpet-bomb the entire eggy battalion. Next, after covering each puddle of egg with a second slice of Wonder Bread, she'd wrap the sandwich in a piece of cellophane and toss the still-warm sandwich into the freezer. Every morning for the next nine months, she'd fill my brother's brown lunch bags with a frozen scrambled egg sandwich, a Capri Sun, and an apple or a bag of celery.

By the time I came of school age, a new school had opened—a new school that, critically, had a cafeteria. But that ethos of efficient parenting that gave rise to the nine-month supply of scrambled egg sandwiches never really went away.

CHAPTER 5

What You Can Expect to Learn in This Chapter:

➤ How not to break up with someone you care about.

➤ Is a first kiss atop a castle, you know, enough?

I had an island. I had a list of books. I had quit my company. Now I just needed to extricate myself from my relationship.

The biggest problem was that there was no problem. There'd been no deceit, no affair, no crushing moment of disappointment. I wasn't eager to be single. Just the opposite. But I wanted to be with someone I could imagine having kids with and living a rich, full life together. And this wasn't it. The other problem was the story of how we'd met. I'd read somewhere that the existence of a romantic story about how a couple met has a crazily disproportionate effect on their long-term prospects. It doesn't matter if that story is fabricated as part of a courtship mythology, just as long as the story is believed by both parties. In our case, we didn't have to fabricate a story. It seemed hard to imagine that a relationship with such a promising start— kisses on castle rooftops and all—wouldn't have an equally happy ending. Or, at least, a happy middle.

I knew that a hundred years ago our comfortable relationship would have been a home run, but today it felt, well, too easy. We never challenged and asked hard questions of each other. Questions like: What kind of life did we want to lead? Who did we want to become?

Instead, we were just a man and a woman going through the motions of a relationship. The sum never seemed greater than the parts.

So, one Saturday morning in early January, the kind of crisp and clear morning when we would normally have headed to the farmers' market in Herald Square to overpay for heirloom tomatoes, I said, "Lorena, can we talk?"

"Sure," she said. We sat down on the bed.

"I don't think this is working," I said.

"What do you mean?" she said.

"This. Our relationship."

"What? What do you mean?"

"It's not working. It's not a good fit," I said, and started to cry. She started to cry too.

"What? Why? What can I do?"

This last question made me so sad. This wasn't about her giving more to the relationship. She had given so much—having left her family, her language, and her culture, there was little more she could give.

"It's not you. Or even me. It's just us," I said.

We both cried for a long stretch until, finally, she looked up and said, "What am I going to do?"

"Oh God, I'm not sure. You can stay here as long as you want. I'm going to leave the United States. The apartment is all yours."

"Why isn't it working?" she said again. "I thought it was working."

I didn't have a tidy answer. "We're just not a great fit," I repeated lamely.

In retrospect, this answer was completely unfair. I'd thought the way to avoid a messy breakup was to be clear and repetitive. At least that seemed the best way to contain the ambiguity I felt about the breakup. But *we're just not a great fit* didn't honor her intelligence or her very real need to understand what had happened.

"My panic attack," I said, "it made me think I need to do things differently. I'm moving to Yap, in the Pacific. Like I mentioned a while back."

"I didn't think you were serious," she said, shaking her head.

I tried to explain some of the reasons, but, being unsure myself, I left her only confused. With so little else to work with, she was left to conclude that I was going crazy. And I started to agree.

CHAPTER 6

What You Can Expect to Learn in This Chapter:

► Assuming you start with the customary two, how many legs can you expect to break if you jump from the top of a coconut tree:
  a) 0
  b) 1
  c) 2

► Why should you always fly out of the country from Newark Airport?

T wo weeks later, in late January, I hailed a taxi and asked to go to Newark Airport. On the way, I tried dropping hints to the driver that I wanted him to ask me where I was heading. Unsubtle hints like "It's strange, you know, leaving a place without knowing if you'll ever be back." But he didn't ask. So I just looked out the window, through oily rain smears, at the barb-wired Northern State Prison, its prisoners hunched in wet groups of two or three near the fence. At the Budweiser building and its brick smokestacks spewing a brown hop-filled haze. At a billboard offering "Newark's Fastest and Cheapest Divorce."

The driver turned down his radio's background squelch and muttered something about which terminal I wanted. "International," I said, looking down at my ticket sleeve. It was then that I first noticed the vacation promotion on the back. In the photo, a woman was lying on the beach, her smug smile barely visible under the thin brim of her improbably flappy hat. Meanwhile, her lover was just down the beach. Wearing only a pair of snug red shorts, he was running toward her, the sun glinting off shallow ripples of turquoise sea, his glossy abs, and his bright, bright teeth. He might even have been skipping.

On the right margin of the sleeve, I wrote what would be my first Life Lesson: "Always leave the country from Newark. No matter where you are going—the South Pacific, Kinshasa, Jakarta—the parting memory of the drive to Newark will be a reminder that you are doing the right thing."

Yet, as we drove, questions swirled. Scary questions like, would I become insane or enlightened after so much time with my own thoughts and a bunch of books? (The books accounted for at least forty pounds of my roller bag's weight.) What if I simply limped home, savings squandered, Paradise unfound, with no further understanding of what had led me to the Pacific to begin with? Or what if I came to know myself better and didn't like what I found? Surely, there are good reasons why more people don't just buy one-way tickets to Yap. For better or worse, I was about to find out.

According to my fifty-page itinerary, I'd be flying from Newark to Houston, Houston to Honolulu, then seven hours farther west to Guam, before flying another five hundred miles southwest to Yap. I usually don't like to talk to people on planes, but the farther west I flew, the worse the movies seemed to become (i.e., *Critters* followed by *Critters II*). By the final leg, I was chatting up the unlucky Guamanian appliance dealer sitting next to me. I mentioned that I might stay in Yap for a long, long time.

"A lot of people think that," he said. "But it doesn't always work out."

He then told me about a U.S. Peace Corps volunteer who'd been stationed on an outer island called Eurapick. After a few months he wanted to come home. When he radioed headquarters requesting a ride home, he was told it would be at least six months till they could send a ship. He radioed a few days later and said he very much wanted to go home and, please, couldn't a ship come any sooner? They again declined his request, citing the expense and distance. They said he would just have to wait.

The volunteer then remembered that the Peace Corp's health insurance plan guaranteed emergency medical evacuations. With a measure of ambition, frustration, and hope that most of us will never experience (and don't normally associate with government employees), he climbed the highest coconut tree on the island and jumped. He broke both legs. But he got a ride home.

STEP 2

SHOW UP

CHAPTER 7

What You Can Expect to Learn in This Chapter:

► When greeted by a topless woman in a grass skirt at the airport, will you:
a) stare?
b) avert your eyes while pretending to look for something in the outside pocket of your suitcase?
c) give her a hug?

► When you find out that the previous occupant of your motel room died in the bed, do you:
a) shrug it off on the basis that death isn't contagious?
b) ask for a clean set of sheets?

It was past one a.m. when the plane landed at Yap International Airport. Simply arriving in such a remote place felt like an accomplishment. How remote? International dialing codes are a pretty good indicator: the United States' code is 1. Antarctica is 672. Yap is 691. The island is served by just two flights a week—both from Guam and both arriving in the middle of the night. I'd quickly learn there isn't demand for much more; with a population of only 6,300, mangrove swamps for beaches, and a growing leprosy problem, Yap simply doesn't brochure well. (Nor does it help that the South Pacific island of Yap isn't even in the South Pacific—technically, Yap is in the *Western* Pacific.) With so few flights, the runway lights at Yap International are kept off until activated by an automated optical system—in theory, when the incoming pilot flashes the plane's lights three times. In recent years, several flights have missed the runway altogether.

Stepping into the humid heat outside made me feel like I'd been given a full-body slap by one of those hand towels they heat up in microwaves at Japanese restaurants. It smelled about the same too. It had just rained, and the smell was of dust and wet concrete.

On the tarmac I joined a line of people waiting to pass through customs in a little open-air metal shed. Planes pause on Yap for such a short time the pilots don't shut down the engines, meaning it was impossible to talk to anyone. I looked behind me. How silly was it to arrive in such a giant machine in search of something as seemingly simple as Paradise? A bit like pulling up to a marina in an aircraft carrier and asking where one might find a Mountain Dew. And would Paradise really just be a place on the standard route system? After all, it didn't seem quite right that I'd be able to just fly away the moment things got difficult.

Yet, almost immediately, I was smitten by Yap. Everyone with me in line was smiling. They weren't strained polite smiles either, but broad glad-to-be-home smiles. Some wore T-shirts; others wore collared shirts. Almost all wore plastic flip-flops. Their thin hair was black and wavy, their skin a light mahogany with an occasional constellation of black freckles. Unlike Americans, who seem to gain weight in their middles, the Yapese, in this line at least, gained weight more evenly, as though their whole bodies were simply swollen. Their faces weren't jowly but rounded, such that the flat disks of their cheeks forced their dark eyebrows and brown eyes into a seemingly permanent but kindly squint.

As I approached the front of the line, a man handed me a customs form. Whatever doubt I still had about buying a one-way ticket to a place with only three letters in its name vanished at the ninth question:

9) Are you bringing prohibited goods such as narcotics?
Yes or No—Circle One. (Remember, honest answers
are important.)

If the charm and optimism of that question wasn't enough to make me burn my passport, the welcoming committee was. After passing through customs, every arriving passenger—whether local or tourist—was given a wreath of flowers by a young topless woman with long braided hair. Sure, I thought, visitors to Honolulu also get leis, but they have to order them for themselves before they arrive. And they're almost never presented by topless women. "Welcome to Yap," the young topless woman said with a smile, and approached to drape the flowers over my head.

I didn't quite know where to direct my eyes as she put the lei on: was it rude to look at her chest? Or rude not to look? I started to give her a hug, but that seemed weird. Then I reached out to shake her hand, but that seemed weirder, so I just smiled dopily and thanked her.

On the curb, I asked the one taxi waiting for arriving passengers to take me to the cheapest hotel in Yap. He obliged. From first appearances, the Ocean View Hotel was nowhere close to the ocean, but it did have a room with a lamp and a thin mattress. I fell deeply asleep.

The following day, I stumbled outside. The light was completely different from back in New York. Perhaps due to Yap's proximity to the equator (just 650 miles) or the humidity (approaching 99 percent), the light made everything appear richer, more vivid, as though a high-contrast filter had been applied to the whole island. The sleepy streets, at least, could use it.

A dog lay in the middle of the road, its long ears slumped on the dirt. Nearby, a cat slipped into the weeds growing around the base of a telephone pole supporting just two drooping wires. The small road in front of the hotel curved by the water's edge, but the motel's view was mostly of mangrove forest—thick, twisting shrubs with spindly roots growing into the mud—and crumbling concrete buttressing a shoulderless road.

I approached a man in his midtwenties painting a thin coat of white paint over the faded white paint of the motel's front entrance.

"Mornin'," I said.

"Hey, you're the guy who just checked in, right?" he said, dipping his brush.

"Yes."

"Into room six?" he said.

"Ya, I think so. Why?" I said.

"A guy died in that room last week. I think he was from Switzerland. Maybe Sweden. No, I think it was Switzerland."

"You know what happened?" I said. The circumstances seemed more important than the country of origin.

"Well, I know it started with an S—"

"Do you know if they threw out the sheets?"

He hunched his shoulders in that way that says, "Not sure, but if I were you, I'd move to room seven."

I thanked him for the update and asked where I might get some breakfast. "Check the store," he said. Before I could ask if there was more than one option, he stepped around the corner, leaving me with the dog on the street and the whines of crickets. In the distance, I could make out a few rolling hills covered in shrubs.

I started walking. An open-air Laundromat next to the motel sat empty and idle, maybe closed permanently. I passed what appeared to be an abandoned house, its tin roof secured with a scattering of discarded tires. A quarter mile or so later, I arrived downtown. It consisted of three concrete buildings: a bar, a small strip-mall kind of thing with a grocery store, and a video store that sold vodka in large plastic bottles. In the distance I could see an empty basketball court with a metal roof, just across the street from a harbor made of faded gray concrete protecting a rotted wooden fishing boat. Plastic bags lined the road, but with no wind to blow them into the sea or against one of what I'd learn were Yap's two stop signs, they simply sat there, the equatorial UV rays breaking the bags down into their most basic elements, just as they appeared to do to most everything else on Yap. At least there are palm trees, I thought.

As I approached the store, I glanced at the eight-and-a-half-by-eleven sheet of paper posted on the Plexiglas door. It was titled "Yap TV Guide" and listed a mix of crime dramas and sports from no particular network, but all American. It wasn't a diverse mix. *COPS!* was broadcast twice a day; *Monday Night Football* on Monday, Wednesday, and Friday. I opened the door, expecting bells to jingle, the way they do in a mom-and-pop drugstore, but the door opened silently. The only person inside was a topless woman of grandmotherly age behind the cash register. She didn't turn as I entered and instead just stared down one of the aisles. Broken fluorescent lights struggled to illuminate half-stocked shelves. A few boxes of frozen chicken wings, some dusty pots and pans, a two-week-old newspaper from Guam, and some gum. I bought a stale Three Musketeers—breakfast—and walked back outside.

In the few minutes I'd been inside, Yap seemed to have become twenty degrees hotter. Heat waves shimmered off every surface—the tin roof of the bar, the cracked asphalt of downtown's road, the top of the phone booth whose receiver dangled limply, as though its last user had just combusted in the concentrated heat of the booth. In the hazy distance, I saw a pickup truck turn down a dirt road. Curious what all the fuss was about, I started walking.

For two or three miles, I passed what had looked like shrubbery from a distance, but now I could see was jungle. Not Amazon jungle with soaring trees and howler monkeys and exotic predatory orchids. Instead, just a tangle of green vines with dull green leaves drooping from a thick coat of beige road dust. So far at least, this wasn't exactly what I'd been expecting, but I didn't want to judge too quickly. Perhaps Yap would just take some getting to know. And its small size made that seem plausible. Just fourteen miles from tip to tip, Yap is roughly the shape of Delaware but, at thirty-eight square miles, less than 2 percent its size. In other words, the entire island of Yap isn't as big as the capital city of America's second-smallest state. More of a suburb, perhaps.

A littler farther along, I passed a small cinder-block house, but it was abandoned. There wasn't broken glass in its window openings—just no glass at all. A wooden fence surrounding the house had long since collapsed. Twenty minutes later I came to a huge white warehouse surrounded by barbed wire and weeds. The gate was padlocked and no cars were parked outside. A small white sign read *Kingtex*. As I'd later find out, Kingtex was Yap's largest—and most illicit—employer, but for now, it didn't seem like much of a destination, so I turned around. On the way back, I was relieved to see motion—a truck trundling toward me. Though it wasn't yet noon, the truck had its headlights on. Or headlight. It had only one functioning light, which, as far I could tell, was one more than needed on Yap—day or night.

CHAPTER 8

What You Can Expect to Learn in This Chapter:

- ➤ Is a coin that weighs four tons convenient or inconvenient?

- ➤ If she'd had one, would Goldilocks have used a guidebook?

A s much as I had dreamed of sitting on a small island and reading all day, after a few weeks I found I simply couldn't. Each day, I'd read for two, maybe three hours, with a warm Diet Pepsi on the wooden bedside table, before needing something else to do. For the first few days, that meant simply watching the fan above me wobble noisily against the faded ceiling. Amazing, I thought late one morning, that ceiling fans get dusty. I guessed there must be little airborne eddies, calm places in a man-made storm, not dissimilar to the one I'd created for myself out here. After the wobbling fan (and the occasional dead-end thought), I'd spend an embarrassing number of minutes watching geckos stalk flies. I loved the drama, however small, of prey and predator. Then I'd go back to reading, pausing occasionally to scratch the early, awkward growth of my mustache and goatee. (Lacking sufficient testosterone or hairy genes, my facial hair grows only around my mouth and on my neck—it isn't nearly as sexy as it sounds.) Eventually, when my eyes blurred and the musty heat of my little room became unbearable, I'd know it was time for the active part of my day.

Around noon, I'd wander to the store, buy some white bread and processed cheese, then walk along the harbor. Most days, I'd see the same ten middle-aged guys sitting on the same rusting patrol boat and drinking beer. I'd stand on the edge of the pier, hoping they might wave me over, but of course they never did. So I'd just walk along the seawall until it ended at a mangrove swamp. There, I'd sit and watch the soaring frigate birds, giant black seagoing birds with a bent wing that looked like a double-jointed elbow. Then, maybe, I'd stare at the water. If I were feeling especially energetic, I'd walk a few of Yap's dirt streets, crickets leaping into the grass as I passed the same empty warehouses and tin houses baking in the equatorial sun, before I turned back to my room to rest up before evening.

On my walks, however, I started noticing something odd: a few of the houses had large round stones leaning up against them. Some of these disks were just a few feet across, others, ten or twelve. They were usually gray in color or, occasionally, a faded white. Almost all had cannonball-sized holes through the center. Figuring these might be examples of Yapese stone money I'd read about in Jungle-Buff27's initial Internet post, I decided to look 'em up in my guide-book.

While rummaging around in my bag, I recalled how I had mixed feelings about even bringing a classic guidebook. I'd brought along a few political and historical books about the Pacific, but an actual guidebook? I hated how they reduced complex cultural moments into tidy consumer experiences: "Hey, honey, if we leave the genocide museum by three p.m., we can still get to the basket market before it closes at five." And I hated the trip-hijacking format of these guides: the concise, spontaneity-smothering itineraries; the tiny stars raising and lowering expectations for every monument, museum, or restaurant; the boxed sidebars flattening cultural quirks into three tidy paragraphs. And I didn't like the way they turned travelers into tourists—with the difference being, as someone said, that the traveler doesn't know what is going to happen next. Most of all, though, I resented how effectively guidebooks punctured the illusion that you were onto something new.

But I also knew that sometimes you don't feel like asking certain questions, such as "Excuse me, stranger. Can you give me a brief history of your country? And I have this exotic rash. . . . Maybe you could take a look. . . ." In the end, I decided that not bringing a guidebook would make me feel principled yet slightly silly, like a movie star addressing the United Nations.

Reluctantly, I opened Lonely Planet's *Micronesia*—a guide to the western Pacific islands of Yap, Guam, Palau, and a scattering of others. It happened to be written by Kate Galbraith, the granddaughter of the famous economist John Kenneth, so I thought her description of Yapese stone money might be especially astute. Turns out, the stones I'd been seeing around were, in fact, Yapese stone money. In use for the last six hundred years, the value of *Rai* is determined not just by the size of the stone, but the difficulty of obtaining each one. They came mostly from Palau, another island located about five hundred miles south. In other words, each stone, some weighing as much as eight thousand pounds, had to be quarried by hand and loaded onto a tippy canoe for the three-week journey home (probably to the great bemusement of the Palauans). The more people who died trying to get each one back, the more valuable it is. Apparently, many *Rai* stones are still used for major purchases, like land and houses. But they're too big to roll around. Instead, everyone simply remembers who owns which one, regardless of whose house it happens to be leaning against.

Hmm, I thought while closing the book, that's kinda interesting. But it also felt disappointing. I wanted this to be one of those instances when you discover how another culture does something better. But four-ton currency isn't better. It's worse. And with people dying to get each piece, stone money isn't even that funny. Then I realized that's not entirely true. It's still kind of funny.

CHAPTER 9

What You Can Expect to Learn in This Chapter:

➤ Why should every relationship be subjected to "The Cleveland Test"?

➤ Why will your search for Paradise require a lot of quarters?

Beyond learning about Yapese stone money, the highlight of most of those early days was laundry. Fortunately, Yap's soaking humidity led to many such opportunities. I came to love the busy purposefulness of it, the dirty beginnings and tidy endings. I started doing smaller and smaller loads. One afternoon, I was walking back to my motel from the store when I saw two women in their fifties at the Laundromat. It would be the day's second load, but up to now, I'd only laundered alone; this was too good an opportunity to pass up. I ran back to my room and grabbed a few clean shirts and a dirty pair of socks I'd missed before.

"Hi," I said, strolling in, with my clothes under my arm. The women sat in plastic chairs. "Just doing some laundry," I said, smiling. They stared at me with small brown eyes—small brown eyes that lacked laugh lines. I put my clothes in a machine.

"Good thing I got quarters," I said.

Silence.

"Just arrived recently," I said chirpily. One of the women spit something red and wet onto the floor. I thought a few drops might have splattered up from the concrete onto her toes.

As I started the machine, I considered asking if they were from around here. Given that they were topless, the odds were good that they were, in fact, from around here. But isn't it bad to make assumptions? I thought. Maybe they were dentists from Boise with a passion for scuba diving and laundering in the buff.

"You live nearby?" I said.

"Yes," the older of the two said. I leaned awkwardly against my machine, crossing, then uncrossing my arms.

"Yup," I said, "as for me, I'm just kind of visiting."

They started to gather their laundry into plastic baskets, faster, in fact, than I would have expected. I wanted to ask them something, anything to keep them from leaving. Before I could, however, they grabbed their tubs and shuffled out, their flip-flops grinding a few grains of loose sand into the concrete floor.

I looked over at my laundry machine—it hadn't started. Given the size of the load, this was both good news and bad news: I lost my quarters, but at least I didn't have to wait forty minutes to wash a pair of dirty socks. I grabbed my clothes and headed back to my motel.

As I walked the now familiar road, I thought that whatever was or wasn't happening here, it wasn't working. Was it me or the place? It wasn't the first time I'd confronted this question. Just after college, I conducted a kind of compatibility test with a woman I was dating. She lived in Boston, and on weekends she'd either come down to New York or I'd go up to Boston. More often, however, we'd meet at a bed-and-breakfast somewhere nearby. Vermont, say. Or the coast of Maine. Once we even met in Bermuda.

"Any couple could get along in these places," I told her early one February day. "But if we could still enjoy one another's company in, say, Cleveland, that would really tell us something." As it happened,

USAir had cheap last-minute tickets. So we went. Though it was dark, cold, and raining, we wandered through the Rock-and-Roll Hall of Fame and an art museum, tried to sneak into a steel factory, got a T-shirt from Hooters—the best of the best of Cleveland, you might say—but neither of us could pretend it was a great weekend. A few weeks later, we broke up. Amicably but definitively.

I'd thought that little test had worked. But now, rounding the final curve to my motel, I worried that I was the weak link, not the place I happened to be. In its way, Yap was perfectly pleasant. The lack of a warm embrace from the locals probably spoke to an intact culture that no doubt was rich and complex, if slightly impenetrable to the outsider. So, clearly, I was the problem. Maybe I just lacked whatever it is inside that allows someone to be happy wherever they are, whether that means being surrounded by people in New York, with a nice woman in Cleveland, or alone in Yap.

On the other hand, perhaps I was being too tough on myself. Most human beings seek out the company of other human beings. Ideally, ones who share a language and culture. Why shouldn't I? So I decided I needed at least one human interaction per day. That interaction could be something short of a new friend, but more than an exchange of money or information. Thus "Is there an ATM nearby?" wouldn't qualify but "Where are you from?" would. With just one of these daily interactions, I hoped I'd have something to look forward to each morning, perhaps reminisce about each evening.

Excited about my new plan, I dropped off my clothes and walked to O'Keefe's Kanteen, Yap's main bar. Surely, I thought, there'd be people there. If O'Keefe's Kanteen had windows, they were covered. Just one bulb provided enough light for me to make out an empty popcorn machine in the corner and an unplugged jukebox in another. I sat on a stool while someone unpacked wilted cardboard boxes in a back room. Before I could say anything, the front door opened, revealing a bulky figure in silhouette. As my eyes adjusted, I saw a Yapese man of about thirty with big eyebrows, bushy hair, and brown eyes. "Are you from the United States?" he said, sitting a discreet-yet-friendly distance away.

"Umm, yes. I am," I said.

"Bartender," he said, "four Bud Lights!" I looked around, not quite able to believe my good fortune.

"You get two. One because you are a guest on my island. The other because you are an American."

He said that his name was Jonathon and that he worked at the dock and had two children.

"I once visited San Francisco," he said. "I couldn't believe the crowds, the stores, the girls."

"In that order?"

"And Wendy's. Man, I loved the drive-thru. Loved it."

"We're lucky that way," I said.

"No, we are the ones who are lucky. My culture exists only because of your country."

"What do you mean?"

He said that during World War II, the Japanese had made his grandfather and others build a huge tunnel. They told them it was to protect the Yapese from an American invasion.

"Actually," he said, "they wanted to put all of us in it—all three thousand of us—and blow the tunnel up. The Americans invaded right before the tunnel was finished. They wanted to save us. To save our culture."

Before I could ask any questions, he stood to leave, saying, "I need to go home and see my daughters. See you here later, right?"

"Of course," I said. He shook my hand, letting our fingers slide away to make that little snapping sound. I came back that night, but didn't see him. In fact, I'd come back many times to O'Keefe's Kanteen, but never again would I see my first friend in the Pacific.

CHAPTER 10

What You Can Expect to Learn in This Chapter:

- ➤ If you have a fire at your house in Yap, how intoxicated can you expect the ax-wielding firemen to be upon arrival?

- ➤ How many packs of cigarettes a day is it reasonable to expect your mother to smoke while pregnant with you? What if they are "low-tar" cigarettes?

While pregnant, some mothers listen to Mozart. Mine smoked four packs of cigarettes a day. Because of a previous miscarriage, my mother was told she had to be on bed rest for five months. She did what anyone else would do in the summer of 1973—she bought a television and a water bed. The comforter was yellow. The carpet, orange. Fortunately, the harsh Texas light coming through the room's many windows was nicely diffused and softened by all the wafting smoke. Sometimes I still imagine her there, the captain of a yellow ship floating on a sea of orange shag: lit cigarette in one hand, Bic lighter in the other, clunky 1970s remote control resting peacefully on her expanding belly. As it happens, the Watergate scandal was at its peak, so she had plenty to watch in this grim pre-cable era.

I once asked her if she ever had doubts about so much prenatal exposure to cigarettes and G. Gordon Liddy.

"Oh," she said, "in those days, I only smoked *lights*."

I didn't say anything—to some arguments, there is no good reply.

"Besides," she added, "you turned out fine."

"Yeah, but how much smarter could I have been?" I asked.

"Well," she said, pausing before her guffaw, "a lot! Probably a lot!"

When I was ten years old, my mother switched addictions from NOW cigarettes to Diet Pepsi. She said she needed the caffeine to stay up late loading the index cards into the computer. "I'm not addicted," she would say, "I just throw up and get migraines when I don't drink enough of it."

With my dad away and my mom at work chugging Pepsi products by the gallon, there was no way for me to get from my elementary school to my after-school program. For most of elementary school, my mother arranged for a taxi to take me. Each day, a bright yellow taxi would pull up, and I'd toss my backpack in. The other kids made fun, but I simply thought I was kinda special. Not in a little-bus kind of way. More a little-yellow-taxi kind of way. And I learned to make the most of the opportunity: eventually, I started asking the drivers to stop at Taco Bell on the way. I liked their Cinnamon Crispas. As far as childhoods go, it could have been much worse.

But now, lying in bed in my Yap motel at ten a.m. reading *War and Peace*, I wondered if that weird childhood had led me here. I didn't really want to send my kids to school in a cab, but why didn't I just go on vacation to a palm-tree-intensive place? That's what most people do. But an open-ended stay on Yap? I certainly didn't have to be so extreme. On the other hand, was I certain that moderation was necessarily the route to happiness? In any case, I could tell all this time alone with my own thoughts wasn't a good thing, so closing my book, I set out in search of my one human interaction per day.

The bar being closed, I headed to my only other choice: the Manta Ray Bay Hotel. I'd avoided the two-story concrete building so far, thinking it was a place just for tourists—at least the few scuba divers who wandered through Yap each year—and I didn't consider myself a tourist. That night, however, its hopped-up air-conditioning and moonlit dolphin art apparently wasn't much of a draw. I was the only one in the dining room. I'd forgotten something to read. So I just watched the condensation slowly sliding down the windows.

Eventually, the cook came out of the kitchen, startled to see someone sitting down. He handed me a menu, poured me a glass of water, and pulled up a chair. He was a Westerner in his late thirties with closely cropped brown hair. Mostly, though, I noticed the bags under his eyes. They were dark, sagging, and huge, especially for a cook in a restaurant without any customers. I asked where he was from.

"Canada," he said.

"You miss it?"

"Oh God, yes," he said. "I came to Paradise to sit on the beach. But there are no beaches here, so I went to work."

"You like it?" I said. Apparently, I hit a sensitive spot because he had a lot to say.

"The work? Yap is a terrible place to be a cook. The worst. Can't get basic things. Like eggs. There's a twenty-five percent protective tariff on imported eggs. But there are no egg farmers here to protect! Same with butter."

"Butter?"

"Yeah, it's more expensive than lobster. But that doesn't mean I'd eat the lobster. Bacteria doubles every twenty minutes here, but the fishermen don't use ice. They eat fish here I wouldn't piss on." I considered interrupting with a question about which fish he *would* piss on, but he'd moved on. "Oh, and the vegetables . . ."

"They're good, I bet. . . ."

"Nonexistent. Too humid. Seeds rot in the ground. No seeds mean no herbs either. You ever been to one of those grocery stores in the United States—sure you have—oh, the herbs you have. The herrrrrrrrbs! The herrrrrrrrrrrrrbs!"

Feeling uncomfortable, I tried changing the subject. "So do you know what Kingtex is? I saw this big building . . ."

"That's a sweatshop," he said, explaining that a loophole in U.S.

regulations allowed the clothes made inside to be labeled *Made in the U.S.A.*

"Oh. But Yap, it's not American, right?"

"Well. Kind of. Yap is part of the Federated States of Micronesia. As a whole, F.S.M. gets a hundred million dollars a year."

"A year?"

"Yup. Part of the Compact Agreement. That's up for renewal this year, though. Got everyone in a flurry."

"Wait. Going back: how do you know it's a sweatshop?"

"They lock the girls inside, take away their passports, and won't give 'em back till they repay their travel and agency fees," he said, pouring himself a glass of water. "Everything's all fucked-up here. Have you seen the fire department?"

"I haven't," I said.

"We had a kitchen fire a few months ago. So we called the fire department. They showed up forty-five minutes later, piss drunk, and broke every window with an ax. You know why?"

"I don't."

"Because the axes were new. They wanted to check them out. To test them."

"And the fire?"

"We'd already put it out. There was just smoke left. Having no windows aired it out quick, though." He stood to leave. "You want a burger?"

I nodded.

"We don't defrost them before cooking them. We just cook it frozen," he said, walking away, before adding with a wave of his hand, "No lettuce either."

When I got back to my motel, I dug around the bottom of the outside pocket of my suitcase and found my original ticket sleeve. Right beside the man in snug red shorts sprinting down the beach, I wrote my second Life Lesson: "Don't become a cook in Yap."

I knew it wouldn't come up often, but vigilance, nonetheless, would be important.

CHAPTER 11

What You Can Expect to Learn in This Chapter:

▶ If you write a book about your search for Paradise, can you begin a chapter with you studying a cultural anthropology textbook in bed and expect anyone to keep reading?

▶ How do you turn twenty-seven feet of light blue fabric into a loincloth without feeling like a prom-night carnation? (Hint: trick question.)

▶ When directed to "present yourself" to the Yap Council of Chiefs, do you:
    a) curtsy?
    b) shake their hands?
    c) shake their hands, but let your fingers slide back into one of those muffled, awkward snaps?

The next morning, I woke up and, without getting out of bed, started flipping through one of my books, *Lamotrek Atoll and Inter-Island Socioeconomic Ties.* Written in 1965 by a cultural anthropologist who'd spent time on Yap's outer islands, the book mostly described technical anthropology research about clan lineage, property rights, and such. But it had a lot of photographs, mostly black-and-white ones showing people in grass skirts standing in front of thatch homes. Clearly, the Yap outer islands were the real thing. Or at least they had been fifty years ago. I wondered if they still were.

Unable to sit in my dank motel room any longer, I grabbed Ms. Galbraith's guidebook and walked to the harbor. With my legs dangling over the brackish brown water, I started flipping through the book to see if she had any advice on the outer islands. Toward the back, she did, in fact, have a small section on an outer Yapese island called Woleai. Unlike the main island of Yap, apparently Woleai had dozens of sand beaches, a reef swarming with fish, a prohibition against Western clothing like T-shirts and caps, a preference for dugout canoes over motorboats, and a reputation for friendliness. She didn't say the word *Paradise* and I wasn't sure she'd actually been there, but Woleai sounded a lot closer than what I'd found so far on Yap.

As it sunk in that I'd be heading to Woleai next, I felt a little bad about moving on from Yap. Though Yap had a certain charm (albeit subtle), it seemed to have picked up a disproportionate share of the bad parts of the modern Western life (alcohol, sweatshops, *COPS*) without the good parts (basil mojitos, cheap T-shirts, everything else on TV). And then there was the lack of a beach. It was hard to shake the idea that Paradise would include an actual white sand beach—or at least less swamp than Yap.

Looking out at the muddy water, I wondered how much a beach *really* mattered. I didn't much enjoy just sitting on beaches, but I liked the feeling of security they offered. A good beach was like the demilitarized zone between North and South Korea: a safe strip of land from which you can see the dangers (sharks, riptides) without actually having to experience them. And since no one really wants to live in either the DMZ or on a beach, they're both generally good places to read a book in relative peace.

Mostly, though, I liked the tidy boundaries of beaches, their simple choices: land or sea, coconut or fish, dry and safe or wet and scared. But a swamp? A swamp wasn't land or sea. It was both and neither. More immediately, a South Pacific island without a beach felt like, well, a South Pacific island without a beach—like a sunroof on a car, it wasn't necessary but better to have than not have.

I opened my guide again and reread the very brief description of Woleai. Though Ms. Galbraith didn't answer most of my questions— What would I eat there? Would I be welcome? Would I be miserable?—she did at least tell me how to get there. Woleai had an old runway left over from World War II. All I had to do was receive permission from the Council of Chiefs, find a *thu*, and get a seat on a plane operated by Pacific Missionary Aviation. It didn't sound easy, but doing laundry twice a day, five times a week, was proving good for the undies, bad for the soul.

I left the harbor and began the few-hundred-foot walk to the pay phone outside the store. My goal: call Pacific Missionary Aviation, get a ride to Woleai, and live happily ever after. But first I had to get to the phone booth, which I could just make out in the hazy distance. After fifty feet, sweat pooled in the small of my back. Salty, dusty sweat seeped into the corners of my eyes. After, maybe, a hundred feet, sweat slid between the soles of my feet and the rubber of my flip-flops, sending my heel over the side and into the dirt with each step. One plodding, sweaty step after another, until I reached the phone booth, slid a quarter in, and called Pacific Missionary Aviation. A man answered. (Luckily, the number hadn't changed since my guidebook was published.)

"Not sure we're flying to Woleai," he said in perfect English.

"Not sure?" I said, exasperated.

"The runway dips badly in the middle. It's old and collects rain . . . and it's been raining a lot there." I looked up. No wind blew. No clouds passed overhead.

"What if there wasn't rain on the runway?" I ventured. "Would I be able to fly there with you?"

"If you pay. But I think there's water on the runway. Woleai called on the radio and said it's fine. But they always say it's fine. We won't know for sure till we try to land."

"But you do have room on the plane? Or you *would* have room on the plane?"

"Probably."

"Should I call back tomorrow?" I said.

"If you want to," he said. Just to be sure, I looked up and down Yap's main street.

"I'm sure," I said. "I'll call back tomorrow."

Inside the store, three topless middle-aged women wearing fabric around their waists were slowly stocking dish towels, glancing at and comparing each one. A musty fluorescent light flickered overhead. "Hello," I said, recalling the list from my guidebook. "I was looking for a *thu*." They glanced at one another and continued stocking.

"Oh, pardon me. Do you know where I might find one? A *thu*?" I asked. They said something to one another in Yapese, then burst out laughing. Two of the women walked away, still giggling. The third woman stayed behind and looked at me. She had brown eyes and a round, young face, her curly black hair pulled tightly behind her head. I'll call her Roberta. "You really want a *thu*?" Roberta said.

"Yes."

She left for a minute and returned with a bright blue bolt of material and a pair of scissors. The other two women also returned and watched. "Take off your shirt," she said. She looked me up and down. "We're going to need three yards." Without pausing, Roberta swept the cloth around my butt and between my pale legs and then back through, around and up the back again. "This may feel a bit uncomfortable," she said, and gave a good yank.

In New York I had worn a button-down shirt with khakis every day for five years. Even on weekends. And on days I had a meeting, I wore a suit. Though Internet start-ups were supposed to be casual, I was young. Had I worn shorts and a T-shirt, I would have looked fourteen. But wearing this tight piece of blue cloth, I felt about two.

Roberta eyed my wobbly legs and glanced at the other women.

They looked like they were about to pee their *thus*. "Three and a half yards would be better," she said.

After another spin and another yank, Roberta cut the cloth the way an artist in peak career signs a painting and said, "You can pay at the front."

I wasn't sure how—or whether—to thank these women, so I just nodded, paid twelve dollars for the humiliation, and, like a pasty, frumpy Smurf, waddled back onto the street.

Out front, a boy of maybe nine was sitting on a small stone ledge. I asked him if he knew where I might find the Council of Chiefs. "Walk toward the sun for ten minutes," he said like a mystical sprite, "and take a right. The second house on the right is the Council of Chiefs." He then leapt off the ledge and ran away.

Those were terrible directions, but I wasn't going back inside for better ones. So I glanced at my watch, then at the sun, and started walking. I passed a few cinder-block houses built on weedy lots and more viny Yapese jungle. For the first few minutes, a mangy dog followed me but then tired in the heat. Sure enough, after ten minutes, I came to an intersection with a small street that did, in fact, have a second house on the right. The house was made of concrete and had faded green window frames.

I approached the wooden door. On the ground was a piece of paper with the handwritten words *Council of Chiefs*. I knocked. No answer. I knocked again.

I was turning away when a blue pickup truck pulled up and a middle-aged man with glasses and round cheeks tumbled out of the driver seat, slamming the door behind him. "Ahh," I thought, Seuss-like, "he too wears little but a blue *thu*."

"Excuse me. Is this the Council of Chiefs?" I said.

"Yes." He carried a blank yellow writing pad, making him the most official person I had met.

"My name is Alex. I was hoping to visit the outer islands."

"Yes, I know. I heard you might be coming, but we're very

busy. Come back tomorrow. You'll need to present yourself to the chiefs."

"About this time?" I asked, as though presenting myself to the chiefs was a standard Tuesday activity.

"Sure," he said. "Just ask for me. My name is Joe."

When I arrived the next day, Joe was sitting at a small desk inside the Council of Chief's house. There was no phone on the desk. Only the same pad of paper, still blank.

"Are you ready?" he said.

"I think so," I said, checking my *thu*. It was wrapped around my waist and privates as a child might wrap a bandage around a hurt ankle: it honored the exercise without providing a lot of actual support.

Joe then led me to a low-ceilinged room lit with fluorescent lights. Scattered about were little Formica tables and little chairs that would have nicely complemented a third-grade classroom, except for the forty or so elderly Yapese men in loincloths sitting in them. All had short gray hair, deep bags under their eyes, and powerful muscles only somewhat hidden by years of slow but steady weight gain.

They stopped talking and stared when I entered. I expected—even hoped for—a little *thu*-induced giggling. But they only stared in silence. Joe whispered to me, "These are the chiefs from all the islands of Yap. I will introduce you." I nodded and smiled as he said something to them in Yapese.

"Alex," he then said, "present yourself to the chiefs." I had no idea how to present myself to a roomful of almost certainly wise but nearly naked men sitting in elementary school chairs.

I gave Joe a confused shrug.

"Alex," he urged, "you need to present yourself to the chiefs."

I still had no idea what he meant. "How do I present myself?"

"Shake their hands," Joe said. Oh, those wacky foreigners.

I shook every hand, beginning with the chief who looked the oldest.

"Why do you want to go?" Joe then asked. I stood in silence for a long moment. Could I really go into everything?

"I want to learn more about your culture," I said lamely, "and maybe someday tell others about it. Maybe in an article." They spoke softly among themselves. Some grimaced; others stared into the middle distance.

"The chiefs want to know where exactly you want to go," Joe said.

I said I was hoping to visit Woleai on Pacific Missionary Aviation. Again, they debated among themselves. Occasionally, I thought I could make out certain words, words like "the American" and "dreadfully pale."

"They want to know if you intend to take a camera," Joe said.

"No," I replied, grateful for another softball. Perhaps some name-dropping might help. "Joe," I said, "please tell them I was hoping to stay at Carmen Rial's house on Woleai. They are cousins of Mike, who works at my motel."

Joe translated, waited for a response, and said, "They say it is customary for the chiefs to determine with whom you stay."

The chiefs again spoke among themselves, but the mood shifted, becoming considerably tenser. Some walked to the corner to confer in private. Another paced over to Joe to ask a question. More whispers.

I asked Joe if I could speak. "The Compact Agreement with the United States is coming up for renewal," I said. "Unless Americans know something of these islands, they will never care about them."

Joe translated, probably saying, "This Smurf says he has the keys to Gargamel's castle."

They talked some more, frequently looking at me. Figuring I had basically squandered whatever chance I had, I swung for the fence. "Joe," I said, "please tell the chiefs that I understand it is customary to bring gifts with me to each island. Would they prefer I bring cigarettes or women?"

He translated. There were discreet chuckles. Then, after more deliberation, the oldest chief spoke. "The high chief grants you permission to go," Joe said, adding, "And he suggests you bring cigarettes."

CHAPTER 12

What You Can Expect to Learn in This Chapter:

➤ How much should you expect to pay, per pound, to fly yourself to the outer islands of Yap?

➤ Upon seeing blue smoke billow out of the engine of the small plane you're about to take off in, do you:
a) panic?
b) hope the priest who is piloting the plane has some healthy doubt about the existence of an afterlife?
c) jot down all the famous people you can think of who have died in a plane crash?
d) most of the above?

The man behind the counter at Pacific Missionary Aviation asked to see my permit. He was tall and thin with blond hair well on its way to becoming gray. He had shorts on but no shirt or shoes. His name tag identified him as *Father Grant, Chief Pilot*.

I handed him my permit. Not unreasonably, he stared at it for a long time. Word for word, it read:

> This is to certify that Alex Fhefhunorze has been granted permission by the Council of Tomol and other traditional island leaders to visit for the purpose of learning other people's culture and other purposes. Meet the chiefs of the island when you get there, present gifts.

"How do you say your last name?" he said.

"Sheshunoff," I said. He looked at the permit, then back at me. "She-Shu-Noff," I said, pausing between each syllable.

"Get on the scale," he said.

"Me?"

"You and your bag."

"I'm supposed to stand on the scale?" I said.

"Who else?" Father Grant said. Having gone to religious schools most of my life, I'd been scolded by plenty of priests, but never one in shorts.

"Two hundred ten pounds," he said, writing on some scratch paper.

"A lot of that is my bag," I said.

"At seventy-five cents a pound that's . . . $157.50."

I generally like pricing by the pound, as it makes comparisons much easier (i.e., "Honey, these tomatoes cost $1.14 a pound. But I think we should get the Corolla. It's only $1.09 per pound."). I had a problem, though. I only had $84 in cash. If I was going to get to Woleai, I'd have to leave all my books behind. *And* lose fifty-three pounds.

"Do you take Visa?" I said.

"No," he said without looking up as he tended to some paperwork. I dug through my wallet and found a crumpled check that had been laundered who knows how many times. It had a New York City address.

"Will you accept a check?" I said, uncurling it. I pressed down the tattered edges and slid it across the counter with a smile. The kind of smile that says, *Ha, isn't this funny? I'm trying to pay a priest to fly me by the pound to a remote Pacific island with half a crumpled check from the Bank of New York.*

"Sure," he said, "we'll take that."

As he wrote something down, he added, "You know, it could be a long time before we can come back."

"How long?"

"Rainy season's coming up. A few months. Give or take."

I asked him to give me a second to think it over. Suddenly, I felt afraid. When is it a good idea to listen to fear and when is it a good idea to fight it? Maybe this was the moment when most people turned back to the deep-cushioned couches of their familiar lives and said, "Nope, not for me." I thought that fear can just as easily keep us from what we really want as from what we really *don't* want, but there was little to pull me to New York, and I loved the possibility, however remote, that I might stay on Woleai forever. After all, on *Fantasy Island*, the tension underlying each shout of "The plane, boss, the plane!" was that arriving guests might return to normal life with their wishes fulfilled or might never leave, their wishes even more fulfilled. *Quién es más macho,* I said to myself, *yo . . . o . . . Ricardo Montalbán?*

I asked to whom I should write out the check.

"Pacific Missionary Aviation."

I watched the three other passengers weigh in. They were Yapese, and, except for their considerable girth, they traveled light. Father Grant then left through a side door and came back a minute later. "Woleai just called on the radio," he said. "Runway's still flooded. We'll have to wait an hour for an update."

With some time to kill (or live), I wandered to the maintenance hangar next door. The PA system was broadcasting a Christian hymn. A bearded man in overalls was fussing with an airplane engine on the floor.

"Hi," I said. "You the mechanic?"

"You bet," he said.

"Is that a good job?"

"Oh yeah. How many jobs out there can you fix planes while doing God's work?" It turned out that Roger had been in Yap for three years, but for seventeen years before, he had farmed eggs in

Ohio. Oh, sure, you know how it goes: one day you're an egg farmer just outside Dayton, and the next, you're screwing in a propeller for Jesus on the island of Yap.

"So, the airline does mostly missionary work then?"

"Sometimes, but Bibles are heavy. Mostly we do medevacs. We picked up a kid a few weeks ago who'd been nailed by a coconut."

"You're kidding."

"No. They have a lot of them on the outer islands, and they're heavy."

"The coconuts, right?"

"Yup. Really heavy. Three weeks before that, we picked up a fisherman who'd been bitten by a shark. That's mostly it. Coconuts and sharks. Sharks and coconuts." I expected a smile, but he just went back to tinkering with the engine. While considering how I'd phrase a question about flying on an airline whose principals had so much faith in the afterlife, Father Grant burst in, still shirtless.

"Woleai says the sun has come out. The runway is dry enough to land. Let's load the weight."

Father Grant and Roger then tossed the three of us passengers and all of the bags into the back of a pickup. The plane had two propellers and an unpainted steel body. From the ground it must have appeared like a silver cross sliding across the broad azure sky. I assumed *John 3:13* was painted underneath.

We wedged ourselves into the plane's tiny seats, and Father Grant started the engines. I thought about a fact I had once heard about flying. Apparently, the number one reason people report wanting to be rich is to better provide for their families. The number two reason? To fly first class. I started to understand why. I peered around the seat in front of me: Father Grant was still barefoot.

We were taxiing to our final run-up when Roger screeched up in a pickup in front of the plane, and jumped out, waving his arms. Generally, this is not something one wants to see the mechanic doing before takeoff. I swear the conversation between Roger and Father Grant went exactly like this:

ROGER: "I see smoke."
FATHER GRANT: "Yeah, I noticed a funny smell."
ROGER: "You shouldn't fly."
FATHER GRANT: "You're right."

Father Grant looks at the gauges.

FATHER GRANT: "What should we do?"
ROGER: "I don't know."

Long pause.

FATHER GRANT: "Me neither."

Long pause.

FATHER GRANT: "We could do nothing?"
ROGER: "Yeah. I suppose, you know, just ignore it."

Long pause.

FATHER GRANT: "We could take off a piece of luggage?"
ROGER: "That might help."

A man in the seat next to mine watched sadly as Roger grabbed a box from the back of the plane and put it in his pickup.

I wondered if I'd go to Hell for bringing twenty pounds of books in my suitcase—that guy's box was probably filled with diphtheria shots—but I'd left at least that weight in books at the Ocean View

Hotel. Some Catholics feel they're supposed to tithe 10 percent. I'd done something like 50 percent. And for all I knew, his box was full of crystal meth. Regardless, having it off must have helped. We took off low and fairly fast over Yap.

From the air, Yap's rolling hills looked lush and lightly populated. I could see just one truck bouncing along a ridgetop's dirt road. The plane turned, passing over Yap's idyllic light blue lagoon, then its little reef, before heading out over the deep dark blue of the ocean. I was wondering why this island wasn't quite right, wasn't good enough, when we popped into the clouds and into the worst turbulence I'd ever felt. Turbulence that didn't stop for two and a half hours as we bounced around in the clouds or banked steeply to avoid rising thunderheads. Reading was impossible. The notes in my journal are brief, the handwriting more vertical than horizontal as my pen slashed up and down with meteorological notes and the names of everyone I could think of who'd died in plane crashes:

> *Rain ... Bumpy. Very bumpy. Buddy Holly ... More rain ...*
> *Thick clouds ... Otis Redding ... John Denver. ... no*
> *GPS. ... Patsy Cline ... pilot just tightened his seat belt ...*
> *Ron Brown.*

Ron Brown, Bill Clinton's former Commerce Secretary, was a peculiar addition, but it was a tense time.

We finally dropped down below the clouds. I leaned around Father Grant's shoulder to glance at the gauges. Our altitude was just five hundred feet. Woleai was directly below. I could see two blue lagoons overlapped in the middle like a cell dividing into two. Each thin, flat island was covered in a thick mat of palms. We flew fast over a village. Just like in the movies, waving children ran out of thatched huts and onto the beach. On a whim, I opened a window and dropped a Coke bottle out and accidentally destroyed their culture. Just kidding—their culture greatly appreciated my bottle of Coke.

Just as I expected the wheels to touch, there was only silence. Instead of landing, we flew down the length of the runway just a few feet above the ground. Over the accelerating engines, Father Grant yelled, "Too much water." We circled the island once and ascended toward the clouds. "We're going back," he yelled again. Two and a half hours of turbulent disappointment later, we landed again on Yap.

CHAPTER 13

What You Can Expect to Learn in This Chapter:

► What kind of suitcase should you not bring and why?

► Which of the following best describes the book *The History of the Catholic Church in Micronesia*?
a) zesty
b) not zesty

he bastards lied to me," Father Grant said, undoing his seat belt after we landed. "They knew there was too much water on the runway. They just wanted me to bring them stuff." When I asked when we might try again, he said, "We're never flying to Woleai. Not Woleai or any island. Never. Never. Ever." I'd never seen such a miffed missionary.

As I'd later read in *The History of the Catholic Church in Micronesia*, Father Grant was another in a long line of disappointed messengers to Micronesia. To save you the time—despite what one might think from the title, it's not a zesty read—here is the only item of interest: the Yapese repelled early Spanish missionaries and colonists by throwing flaming coconuts at their houses. Each time the Spanish rebuilt, the Yapese would throw more flaming coconuts. Eventually, the Spaniards grew weary of all the flaming coconuts being thrown on their houses and went back to Spain.

Father Grant gave me back my check. I went out to the street and sat on the curb. Even before sadness or anger sets in, failure often evokes the question: what the hell am I going to do now? I considered getting a job in a restaurant, maybe teaching in a school. Or perhaps I should just chill out, see what happens, let go, and stop trying to control everything.

So I waited. A lone chicken settled into a brittle pile of leaves. A new white pickup marked *Kingtex* drove by, adding another gritty layer of beige dust to the bushes, to the airport's rusting tin roof, to the mess of my hair.

This wasn't the Delta Dream Vacation brochure life I'd imagined. Creating an ideal life from scratch—instead of backing into a life created by chance and momentum—sounded nice, but what if you ended up here? So I waited twenty minutes. Maybe another truck would pass? None did. I pulled out the handle of my roller bag and started walking back to town.

Before coming, I'd put an embarrassingly large amount of thought into which bag to bring. A backpack had felt too young, too transient. A duffel too inconvenient. That pretty much left a roller bag. Though a tad too flight-attendanty, I liked the compromise the roller bag represented between mobility and permanence. After all, I wasn't traveling around the world; I was looking for a place to stay. Yet now, as I bumped over the broken gravel, dusty sand, and deep potholes of Yap's few streets, it just felt dumb. In retrospect, I should have considered that maybe the rest of the world, or at least the islands of the western Pacific, might not be surfaced as smoothly as home.

I picked up the bag by a handle on the side and within twenty yards felt my shoulder start to strain. I thought of my dad's own broken shoulder. As bad as I felt, it was much better to be carrying a heavy bag on the way to Woleai than to a bank convention in Omaha. On the other hand, I wasn't actually on my way to Woleai. I was stuck in Yap. As I walked toward town, I thought back to that brief flyover, of those children waving and splashing into the lagoon. I knew Woleai was the closest I'd ever come to Michener's Bali Hai, Gauguin's Tahiti, my own, luscious, palm-tree-intensive Paradise. It had seemed so perfect, so un-Omaha. I had to get there. I just needed to find a way to get across five hundred miles of open ocean. If I didn't, who knows, maybe someday I'd too find myself racing through airports to get to some place I didn't want to go.

That afternoon I ran into Joe from the Council of Chiefs at the grocery store. He was buying a giant jar of aspirin and a can of corned beef. I told him about the flight and asked if he knew of another way to get to Woleai.

"The field ship," he said. "It goes to all the outer islands." Perfect. "But there's no money for fuel."

"Any idea when they'll get some?" I said.

He shrugged. "Maybe a month. Maybe more. Go talk to Moses."

Excited, I walked as quickly as I could in the heat to the Micro-spirit Shipping Office, a small metal building struggling to retain its last flakes of dark blue paint. I found Moses, a large, serious-looking man, seated behind a metal desk. Faded marine-safety posters and handwritten boat schedules covered the walls. He wore a short-sleeved collared shirt. He was the only person in the office.

"Sorry. No fuel," he said. "But even when we get it, there's no room. We have three funerals and their families on board. They have priority."

"But there might be room?" I asked.

"Do you have permission from the chiefs?"

"I do. I'll sleep on the deck."

"Everyone sleeps on the deck," he said. "There are only three cabins—and they're reserved for family members of the deceased. Now, no space and no fuel. Check back in a month."

CHAPTER 14

What You Can Expect to Learn in This Chapter:

► When offered the chance to coach the Yap Olympic baseball team, should you accept? What if you have never, technically speaking, played baseball?

► What should be the next phase of the women's suffrage movement?

For the next few weeks in Yap, time didn't fly. It oozed. My days were largely dictated by the course of the sun. The most difficult time started around eleven a.m. and ended about four p.m. Before eleven, the sun's low angle lent just enough ambition to the day for a morning walk. I'd amble past the scrappy restaurant serving frozen sushi, the liquor store that stocked only beer and vodka, the empty basketball court, and the nearly empty grocery store. I'd usually pause in front of one of Yap's two stop signs. I'd look left, then right, waiting for traffic that rarely came. In the distance, a dog might twitch an ear, perhaps even raise an eyebrow.

By eleven, the sun's rays would be filtered through so much evaporating water vapor that the light's earlier crispness became muffled and heavy. I'd then retreat into my nearly windowless motel room, where I'd try to read, but lying down amid so much heat and so little wind, I'd fall asleep. Almost always while reading *The Making of the Atomic Bomb*.

To save you the trouble of reading a 928-page book with a lot of equations and diagrams, I'll relay the very best part here. Two and a half years before "Little Boy" was dropped on Hiroshima, an Italian physicist named Enrico Fermi and a couple of colleagues were experimenting with uranium in the squash courts of the University of Chicago. His goal: to create the world's first self-sustaining nuclear reaction. But as is often the case when a bunch of guys start fiddling around with eighty-six thousand pounds of uranium oxide, there was a catch: in this case, the possibility that the reaction might spiral out of control and blow up the world. The chance was small—they figured about one percent—yet . . . and I pause for emphasis . . . they did it anyway. You know, just to see what would happen. The moral? Science cannot be stopped. That and the next phase of the women's suffrage movement should be about exclusivity.

After my nap, I'd usually drop off some clothes at the Laundromat before heading to the store to buy a soda and something to eat. Then I'd walk the few hundred dusty yards back to the Laundromat and, while waiting for my wash to finish, sit on a dryer, read, and eat my snack. I would have liked to listen to the waves in the distance, but there are no waves in Yap—just swamp. Not that waves could have drowned out the thumping and swirling of the laundry machines anyway. The load done, I'd hop off the dryer, fold my clothes, and walk back to my motel . . . concluding the busiest part of the day. To say it was less hectic than my life in New York would be pretty accurate. Check *that* problem off the list.

Then, at my motel, I'd read, then perhaps fall asleep again, neither particularly easy in the humidity. Yap's steaming, still climate made everything stick together. It made the pages of my books stick together. It made my back stick to my shirt. And my shirt stick to my sheets. Even the keys of my laptop, like the neurons in my brain, had a sticky inertia about them. How much better would the world be, I sometimes wondered, if everyone lived in a place with such weather? There is no way, for example, that Fermi and his buddies would have tinkered around with so much uranium in 90 degree weather with 95 percent humidity. Instead, they would have just taken a nap. And voilà! No nuclear weapons.

Most evenings, I'd head to a bar for dinner and my daily dose of human contact, but I was finding that people didn't quite know what to make of the tourist who didn't scuba dive and who didn't leave. Often I'd eat alone.

One night, though, at O'Keefe's Kanteen, I got lucky—not *lucky* lucky, just lucky in that I had an actual conversation with another human being.

"So, you play baseball?" Jeb said in a nasally, high-pitched Southern accent after we'd spoken for maybe three minutes. A bearded American expat in his midfifties, Jeb was Yap's director of wastewater and utilities.

"Not really," I said. "Why?"

"Because we're looking for a coach for the Yapese Olympic team."

I told him I'd have to learn the rules first. "Wait. Do they even have baseball in the Olympics?" I asked.

"Not those Olympics," he said. "Micronesian Olympics. Last time they were in Kosrae. This time it's Yap's turn."

"So they take turns hosting. That seems fair. . . ."

"Unless you're in charge of Yap's wastewater," he said starkly, staring into my eyes. "We'll have five thousand extra people on the island. Don't you think they're gonna wanna poop?" I had a hunch they would. "You bet they will," he said without waiting. "You bet they will."

I asked him what other events were in the Olympics.

"Oh, all sorts. Basketball. Spearfishing. Coconut-tree climbing. You name it."

"You're kidding."

"No, sireee. Coconut-tree climbing. Winner is the fastest to the top."

A deeply tanned man then sat down with us and said, "Good evening, mates."

"Hey, Anton," Jeb said wearily. Anton was a tanned man also in his midfifties, with receding but well-coifed hair. Apparently, he wasn't the type to waste time on buttons.

"Anton is a surgeon," Jeb said.

"Brain surgeon," Anton said, gesturing for another beer.

"Before that, Anton was an athlete," Jeb said as though hurrying to get through topics he knew would be coming up.

"Olympic athlete," Anton clarified. "Gold medal winner. The real Olympics."

"The luge, was it?" Jeb said. "Or figure skating?"

"Downhill, my boy. Downhill."

I believe you always give people with outlandish claims the benefit of the doubt. If, for example, a man says he's Jesus Christ, I tend to think, *Well, maybe he is. If Jesus Christ did return, who else would he say he was?* So perhaps Anton was a former brain surgeon and Olympic skier.

"With all of that, what brought you to Yap?" I said.

"The native girls. Why else would you be here?" I thought of the women in the Laundromat. "Not that we don't have lovely ladies in Switzerland. We used to ski with them every afternoon, down those treeless slopes. Then there were the Jacuzzis. Those girls loved the Jacuzzis."

"I'm sure—"

"Nothing compares to the girls here, though," he said.

"Anton married a cranky Filipina prostitute," Jeb offered.

"Dancer. She was a dancer before we met," he said, "though I agree on the cranky."

"Speaking of cranky," Jeb said, "this pump, over at station three, it needs to be retooled if . . ."

At that, Anton stood to leave. Shaking our hands, he told the bartender in a voice loud enough for the room to hear, "Put their drinks on my tab."

Jeb waited for him to leave before speaking. "Every expat here is running from something," he said.

"What's he running from?" I said.

"No one knows. Ex-wife, probably."

"Can't be much brain surgery to keep him busy here," I said.

"Or skiing."

We both took long sips from our beers.

"Surprised he didn't go with race car driver," I said.

"That's his problem," Jeb said. "He thinks he's a modern O'Keefe."

"He likes to paint cow skulls too?" I said.

"David O'Keefe. His Majesty O'Keefe." I looked confused. "You haven't heard of him? Should read the book. It's a true story. They even made a movie." He pointed to a poster on the wall for *His Majesty O'Keefe*. It starred Burt Lancaster.

"How was it?"

"Excellent, except they filmed it in Fiji. Really pissed off the Yapese. Fijians have Afros. Most Yapese don't." Having never been portrayed in film with a hairstyle I didn't have, I couldn't relate very well, but no doubt the slight was aggravating. "The book also has a few mistakes, but it's better. They sell it here at the bar."

We chatted for a few more minutes about pump 3 before Jeb too excused himself. Eager to read the first book recommended to me since arriving, I bought *His Majesty O'Keefe* and went back to my motel to read. It seems Yap has been attracting scrappy schemers for a long time, the most famous of whom was David Dean O'Keefe, a big redhead from Savannah, Georgia. He landed in Yap in 1871 and immediately figured out an arbitrage opportunity: namely, the Yapese would give him coconuts in exchange for steamship rides to their stone money quarries in Palau. O'Keefe would then give the carvers (and their unwieldy coinage) a ride home before heading to Hong Kong to sell the coconuts. It worked. So he repeated the circuit again and again. Despite having a wife and family back home in Georgia, he married a Yapese woman and was crowned, perhaps jokingly, the King of Yap.

But like most great empires, I'd later learn, his was undone by inflation. With so much stone money in circulation, the currency's value collapsed. Among Yapese today, he is blamed for almost destroying the traditional use of stone money—only the distinction between pre-O'Keefe and post-O'Keefe coinage saved it.

I lay on my bed and wondered how many others had come here with modest intentions, only to see those intentions metastasize in inverse proportion to the size of this little island. Anton was a good candidate. Father Grant another. Perhaps Jeb, with his water and his electricity, also thought of himself that way. In fact, nearly all the expats I'd met had a hero-to-the-people-even-if-the-people-don't-know-it-yet way about them. What was it about this place that reduced so many dreams to schemes?

Maybe the problem stemmed from the kind of wanderers attracted to such islands in the first place, the kind of people who assume deep topsoil means lush fruit and vegetables, who mistake sunny skies for good weather and generosity for opportunity. I didn't feel much of a need to change the world anymore, much less these islands. But was it inevitable, I wondered, that after enough midday beers in window-less bars, I too would stop bothering with my shirt buttons and start imagining the size of the ripple I could make in such a small, small pond? Better, I figured, to stick with my box of books.

CHAPTER 15

What You Can Expect to Learn in This Chapter:

► What is the relationship between accidentally helping George W. Bush get elected governor of Texas and needing to escape to a small Pacific island?

► If a U.S. Senator offers to let you rummage around in his pocket for candy, should you accept?

Until coming to Yap, I'd done just about everything that was expected of an ambitious kid of upper-middle-class parents, including starting a school newspaper in the fifth grade. By the tenth grade, I'd become a news junkie and gotten it into my idealistic young mind that the world's problems could be solved through politics, a notion that would take an embarrassingly long time to shake.

After serving as tenth-grade class president (no one else wanted the job), I worked in Washington, D.C., as a summer page for the U.S. Senate. There, I learned the two main responsibilities of pages are 1) to run around with copies of legislation no one, not even the people who wrote it, actually read; and 2) to not get molested. The latter was surprisingly difficult. About once a week, Senator Strom Thurmond would ask us pages to reach in his pocket for candy. "It's from the Senate dining room," he'd say with a wink. Wanting the candy and not wanting to be discourteous, I'd reach in and pick out a few, always careful not to rummage around too much.

But I suppose the low-water mark of my political education—other than when Ted Kennedy snapped his fingers at me for water ("Water, page! Water, page!")—was the day that Bob Dole stole my ice cream.

Like most people in the Capitol Building that day, I was excited when I heard the U.S. Dairy Association would be handing out free ice cream, you know, as a community service for U.S. senators about to vote on extending agricultural subsidies.

"Vanilla or chocolate?" a man behind the counter had asked.

"Chocolate," I said.

"You're lucky," he said. "You got the last chocolate."

"No," I heard a familiar voice from behind me say, "I'll have that chocolate."

Turning around, I saw it was Senator Bob Dole. The man handed him my chocolate ice cream. The senator walked away without a word.

Years later, when he was running for president, I considered telling the world my little Bob Dole story, figuring it shed considerable light on his character. But there was a chance it said more about power than it did about Bob Dole, so I just kept it to myself.

Yet I was still sufficiently optimistic about politics that I later got a summer job in the press office of Ann Richards' reelection campaign. There, between my freshman and sophomore years of college, I made what I'm sure will be my only contribution to world history. Ann Richards was the governor of Texas; her opponent, a failed Midland oil executive whose friends had given him a symbolic one percent of the Texas Rangers baseball team because he liked baseball and needed a job. That and his father's connections might help them build a new stadium. Anyway, one day in mid-July, I happened to answer the phone. That call—and my response to it—probably cost the governor half of the margin she'd eventually lose by. Maybe more.

To my credit, I wasn't really a press person. I was supposed to be doing opposition research. Not that I was very good at that job, either.

The other guy doing research and I found mostly suspicious-sounding relationships between George W. Bush, his father, and Bahrain oil companies that no one much cared about. So we chatted, read the newspaper, and answered the phone when it rang.

That particular day, the call came from a representative of the nonpartisan group Project Vote Smart. He told me they'd sent us a candidate survey asking our position on various issues. He said we hadn't sent it in, but George W.'s campaign had. Not filling it in, he warned, would make the Richards campaign seem evasive on the issues. I said I'd call him right back.

I told the head of the press office about the call. "We don't fill out candidate surveys," he said, "because we can't articulate nuanced positions in a generic yes-or-no survey." I told him I thought we'd been getting some negative press about not being clear about our positions, and that we should fill it out. After all, the other side had. He told me if I felt so strongly about it, I should talk to the head of the campaign.

She, in turn, informed me, "We don't fill out candidate surveys because we can't articulate nuanced positions to complicated issues in a generic yes-or-no survey." Undeterred, I explained my view. She said if I felt so strongly about it, I should talk to the governor's head legal counsel. I did. He said the same thing, but if I felt so strongly, I should talk to the governor herself. I did, and she said the same thing, albeit in a charming Texas drawl. Yet still I pushed.

"OK," she finally said. "Answer the questions and have the lawyers review it."

Among many other questions, there was this: "Do you support an increase in state spending?"

We circled *Yes*, and wrote in the margin, "but only for education."

Turns out, Project Vote Smart lied. George W.'s campaign didn't fill the survey out. But his campaign did see our responses. A few weeks before the election, they sent three million fliers to Texas voters. The headline: "Governor Richards Pledges to Increase State

Spending." We lost by 334,066 votes. That it took me so long to buy a one-way ticket to Yap is really the shocking thing.

Now, alone in my motel and watching geckos lunge at flies, I'd certainly deviated from the expected trajectory of my life. As I saw it, I had two options: return to New York and write this time off as a strange vacation, or stay on mission and continue ahead. I did know I couldn't stay on Yap, its people too difficult to reach, its shores beachless, and its interior dusty and sweatshop-filled. But going back to New York now would feel like a defeat, a submission to a path and a life dictated by momentum instead of choice. So, for now, Yap it was.

As the weeks slowly passed, however, I started to feel lonely. Not in a soul-searching, oh-my-God kind of loneliness, just a little, annoying, nagging feeling, like a foot that has fallen asleep. I didn't exactly fit in here. To the Yapese, I was a tourist. To the expats, I was like a companion on a lifeboat: good for company, but also a drain on limited resources—such as the goodwill of the locals or, if I were to stay, one of the limited jobs open to foreigners. Whatever cultural experience they were having was, by definition, diluted by my presence.

Perhaps out of pity, Jeb invited me to his house for dinner one night. It would prove to be the social highlight of my month on the main island of Yap. As soon as I arrived, he directed me to a couch where I sat between him and his wife, and passed a perfectly pleasant evening eating frozen pizza and watching reruns of *COPS*.

The next morning, based on a tip from Jeb, I went to see Moses at the Microspirit Shipping Office to see if they'd found money for fuel. They had. The boat was leaving that evening but, he reported, it was still full. He was distracted by paperwork but I begged. I groveled. I told him I had permission from the Council of Chiefs. I promised to wear a *thu*. Finally, he relented, mostly because my lack of dignity was starting to compromise his own. He said he'd sell me a ticket. The cost of this life-changing little piece of paper? $16.

I raced to the store to load up on supplies—gifts and backup food for myself. Though choices were limited, I managed to spend a hundred dollars: half on Lucky Strike cigarettes, half on frosted strawberry Pop-Tarts. I wasn't proud of my choices, but at least I was prepared.

CHAPTER 16

What You Can Expect to Learn in This Chapter:

► When looking for a place to sleep on the deck of a small freighter, are you better off:
   a) on a giant pile of rope?
   b) under a dripping air conditioner?
   c) beside three coffins?

► How seaworthy are onions?

L ate that afternoon, I watched a crane hoist the first of three flower-covered coffins onto the deck of the *Microspirit*. Each twisted slowly in the light wind, sending yellow petals into the sea. I expected the coffins to be placed somewhere in the hold of the ship but instead watched as each was lowered to the center of the top deck—right where the pool might be on the *Love Boat*.

A few hundred people had gathered to watch the *Microspirit* prepare to depart. Most were women whose purple and pink sarongs contrasted sharply with the anxious looks on their faces. Young women crossed their arms and stared at their feet. Middle-aged women made slow windmill waves of good-bye as they searched for eye contact with friends or relatives. Older women with deep-set eyes held their hands tightly in front of their mouths. In the distance, a child noisily, and perhaps angrily, kicked a soccer ball against the metal wall of a warehouse.

Out of nowhere, a bucket brigade of shirtless men formed to load the boat. I joined in the middle, helping to pass up Adidas bags of taro, Tupperware containers of tapioca, fraying reed baskets of fish, plastic tubs filled with old blankets and clothes, and old boxes of who knows what.

There is still drama to boat travel. Anything could happen on a boat. Icebergs, romance, murder: they're almost expected. Because unlike a plane or car, on a boat you are stuck. Especially on the *Microspirit*. It takes about two and a half weeks to make the twelve-hundred-mile circuit through Yap's eighteen inhabited outer islands. The ship stops twice at each island, dropping off people and supplies the first time, picking up passengers, fish, and coconuts the second. The advantage of this route—at least for me—was that I could potentially be dropped off at any island on the way out and picked up the next week on the boat's return journey. Or, failing that, on a later circuit, months or even years later.

The supplies mostly loaded, I shuffled up the *Microspirit*'s metal gangway with my heavy suitcase rolling behind me, using my other hand to hold up my *thu* while balancing a fraying cardboard box of cigarettes, Pop-Tarts, snorkels, and T-shirts awkwardly under my arm. I tried to appear as natural as possible, but I felt like I was walking in to the first day of junior high, only with more books, fewer friends, and in a loincloth. Each step was a challenge. My box was falling apart. My *thu* was slipping down my hip. My bag's wheels were getting stuck in the ruts of the metal grates. I glanced down the length of the ship. It wasn't big—maybe sixty yards—but it *was* rusty. I saw someone open a window, causing a napkin-sized sheath of rust to slide into the water. Oh, my God, I thought, I'm about to make a trans-Pacific crossing aboard a rotting onion.

At the top of the ramp, I looked around for a place to put my things, but every square inch seemed spoken for. The main deck was fully occupied by women, children, and the three coffins. The second deck, not much larger than an average living room, appeared to be reserved for elderly men. Curiously, several of them were already lounging in a giant box of rope and lumpy life preservers. The top deck was occupied only by women. Just as the engines started, I found a lovely spot back on the second deck outside the captain's quarters. It even had an overhang to protect me from rain. I felt the boat moving and went to the railing to look back at the harbor. Our departure wasn't announced with streamers or even horn blasts. Just the muffled rumble of the engine and the thuds of thick ropes hitting the concrete sides of the harbor wall.

The atmosphere on board was subdued. Many people were heading to their outer-island homes and probably would not return for years. Others were making the round-trip to attend funerals. (An elderly chief who'd die en route would be attending his own. Our net gain and loss, however, would be zero, as, a few days out of port, a woman on the third deck would give birth to a baby girl.)

I watched Yap's silhouetted hills slide behind us. Was I taking this idea of Paradise too literally? Could a remote island and a bunch of books make me happy? Could I really find out what was important by just taking everything away? Would I fall in love and never return? Or, after a week, would I start looking for my own tall coconut tree to jump out of? In fact, I would later find that there *was* one thing I'd miss more than anything else; one thing that would come to represent both the good and the bad of life on a remote island. What it was I never could have guessed.

I sat down and leaned against the bridge of the ship. Ahead of us, to the east, the stars seemed to reveal themselves a bit earlier and clearer than they ever had in the dusty haze of Yap's sky. Slipping through a break in the reef, the *Microspirit* began to sway, a gentle roll to the rhythm of the ocean and the soft moans of women slumped beside closed coffins. I unfurled my sleeping bag, wound a T-shirt around my flip-flops for a pillow, and fell asleep, thinking that this was the most adventurous thing I'd ever done.

STEP 3

FIND THE RIGHT ISLAND

CHAPTER 17

What You Can Expect to Learn in This Chapter:

► What is the principal problem associated with certain cabinmates' ear-cleaning habits?

► Do sarcasm and the Yap outer islands go together like:
(a) peanut butter and jelly?
(b) peanut butter and salmonella?

An hour later, I woke up to air-conditioning condensation dripping on my face. I rolled to the side, but it dripped down my neck. I rolled to the other side. Cold water then dripped into my ear before sliding down my neck. So, like Linus and his blanket, I slung my sleeping bag over my shoulder and went in search of another place. To my surprise, the bow was fabulously empty. I spread out my sleeping bag and snuggled in. A minute later, the first wave struck. Nothing dangerous—just a bucket or so of salt water sloshed onto my sleeping bag—but enough to make me reevaluate. I finally settled for a spot in front of the door to the engine room at about three a.m. Not that I fell asleep. The engine vibrations made my body hurt and my eyes blur, a bit like trying to sleep in a juicer.

I was, not surprisingly, the first one to arrive for breakfast. The boat's exceedingly small galley had just a two-burner stove, a tiny counter, and a narrow shelf with a toaster and a shaker of salt. A small sea-sprayed porthole cast an opaque light over the room's only table, a kindergartner-sized booth whose slick orange Formica surface was made slicker by a film of grease. Most people on board had brought along their own food, but those willing to pay $1.25 could choose between a fried egg and a slice of Spam over frozen white bread or a fried egg and a slice of Spam over cold rice.

"Wait for the egg," the cook said, handing me an empty bowl. He was probably in his early fifties. A deep-set frown permanently creased his forehead. He leaned against the wall and watched as I put the bread in the toaster.

"Hi. I'm Alex," I said. He simply stared.

"Are you from one of the outer islands?" I asked.

"Yes."

"Oh. Which one?"

"Woleai," he said. I nodded and waited for him to add something.

"A good island, that Woleai?" I said, pretending that I hadn't flown over it once. Just then, a middle-aged man wearing flip-flops and a blue loincloth walked around the counter and poured himself a coffee.

"Good morning," I said.

"Morning." He nodded. "What island are you going to?"

I smiled. "Not sure yet," I said. "What about you?"

"Not going to an island. I'm Cargomaster," he said.

"Oh really," I said, checking my toast, "what does the Cargomaster do?"

"Master cargo."

"I see," I said, though I didn't. "Well, maybe you have some advice. I was sleeping outside the captain's quarters but the air conditioner drips a bit. . . ."

"Do you want a cabin?"

"You have one available? Yes," I said. "I mean, aren't the people from the funeral—"

"They don't want it."

"Well, yes, then. Do you know how much it would cost?"

"Sixteen cents a mile."

"Really?"

"Yes."

I asked how many miles it was to Woleai.

The cook raised an eyebrow. "360 miles."

He grabbed some coffee and, as he left, told me to stop by the bridge later to get a key. As soon as I sat down, the cook held up a spatula with a slippery sunny-side-all-over egg. "Your egg," he said.

"Oh, one second," I said, turning to get my toast. It was still frozen. I looked at the back of the toaster. It was unplugged.

"Ahh," I said, "toaster toasts faster when it's plugged in." I smiled, holding the end of the plug up for the cook to see.

"Yes," he said, "it does." I waited for him to smile, but he didn't. I could only assume he was being sincere: the toaster toasts faster when plugged in.

"Cold bread is fine," I said, gesturing for him to slide the egg into my bowl. I sat down at the table, the top of my knees grating against the hard gum stuck to the underside. I turned to ask him for a spoon—the runny egg kept slipping through the bent tines of my fork—but the cook was focused on smothering a bowl of white rice in Karo corn syrup. I wondered if he might sit down with me to eat. Instead, he stepped into a storage closet to the side of the grill. I could see only the knobs of his knees and the edge of the cardboard box he was sitting on. Separated by three feet, we finished our breakfasts together, yet utterly apart.

As the Cargomaster led me down a narrow hall to my cabin, I thought about how good it would be to have my own space, a place I could escape the swirl of people and coconuts up on deck. He opened the door, revealing not so much a cabin as an oversized oven. The walls were metal. So was the bunk bed. A small, grimy porthole looked out onto the outside passageway and the ocean beyond but let in little light.

In the middle of the floor lay a waist-high pile of blankets, baskets, and a basket of fish swarming with flies. "Hope you don't mind sharing," he said, leaving. It might be good to have a roommate, I thought. We might get to know each another. Even become friends.

Just then, a man in a snug white loincloth walked through the door. Actually, he didn't so much walk as wedge his way through. I had a roommate. And at six and a half feet tall and about the same girth around, he was big. He stooped to avoid hitting his head on the disturbingly low ceiling.

"Hi. I'm Alex," I said. "Seems we're cabinmates."

He tilted his head and, without a word, got down on all fours and began to dig into his pile, occasionally tossing a container of Tupperware between his legs as a giant gopher might toss dirt. Every now and then he'd eject a coconut or a blanket that, after a brief flight, landed on the bottom bunk. Guess I'm on the top bunk, I thought. Though only a foot from the ceiling, at least it was closer to the window—a window that even opened. Finally, he emerged holding a comb.

"I'm Chuck," he said as he faced the mildewed mirror on the wall and began to coif his fluffy black hair. I wasn't sure if he was talking to me or the person in the mirror. Then he said, "I'm Chuck. Chief Chuck of Chuuk." Chuuk being an island group to the east of Yap's outer islands and home to at least one pair of parents with a sense of humor.

Chief Chuck would prove to be a peculiar, if occasionally helpful, cabinmate, but mostly he just left me baffled. One afternoon, for example, I came back to the cabin and found him asleep on my bunk. Apparently, he found his too hot and had moved to mine.

"Chief Chuck," I said trying to be cool about it, "I brought you this." Without moving his head, he looked down at my plate of cooked fish. "Someone gave this to me. Would you like some?" He leaned on one elbow and took one of the two large pieces into his fleshy fingers. Slowly, he swung his legs around and peeled himself down.

I then showed him a dear tube of wasabi that, for some reason, I had picked up in Honolulu. "Would you like some of this? It's spicy."

Apparently, he liked it. After trying a dab on the other large piece, he examined the tube and, without comment, snapped it into one of his Tupperware containers.

I knew if I was going to learn anything out here, I'd have to leave my own expectations behind. But some, like those involving privacy and personal space, were harder to shake than others. Each morning, for example, Chief Chuck used my razor. More concerning was his ear-cleaning habit. Twice a day, Chief Chuck would wrap the corner of a paper towel around his right index finger and start digging in. The right ear, then the left, then the right ear again before returning to the left. I found the vigor with which he cleaned deeply concerning, if not actually violent.

"Chief Chuck," I said once, "you might have the cleanest ears in the Pacific."

He nodded, I assume thinking proudly, Indeed, I might have the cleanest ears in the Pacific.

From a cabinmate's perspective, however, the central problem with his ear-cleaning habit was the paper towel. After each purging, he would toss the towel out the window. From there it'd either blow out to sea or float down on the walkway outside our window, perhaps onto the face of a sleeping baby. But sometimes it wouldn't blow out the window at all. Sometimes it would just roll off the window's rim . . . before coming to a waxy rest on my pillow.

CHAPTER 18

What You Can Expect to Learn in This Chapter:

> ► Is the willingness to fly a kite from a rooftop at night a reasonable litmus test for a friend or girlfriend?

> ► Are sextants still handy navigational tools? Why or why not?

On our third day at sea, the wind shifted. The sky grew gray and billowy. A light rain fell. The swells too had increased in size. When we hit them straight on, the hull shuddered. When we were hit from the side, the boat leaned extravagantly, then righted itself before leaning again to the other side. In weather so rough, no one walked the decks. So I sat on my top bunk and read. Or just watched the rain fall into the ocean.

I'd begun to notice a disturbing pattern among the books I'd chosen: many had unapologetically despicable protagonists. Ignatius J. Reilly in *A Confederacy of Dunces*. Yossarian in *Catch-22*. Most disturbingly, I saw aspects of myself in all of them. Especially in Sinclair Lewis' character Babbitt in a novel by the same name that I'd started in New York but never finished.

Babbitt was a real estate agent, or as Lewis describes it: "He made nothing in particular, neither butter nor shoes, nor poetry, but he was nimble in the calling of selling houses for more than people could afford to pay." From a considerable distance, he could spot a quality watch or a member of the Rotary Club or the Elks. And, though sometimes wrong, Babbitt was never in doubt. It was in Babbitt that I saw how much I too defined my New York self by the exquisite collection of my own opinions.

I took a break from reading, but the book stuck with me. I thought back to an evening I'd had in New York a few months before leaving. More than any other, that Wednesday night captured what was wrong about New York for me. Lorena and I had met my friend Tyler and his new girlfriend, Marissa, for dinner at a crowded restaurant in the East Village. Tyler was a friend from college. He worked in finance. He said we'd have to meet late since he'd be coming from work.

When we walked into the restaurant, I saw Tyler in a dark blue suit pacing in front of the hostess' stand. Tall and slender, Tyler wore his brown hair a little longer than you'd expect, given his job, as though in a delicate compromise between his daytime and nighttime selves. Just as we approached, I noticed him handing a folded bill to the hostess. She took it, albeit awkwardly.

"Our table is almost ready," he said, kissing Lorena on each cheek in the European fashion. He then introduced us to Marissa, a pretty woman in her late twenties with curly brown hair. I asked what she did for work, but Tyler answered for her. "She's a moa."

"Moa? She's an extinct New Zealand bird?"

"Moa. M-O-A," he said, spelling loudly over the music. "Model or actress."

Marissa punched him playfully on the soft shoulder pad of his suit. While a hostess in a small black dress led us to our table— a tiny table that in any other American city would have been set for two, maybe even one—I wondered if someday they'd make a nice S.I.T.C.O.M. (Single Income, Two Children, Outrageous Mortgage.)

Upon seeing the table, Tyler turned to the hostess. "No," he said, "no way."

"It's fine," Lorena said.

"If you can wait ten minutes, we can get you a bigger table," the hostess said.

"This place blows," he said loud enough for her to hear. "Let's go somewhere else." With a shrug, she walked away with the menus. Tyler led us across the street to another restaurant, this one only slightly less crowded and loud than the previous. The only space available was at the bar. "Two calamaris!" he said to the bartender without bothering with a *please* or *could we have*. "And four Russian standards."

Turning back to us, he said, "I'm glad we're here. This place has the best calamari with aioli sauce in the East Village."

"I think third best," I said.

"No way. The VERY BEST."

"I'm just joking," I said. "I have no idea." (I'm embarrassed to admit that I actually did have an idea. I had had better calamari with aioli sauce in at least two other places in the East Village.)

Lorena tried her best to follow as the conversation turned to the usual Manhattan banter in which people argued about cupcakes from Magnolia Bakery compared to those from Fat Witch, Korean barbecue versus Japanese Yakiniku, the best route to J.F.K., the temporary exhibit space at the Whitney versus the MoMA, how best to manage the taxicab medallion system. For her part, Marissa argued passionately for a vegan restaurant in TriBeCa.

Despite the noise and the cramped space and the translation problems with Lorena, I enjoyed our dinner and how the conversation made me feel if not hip, at least informed. To us, these opinions were the Rolex watches of millennial New York. We'd worked hard for them and wanted to show them off. After all, what good is a fancy watch hidden under the sleeve? But then something happened that really startled me. Just as dinner was coming to an end, Tyler said, "OK, let's go," then dropped two one-hundred-dollar bills on the table.

"Umm, don't we want to wait for the check?" I said.

"Nah. That dude will take forever to come back to us. He sucks." While Tyler helped Lorena and then Marissa with their coats, I wondered, if the waiter sucked, why would you leave him what was probably an enormous tip? And since when had people in New York—or at least Tyler—become too obnoxiously busy, too obnoxiously rich, to wait for the bill?

"Let's go to Bowery Bar," he said as we walked out on the sidewalk.

"Actually," I said, "what about something different?" Marissa and Tyler stared at me, confused. "You know, something new."

"I guess we could go to Zoe. . . ."

"I dunno," I said. "It's windy. We could make a kite and try to fly it from some rooftop or something." I knew this came out of left field: in New York you either pay for entertainment or you meet people for drinks and dinner. (If you know someone really well, you risk being seen in daylight and meet for brunch.)

"Dude, we are not making a kite," Tyler said. "Let's just go to the Bowery."

"No, really. Flying a kite could be amazing. Come on. Worst case, it doesn't fly."

"I think they want to get a drink," Lorena said.

"OK, we don't have to make it. We can buy it. I think Kmart at Astor Place might still be open."

"Whatever you like," Marissa said to Tyler. Reluctantly, he agreed.

We slipped into Kmart just before it closed. While the others waited by the door, I ran to the toy section and grabbed a Spider-Man kite and a spool of string. When I returned, triumphant, holding both above my head, I found Tyler on his cell phone and Marissa checking her BlackBerry. Lorena just looked nervous. "Sergio!" Tyler was saying. "Where are you guys?"

"So," I said as we walked outside, "I was thinking we can get to the top of—"

"Hey, Alex," Tyler said, without hanging up his phone, "I think we're going to peel off."

"Oh," I said.

"Maybe we'll catch up later. How long do you think you'll be flying your kite for?"

"Not sure," I said. I didn't like the way he said *your kite*.

"That was really fun," Tyler said before turning back to his phone. "Serg, I'll call a car. We'll be there in seven minutes."

"Yeah, it was fun," I said as we all hugged and kissed good-bye.

Lorena and I walked slowly west toward Broadway. I felt like I needed to take a long shower. What had I ever found appealing about him? I thought. In college, he had seemed to have an active, mischievous mind, but now he just seemed like a run-of-the-mill asshole.

"Are you sure you don't want to go with them?" she said. "We could still—"

"I'm sure," I said.

After turning north on Broadway, we stopped in front of a nondescript office building. "Let's try this one," I said. Inside, we found a security guard behind a podium reading the *New York Daily News*.

"Excuse me," I said. "I know this is a strange question, but my girlfriend and I have a kite and were looking for a roof . . ."

"No way, man," he said before turning a page of his paper.

Back on the street, Lorena again suggested we reconsider. "You sure you don't want to catch up with Tyler?" she said. "Or we could just go home."

"Let's keep trying," I said. We walked another block or two in search of a building that seemed open. "Do you think New York attracts people like Tyler, or does it just turn them into him?"

"What do you mean? I think Tyler is a gentleman." I realized Lorena had missed much of the subtext of the evening, not that the actual text was all that great.

"Well, there is something about this city," I said. "Maybe it's the density. You know, rent is so expensive that you have to maximize every square foot. So you get tiny apartments, tiny restaurant tables, and businesses that demand their employees create as much revenue as possible—per square foot."

"Not sure," she said, "but I think he can do much better than Marissa." I had no idea if he could or couldn't, but Lorena and I were clearly speaking past each other. I stopped in front of another building. "Maybe this one," I said. Inside, a security guard sat at a desk and stared at some black-and-white video monitors.

"Just left some papers," I said as we walked past him to the elevators. He waved without looking up. Evidently, not many people tried to sneak onto the roof of this medium-sized office building on Wednesday nights. We stepped into the elevator. The top floors, twenty-five and twenty-six, required a key, but not the twenty-fourth. I pressed twenty-four.

"This isn't a good idea," Lorena said.

"I think it is," I said.

The elevator opened in front of the wooden doors of what appeared to be a law firm. We found the emergency exit stairs and walked right past the doors to the twenty-fifth and twenty-sixth floors. Arriving at what would have been the twenty-seventh floor, we found a door propped open. Cigarette butts were strewn across the floor. We opened the door and stepped outside to a large, flat roof with big steel boxes of mechanical equipment scattered about. The building was a peculiar height: tall enough to muffle the street sounds below, but with other buildings towering around us, not tall enough to offer any kind of long-distance cityscape. Carefully, we walked to the edge, where a low wall gave only a marginal feeling of safety.

I set up the kite and, holding it up, slowly let out string. Catching a gust, it soared. First, up ten stories. Then down five. Then up another fifteen.

"It's working!" I said. The kite flew around the corner of a building, and just when we thought we'd never see it again, it swung back around. The kite was beautiful and incongruous: a frivolous piece of plastic floating, unnoticed, through a valley of office buildings full of analysts and attorneys tweaking Excel models and purchase agreements late into the night.

Lorena put her arm around my waist. I rested my head on hers. But just as quickly as the wind picked up, it died. Spidey fell limply down the side of the building. I started to wind up the string, but the kite must have gotten snagged on something. I gave it a little tug, only to find myself holding a long piece of limp string.

Back downstairs, I called Tyler to see where he'd ended up. The call went straight to voice mail.

Now, lying on the top bunk in my cabin, halfway to Woleai aboard the *Microspirit*, I wondered how I'd allowed myself to spend five years jockeying for space in a city teeming with Tylers. What had I hoped to learn the fifth year that I'd somehow missed in years one through four? Was it just to add more to my collection of opinions? So I could spout off about the best bagels in the city in addition to the best brownies? At first, I thought New York was to blame. I'd been sucked in. After all, how could anyone stand up to the colossus that is New York City? But I was the one who had moved to New York, who had moved into an apartment I couldn't afford, who'd started a relationship I couldn't commit to. I was the one who'd made time for Tyler and his various girlfriends, all so I could feel I was in a club whose members whiled away their days—or at least evenings—in the lavender-scented bath of their own opinions. Thinking back to the person I was in New York, or to the person I almost became, I didn't know what to do. Except wince.

When the rain let up, I worked my way to the bridge of the ship and introduced myself to the captain. He was about sixty years old and heavyset with focused dark brown eyes. To thank him for having me on board, I gave him a pack of cigarettes. He nodded and put them on the dash, then turned to face the sea. Huge waves swept the bow at an angle, forcing him to turn the wheel constantly just to maintain a straight heading. He looked about as serious as a sea captain can look in shorts.

I asked him how long he'd been the captain of the *Microspirit*.

"Thirty years," he said without turning to me.

"Seems like a good ship," I said, lying.

"A great ship," he corrected. "Seven hundred and ninety tons but only a hundred and seventy-eight feet long." I just nodded, my nautical ratios not being what they used to be.

"Has anything, you know, exciting ever happened on board?" I said. Before leaving New York, my mother had forwarded me a long article about the rise of piracy in the western Pacific. Ships were now arming themselves with guards and high-powered water cannons.

"No," he said. The hull shuddered as a large wave hit the boat's starboard side, which is, technically speaking, the right side.

"What about pirates? You see many of those?" I said, straining to sound casual. He didn't respond. He must not have heard. "Ever had any trouble with—"

"No," he said.

"So probably no need for water cannons and such . . ."

He turned, looking me in the eye for the first time since I'd given him the cigarettes, and said, very slowly so I would understand every word, "We used a sextant for navigation until 1985."

"What would you do if it was cloudy?" I said.

"Hope," he said, "and wait." I nodded in agreement, those being two things I'd become very good at.

CHAPTER 19

What You Can Expect to Learn in This Chapter:

► You will have about an hour to decide whether you want to stay on each island potentially forever and ever. But the more islands you visit, the fewer choices you will have. How do you decide?

► When inhaled as part of a cigarette, what section of the newspaper tastes the best? (Hint: not the classifieds.)

A s the dinghy sped toward the *Microspirit*'s first stop, the island of Ulithi, the dark blue of the open ocean lost its color one pixel at a time before finally turning almost clear. Fish flashed away, sliding under coral or disappearing into the sun's glare. The bay in the center of the atoll was huge, miles across, and made the surrounding islands seem slim and distant. Most of all, though, I was struck by the islands' tiny size. They looked even smaller up close than they had from the boat. In fact, all the islands of Yap, hundreds of islets both inhabited and uninhabited, add up to only forty-five square miles. By way of comparison, that's about the same size as Johnston Atoll, the island group that Fermi's colleagues at the U.S. Defense Nuclear Agency felt compelled to remove from the earth just, you know, to see what would happen.

Approaching my first outer island and potentially my home for the rest of my life, I was about as nervous as I'd ever been. I looked over at Chief Chuck. His eyes were closed. As far as I could tell, he was sleeping. Even when the dinghy's fiberglass side scratched noisily against the crumbling concrete dock, his eyes stayed shut. I glanced back at the driver. His face suggested that a shredded hull was a standard by-product of proper boat parking. And ropes an unnecessary encumbrance while the boat bobbed about, passengers leaping onto the slippery stairs. Chief Chuck was the last one up.

As I found my land legs, I noticed only men were there to meet us, and they came without ceremony: men slumped in the back of trucks, men under trees, men leaning against a faded yellow bulldozer stripped of treads or wheels. Half a dozen pickups were parked near the dock, some old and silent, others shiny and new with doors open, stereos thumping with competing rap beats that contrasted awkwardly with the heavy stillness of the place. It looked much like the main island of Yap, except flatter, hotter, and rustier.

I looked over at Chief Chuck again. He stood alone and stared into the middle distance, thinking perhaps of his family in Chuuk. Or more likely, of his hair curling in the humidity. I kicked a fly away from a cut on my foot and walked over to him.

"Chief Chuck," I said, "you know many people here?" He didn't respond. "Do you think I should introduce myself to someone?" He gave me the slightest of nods and started walking. I followed him along a dirt path that paralleled the coast, the water just out of sight. Chickens chased one another in and out of bushes. A fist-sized crab dropped into a dirt hole. A lizard eyed us from the trunk of a coconut tree. A few side paths led inland toward concrete houses, their white paint barely visible through the dark green of the underbrush and a faint haze of smoke. In the distance, a few women carried plastic tubs among the palms.

We turned toward the water. Three elderly full-figured men sat in a loose circle on a patch of shaded sand strewn with spiky palm fronds. They wore bright blue *thus*, like mine. Chief Chuck gestured for me to join them. "Hello," I said, sitting. "My name is Alex. I'm just visiting." Maybe I started this way because the question of whether I'd decide to stay here was at the top of my mind. The oldest of the three nodded slightly. Only later did I wonder how I'd feel if, say, a tourist stopped me on the street and, before asking for directions, explained that he didn't intend to live here.

The flies were driving me crazy, attracted perhaps to the salt beading on my sweating body. "Yup . . . just passing through," I said.

I'd read that they spoke English on the outer islands for the same reason they did on the main island of Yap—the whole group having once been administered by the U.S. Department of the Interior—but the chiefs' expressions, somewhere between aloof and bored, didn't change. I noticed one of the men stared out to sea. Another watched the boys unload the dinghy far down the coast. The youngest, a man with thick cheeks and a graying goatee, watched a fly circle. At least half a dozen were circling his hairless calves as if they were shucked corn on the cob. Either his eyes were bad or he wasn't that interested, because his gaze lagged at least half a loop behind. I didn't want to be one of those blabbering Americans who can't appreciate a few quiet moments among men, so I decided not to talk, just play it cool. The conversation in my head, on the other hand, went like this:

ME: I wonder how old *that* chief is. Maybe sixty. Maybe a hundred.

ME: There aren't many birds here. I wonder why.

ME: I like birds. I don't love them but . . . Wait. Did that chief just change positions?

ME: False alarm. He just shifted his weight a little. I mean, all things being equal, I'd rather there be birds than there not be birds.

ME: Is that a crab in the bushes?

ME: Fuck it, I have to say something.

I cleared my throat. But sensing the commotion, the youngest chief spoke first. "Why are you here?" he said. His English was clear, if accented, his tone more confused than confrontational.

"Well," I said, "I know very little about your islands, and I want to learn more. The best way seemed to be to come in person. I hope I'm not a burden." No one responded.

I turned to look at Chief Chuck, but he was just watching me. I then noticed one of the chiefs was looking at my Ziploc bag. The cigarettes!

"Oh, I brought these," I said, and placed the bag on the sand in the middle of the circle.

They all smiled. "Are those Lucky Strikes?" someone asked.

"Yes, someone in Yap told me they're appreciated."

"Lucky Strikes," the oldest chief said, reaching for one. "Fantastic."

He clapped his hands and a boy ran out of the palms. They spoke in Yapese. The boy wore a blue *thu* like the men. His must have been the same size as mine because both ends dangled awkwardly around his ankles.

"We have something for you," the oldest chief said as they passed around the cigarette packs and twirled them in their hands.

A minute later, the boy returned with a cardboard box. Inside: a canister of Pringles, a green plastic Tupperware container, and a folded newspaper.

The oldest chief sent the boy away and opened the Tupperware, revealing a soupy brown liquid. White flecks floated on top. He took a long sip and passed it to me. It tasted like coconut milk, if that coconut milk had first been mixed with a squirt of rubbing alcohol and a handful of dirt. After the Tupperware was passed around, one of the chiefs left it open in the middle of our little circle. Flies, I noticed, struggled in its filmy surface. I started to feel sick—in other words, the perfect time to take up smoking.

The eldest chief opened the newspaper up. There was a mound of tobacco and a box of matches. "From Fais," he said. "They grow the best tobacco."

The youngest chief tilted the can of Pringles toward me. I took a short stack. Then, he ripped off a piece of the *Pacific Daily News* from Guam, tapped two fingers of Fais tobacco inside, rolled up the paper, lit it, and passed me my first cigarette since junior high.

I inhaled deeply. Smokers will debate the exact breakdown, but I think 50 percent of the appeal is having something to do with your hands, 25 percent the nicotine high, and 25 percent the controlled flame and smoke, both of which make you feel vaguely like an Aztec.

The smoke scratched down my throat, coating my esophagus with newspaper advertisements for used cars. I'd hoped that this moment might bring us together. Perhaps someday the chiefs and I would reminisce about these first uncomfortable moments and punch one another on the arm, as they imitated my first few puffs. In the meantime, however, they simply watched, their eyes heavy with indifference, as I wheezed and coughed and gasped for life itself. I felt like I'd been through a fraternity hazing, only somber and carcinogenic.

"Fais tobacco," the oldest chief finally repeated. "The very best." Finally, Chief Chuck nodded to me that it was time to head back to the boat. I gladly assented. Instead of finding my future home in Paradise, I'd found what, at first glance, felt more rusting and sullen than sunny and, well, unrusty. Perhaps Ulithi was both too far from and too close to the relative metropolis of Yap? In any case, Goldilocks style, I decided to take my chances and continue on to the next island.

CHAPTER 20

What You Can Expect to Learn in This Chapter:

► How sticky, exactly, is orange Gatorade when poured, by the gallon, on a set of sheets?

► In a boat traveling at approximately ten mph, how tightly must you tie your roommate's sheets to the stern to ensure they don't fall off? Can any human really be expected to tie sheets that tightly?

B ack on the boat, I found Chief Chuck snoring on his bunk bed, one hand buried deep inside his *thu*. The *Microspirit*'s mighty engines started up, sending a shudder through the boat. Not sure what else to do, I climbed up to my bunk with my anthropology book about Lamotrek, an island another two days farther west. We had several more stops before Lamotrek—including Fais and Pig— but my Lamotrek book was the only one I'd been able to find about the outer islands of Yap. I tried reading, but the heat of the little metal room, the rocking of the ship, and the academic writing of the book made it impossible not to sleep. A moment later, however, I was woken up by my first porthole visitor (not a euphemism, an actual visitor to my porthole). Apparently while I was onshore, word had spread that the *haoli*—the white guy—in cabin three had Pop-Tarts— frosted strawberry Pop-Tarts—because for the next few hours, I received a steady stream of pastry seekers. My bunk being so close to the window, the conversation usually went, nose to nose:

MAN: Hello.
ME: Hello.
MAN: Hi.
ME: Hi.
MAN: I hear you have Pop-Tarts.
ME: I do. Would you like one?
MAN: Yes.

I'd then swing down from the bunk, grab a package of Pop-Tarts from my suitcase, clamber back up, and hand it out through the porthole. The man—it was only men who visited—would then look me in the eyes, thank me, and walk away. Sometimes, however, they would linger to ask questions about my Pop-Tarts: where had I bought them? How much had they cost? How many came in a box? And so on. I'd try my best to answer, happy for the conversation and the culture-bridging quality of sugar and saturated fat.

One visitor, a slender man with long hair and in his early twenties, paused long enough to notice the title of my book: *Lamotrek Atoll and Inter-Island Socioeconomic Ties.*

"Lamotrek," he said. "That's my island."

"Oh," I said, "do you know this book?"

He shook his head and then asked to take a look.

"Sure," I said.

"I'll come around."

As I started to climb down from my bunk so I could properly greet my first houseguest, I noticed that Chief Chuck was gone. That was good news. Getting down from the bunk had always been a little tricky since it meant stepping on his mattress and, therefore, waking him up. But just as I stepped, I noticed that he'd left a nearly full open bottle of orange Gatorade on his bed. It was right in the middle, as though Chief Chuck himself had been transformed into a sports drink.

The side of the thin mattress depressed just enough to tip the bottle over. Within one second, all of the contents had spilled through the bottle's extra-wide opening. Before I could even make a plan for righting the bottle, a good quarter gallon of sticky liquid pooled in the center of his mattress.

I heard a knock on the door. My visitor. Shit. Flustered, I knocked over a suitcase on my way to the door. The suitcase, in turn, knocked over a half-eaten bowl of ramen noodle soup that Chief Chuck had left on the floor. Lukewarm, MSG-laden noodles sloshed into the dusty pile of the Chief's blankets.

"Welcome," I said, my voice cracking a bit as I rummaged around for something to soak up my messes with. "So . . . you're from Lamotrek?"

"Yes," he said. "My name is Isadore."

"Hi. I'm Alex."

I must have looked flustered. "Do you need a hand?"

"Maybe," I said. "Maybe." The sheet was the first priority. "Do you know if there's, you know, a dryer on board?"

"Give me the sheet," he said.

"Where are you going to take it?"

"Hang it off the back of the boat." He disappeared, returning moments later.

"Will that work?" I said

"Why wouldn't it?" he said.

"Did you tie it tightly?"

"Of course," he said. "It will be fine." Isadore then picked up the book and sat on the Chief's bare mattress, reading while I picked noodles out of the blankets.

"This map is no longer accurate," he said. "This coconut tree now belongs to a different family."

"Hmm," I said. "What about the villages? They get along now?" According to the book, Lamotrek's two villages hated each other.

Even though they shared a 158-acre island, they'd grown far apart, eventually even speaking different languages. War over women was common.

"They get along now," he said, "but there are differences between them."

"Between the villages?"

"Yes," he said. "The two villages are actually very different."

I was thinking about how we humans reserve our most serious hate for those who are nearest geographically, when Isadore showed me a photograph from the book. "This boy," he said, pointing, "he became chief. His son is on the boat."

"That's interesting," I said. It made me think of the Irish and the English, the Chinese and the Japanese, the Indians and the Pakistanis.

"If you go to Lamotrek, you should meet my uncle," he said.

"OK," I said. And then there was America's bloodiest war, the one between North and South.

"He has an octopus call."

"An octopus call?" I said, looking up.

"Yes. He is magic. He can call all the octopus in the area to his island."

"Is that so?" I said. Isadore wasn't smiling.

"Yes. He also can make thunder."

"How is he with lightning?"

"He doesn't do lightning," Isadore said, adding that he needed to get going. As far as I could tell, he was completely serious: he needed to get going and his uncle didn't do lightning, just thunder.

After he left, I went to the back of the boat. Amazingly, the sheets were still tied on, fluttering in the wind as though the *Microspirit* was declaring defeat. As discreetly as you can do such a thing, I hauled the sheets in. Isadore's system had worked . . . in a way. The sheets were orange and sticky, but at least they were dry, orange, and sticky. I got the sheets back on Chief Chuck's bed before he returned; he never said anything about them.

That night I dreamed I was inside an aircraft carrier and threw a rubber bouncy ball as hard as I could. It bounced off the walls, off planes, off tanks, and off random pipes before disappearing in the darkness. This was funny. Really funny, apparently. I woke up not just laughing, but laughing hysterically. I looked at my watch: three fifteen a.m. Still giggling, I glanced down at Chief Chuck. I could just make out the whites of his eyes as he stared up at me, no doubt—and not unreasonably—concerned.

CHAPTER 21

What You Can Expect to Learn in This Chapter:

► Under what circumstances is it appropriate to take a photograph of a woman while she is giving birth?

► If you give birth to a baby while at sea, are you obligated to name that baby after the boat?

After getting all *thu*'ed up in my cabin, I climbed down the *Microspirit*'s ladder and took the dinghy to our next stop, Fais, the island regionally famous for its tobacco. After a brief tour led by some local children, I quickly decided Fais wasn't for me. Though I liked that it didn't have cars or mountains of trash piling up, it did have a runway. I asked one of the chiefs if it ever held rainwater in the middle.

"No," he said, "no problems with that."

Before, I was OK with an island having a runway, but now, having worked so hard to get here, I didn't want to move to an island where a missionary and a plane could simply fly me away the moment things got tough. A runway would make life here too easy and uncommitted, almost touristy—if a place can feel touristy without any tourists. I returned to the *Microspirit* and ran into the Cargomaster. He said his favorite outer island was Pig, our next stop. Before he could explain why, a boy interrupted, speaking Yapese.

"Excuse me," the Cargomaster said, turning back to me. "A woman is having a baby. I should tell the captain." His tone was more matter-of-fact than panicked, the same one might use to say, *There's more mustard in the refrigerator if you need some.*

"Are we going to turn around?" I said as he walked away.

"Why would we?" he said.

I could think of a hundred reasons but just kind of stood there, slack-jawed.

"Check it out, if you like," he said. "She's on the top deck."

The top deck was the only place on board that I hadn't visited. Whether formally or informally, it was home to just women. But now with permission, at least from the Cargomaster, I ascended the two steep flights of metal stairs. There, I found two dozen topless women on a thick carpet of blankets, baskets, and coconut bundles. Most were dozing or chatting softly. Some sat with their legs crossed; others rocked from side to side with the boat or leaned against emergency rafts. I approached a clean-shaven man in a bright red *thu* who stood near the railing.

"Hi," I said. "Is a woman having a baby up here?"

He pointed to one corner where a dark green tarp had been strung between two posts at about shoulder height.

"Is there a doctor on board?" I said.

"I'm a registered nurse."

"Oh."

"Would you like some taro?" he said, peeling back the tinfoil of a paper plate holding a large portion of the almost inedible tuber.

"Umm, no, thank you. How much longer do you think before she has the baby?"

"Not sure. Probably a few hours."

"And you just happened to be on board?"

"I'm giving vaccine shots on all the outer islands."

"Well, does she need anything?" I said. "Can I help? You know, like, boil some water?" I had no idea what I was talking about, but just as I said the word *water*, I heard screaming. Several women stopped weaving and looked up. Two teenage girls in blue-flowered *thus* tiptoed toward the tarp and pulled it slightly down to get a peek. I wasn't sure why, but I got out my camera and took a picture of one of the girls as she walked away. She was looking toward her feet, her long black hair barely concealing an expression at once nervous and demure. You could almost see the beginning of a smile as well.

I loved the resulting photograph. Or I did, until a few weeks later when I read *On Photography* by Susan Sontag. Sontag is to photography what the *MacNeil-Lehrer Report* was to television: namely, a fun sponge. Photography, she says, is predatory. "To photograph people is to violate them," she writes, "by seeing them as they never see themselves, by having knowledge of them they can never have."

Oh, jeez, I thought. I'd only taken that one picture almost instinctively. But I also know that instinct is one of those words we use to describe behavior we don't really understand. I'd later look back and realize that, in a way, she was right. I did feel like I'd somehow violated if not the person, then at least the moment. I'd taken this young woman's photograph just as I would have taken a photograph of the Grand Canyon. It felt important, and I wanted to remember the experience. In that sense, it was like all travel photography, which, as Sontag says, converts "experience into an image, a souvenir." See? I could say, I really was on a small boat where a young woman gave birth to a baby girl on the top deck.

I later sent the camera home. Looking back, that was a mistake. Because of Susan Sontag, I have few photographs of my time in the outer islands of Yap. In fact, just a few dozen "exploitive" ones "soaked in pathos" giving the "appearance of participation."

After a few moments of screaming, the woman had the baby. The tarp came down and women calmly gathered around the two of them.

"Are they OK?" I asked the nurse, who hadn't left his perch near the railing.

"They're both fine," he said.

"Do you know what the baby's name is?"

"Microspirit."

"Really?" I said.

"She's at least the third Microspirit I know of." While there are worse names, at that particular moment, I couldn't think of a single one.

Late that night, I was woken up by the loud rattling of the *Microspirit*'s unfurling anchor chain. We'd arrived at Pig, one of my last chances of finding Paradise in the outer islands of Yap—assuming, of course, they'd even have me. I looked out the porthole from my bunk, expecting to see fire or lights. Instead, only a thin dark line of silhouetted palms, their fronds slightly shaking against a moonless, star-filled sky.

CHAPTER 22

What You Can Expect to Learn in This Chapter:

➤ How will you know if you've found Paradise?

➤ Are cigarettes really the best way to the heart of the Outer Yapese?

Around nine a.m., the *Microspirit*'s dinghy, the *Nanospirit*, whisked me, Chief Chuck, plastic containers of food, and a coffin toward the shore of Pig. In daylight, Pig certainly looked the part of Paradise. Palm trees stretched out over a long sandy beach, a few older ones even over the bright turquoise water. Waves crashed over a distant reef. Puffy clouds, as if drawn by a seven-year-old, filled the horizon. The boat nudged into the soft white sand of the beach, and the driver cut the engine. Pig, at least at first sight, was so far out of a *Far Side* cartoon that had I come across two sharks lying on the beach telling jokes to each other, I probably would have just stepped around them, looking instead to help the guy in rags sitting below a coconut tree playing checkers by himself.

As he was wont to do, Chief Chuck snapped me out of it. "Your *thu*," he said. Several of my half dozen ropey knots had come untied, leading me to reveal more thigh than I typically do.

"Thank you," I replied just as kids emerged from the forest of coconut trees and ran toward our boat. Soon adults emerged as well. Relatives and friends who hadn't seen one another in who knows how long embraced, kissed, and laughed. Having neither relatives nor friends for a thousand miles, much less on Pig, I started unloading some of the containers and baskets, grateful for a busy, purposeful-looking job. I'd finished just one load, however, before Chief Chuck tapped me on the shoulder and pointed inland.

Together, we walked in silence through a dense grove of palms along a faint sandy path. I could see only palm trees and the occasional chicken sprinting into the spare underbrush. But each time, we could still see the chicken peering back. On Pig, it didn't seem there were many places to hide. After only a few minutes, we approached a thatched structure set in a small clearing not far from the water.

"Men's house," Chief Chuck said.

"Men's house," I said, nodding even though I had no idea what that actually meant.

About the size of a small home, the men's house had no walls—just posts supporting a peaked roof made either of palm fronds or the dried leaves of the pandanus plant, a squat, spiky relative of the coconut palm. Nor was there a door for Chief Chuck to knock on, not that he was the kind to knock. Instead, he simply hunched below the rough thatch mustache that marked the roofline and walked in. I followed.

As my eyes adjusted to the dimmer interior, I could see a dozen children clambering over two dozen men, all of whom were dozing on the woven-mat floor. They formed a loose circle around a central clutch of older, plump men lying on their sides or propped up on their elbows. One of the men in the middle waved a small handwoven fan. Another rolled onto his stomach, the palm of his foot facing skyward, occasionally twitching at a passing fly. From the ceiling dangled shark fins, tangled nets, and Japanese glass fishing buoys. It was like being in a Skippers Seafood & Chowder House. Or Disney's Polynesian Village Resort. But with one big difference: except for their digital watches, the pink flowers in their hair, and wispy *thu*s, everyone was, essentially, naked.

The men's skin was a dark bronze, if slightly fairer than that of the women I had seen on the beach. And there was a lot of it. Like tectonic plates, the men's bellies and boobs seemed to be slowly colliding, the former oozing into some dark subduction zone as the latter gradually formed a new layer over the top. Here in Pig's men's house, I felt less self-conscious about exposing such quantities of my own flesh. I supposed that's part of what a men's house was about: a semi-private space, a locker room of sorts, in a place with almost no privacy. (If there was a women's house on any of these islands, I certainly hadn't been invited to it.)

I watched Chief Chuck find a place on the edge of this mass of men and sit down. He didn't gesture for me to follow, so I stood awkwardly, arguably the most awkwardly I'd ever stood. I'd just invited myself into these nice people's lives and, understandably, they had no idea what to do with me. Just before I turned to leave, however, a man on the floor made eye contact and smiled. Rising slowly with a tangle of children still clinging to his arms and legs, he introduced himself. "Hello, my name is Paul," he said, holding out large fleshy fingers. "Welcome to Pig."

I loved his sonorous voice, which was deep but gentle; he sounded like James Earl Jones, only speaking to a friend instead of, say, on behalf of the Death Star.

"Good to be here, Chief Paul," I said. Not wanting to offend, I assumed every man on the island was a chief.

"Welcome," he said again, smiling. He was at least six feet tall and had a broad, flat nose, slightly graying hair and a beard no longer than a pencil eraser. His short hair and short beard made me think his face would look exactly the same if it were turned upside down.

"Are you Eric? We heard a rumor you might be coming," he said with a warm smile that forced his cheeks upward and his eyelids into narrow slits.

"Umm. It's Alex. Yes, I was coming. I am coming. I mean, I'm here. And I'm thrilled."

Chief Paul tilted his head to the side and gave me a confused look before gesturing for me to sit. Being remarkably inflexible—I can barely touch my knees, much less my toes—I splayed my legs uncomfortably to one side. Chief Paul smiled at me. I smiled back. I looked around. The whole room was smiling back. Was it the way I was sitting? I wondered. Surely I shouldn't just sprawl out and start fanning myself?

Then I remembered the cigarettes. A bit frantically, I took all four packs out of my Ziploc bag. "I brought you these," I said, placing them on that mat in the center of the chiefs. No one touched them. Their smiles became stares as they looked back and forth between me and the Lucky Strikes. I worried I'd made a frightful mistake, not just in timing but also in kind. Maybe Pig was more traditional than Ulithi. Maybe I'd misjudged where cigarettes fell in that confusing continuum of things the Outer Yapese wanted and didn't want—gasoline engines were OK, but not T-shirts; electricity but not air-conditioning; fishing hooks but not fishing reels. Clearly, they couldn't stop all modernity from washing up on their shores. Or could they?

Chief Paul looked at the cigarettes.

"Wonderful!" he said, and distributed them in pairs to the adults. "We ran out of cigarettes six months ago. I don't think we've seen Lucky Strikes since the American GIs brought them during the war—isn't that right?" he asked an older man squatting alone in the corner. The older man nodded and stared at the cigarettes.

Chief Paul offered me a pair of cigarettes. I accepted and wheezed my way through both. The top of the men's house filled with cigarette smoke for the first time in six months and with Lucky Strike smoke for the first time in sixty years. The sun dipped below the crown of palm trees just beyond the men's house and half the room began to glow in a hazy late-afternoon light. The other half, however, remained deeply in the shadows.

With singed lungs, I asked Chief Paul about the shark fins hanging from the ceiling.

"Oh, a man from Korea came and told us we should collect shark fins and that he would come back to buy them. We have been collecting them ever since."

"How long ago was that?"

"Seventeen years ago."

"Seventeen years?"

"Yes, we are beginning to think this man from Korea is not coming back," Chief Paul said with a smile.

I then watched one of the chiefs give a handful of cigarettes to a boy, who delivered them to a small group of women who'd gathered outside. They secreted them away and disappeared into a thick grove of palm trees and pokey pandanus plants.

Chief Paul suggested we have a walk around the village, which was made up of a dozen thatched huts. Each stood on a raised foundation of white crushed coral boxed in by large, rounded gray stones. A clothesline had been suspended between two nearby palm trees. It supported a single yellow *thu*.

As we passed, a woman looked up from a plastic bowl of murky water. Smoke from early-evening fires of palm fronds wisped gently through the canopy above, while black chickens prattled below.

Well-worn sandy paths, marked with clean rows of bleached coral, threaded between each house, various strands leading into the interior. The paths were most helpful—despite the lack of undergrowth, the palm trees grew so thickly that walking between them would have been difficult.

"Chief Paul, thank you for having me," I said, before realizing he hadn't had much choice in the matter. I had just shown up.

"Happy to have you, Eric."

"Umm. It's Alex."

"No problem. Happy to have you." That made me feel less awkward, but I still felt like I was imposing.

The first path took us to a one-story church not much longer than a school bus, painted a light blue faded to almost white. A cross stood at one end.

"Church," he said.

"Church," I said.

Farther down the path, Chief Paul pointed proudly to a barely discernible clump of broad green leaves connected to the ground by thick stalks.

"Taro patch," he said.

"Taro patch." I nodded solemnly.

The fact that anything grew in this sandy, salty place was a bit of a miracle. Only forty or so species of plants grow in the Yap outer islands, making this ecosystem one of the least biologically diverse on earth. But that's only the land; the sea is incredibly rich. In that way, Pig was like a grocery store with aisles stocked high with the same few choices but with a nearly endless fish department.

"Does Pig have any, you know, pigs?" I asked.

"Michelle and Johnny have one. I can show it to you if you like. But let me show you the power plant."

A couple of minutes down the path, we came to the power plant: a few rusting solar panels, a cracked wooden box, and a wheel of loosely wound cable. I asked when they'd first gotten electricity.

"Nine months ago," he said. "The last time the ship came."

"What do you use it for?"

"Movies. Mostly to watch movies."

I asked if things had changed much since he was a boy. He stopped to consider. "No," he said, "they haven't."

I kept pressing. "Are you scared that some of these things—these cigarettes, movies, foreign fishing boats—that they will change things too much?"

"These islands are small. Those that don't like it can leave." He wasn't exactly answering my question, but he wasn't not answering it either.

As if to show that they knew changes were coming, Chief Paul said, "I want to show you the cultural hut." We concluded our tour at a small version of the men's house built near the school. He explained that students spent half their days learning reading and math inside the thatched schoolhouse and the other half in the cultural hut. There, they studied basket tying, fishing, and ocean navigation using the stars. I thought about what a cultural hut would look like in America before remembering we already had one: television. A communal cultural hut that not only shapes our culture but spreads it too.

"Chief Paul, what's it like living here?" I immediately regretted the question. What is it like living anywhere? And compared to what?

"It's OK, but sometimes you feel"—he paused and stopped walking—"alone."

"Really?"

"No." He shook his head. "I'm just kidding."

It took me a minute to get the joke: if there is anything you don't feel on an absurdly small island surrounded by family and neighbors, it's alone.

CHAPTER 23

What You Can Expect to Learn in This Chapter:

► What is the best way to tell the chiefs of an island you've spent an hour on that you'd like to stay, potentially forever and ever?

► Can you catch a marlin with a spoon?

fter Chief Paul retired for an afternoon nap, I went for a walk down the beach, only to be swarmed moments later by at least a dozen children. They'd burst out of the undergrowth and formed a tight, menacing circle around me. I was already a bit nervous around children, especially wild-eyed, potentially cannibalistic children whose eyes seem to say, "What are we going to do with him now?"

They must have sensed my fear, because as I turned my back to continue walking a coconut whizzed past my head. This is it. Just like they did to Piggy in *Lord of the Flies*, they are going to break my spectacles and make me into taro soup. Best case, my head would end up on a stake to warn others.

I spun around. Several of the children were laughing. I had no choice but to throw a coconut back at the smallest of them, only harder and with better aim. If only I had the guts.

Instead, I did what anyone would do under such trying circumstances: introduced the dizzy-bat game.

Done well, there is perhaps no higher form of humor than slapstick, and the dizzy-bat game is perhaps slapstick's ultimate expression. Here's how you play: you and your opponent plant your baseball bat on the ground out in front of you, lean over, and place your forehead on the end of the bat. Then you run around it ten times, so you're really dizzy, and race toward a predetermined goal, usually a Ford truck. This is an activity common at Little League and minor-league baseball games; it is popular because it's the only time baseball players, technically speaking, move.

If you have never played dizzy bat, I suggest you try it right now, but instead of a bat, use this book. Being shorter than a typical bat, it will induce nausea much faster (and without even reading it!). Better yet, get a friend to do it, because as my grandmother always used to say, "The only thing better than a good slip and barf is watching your friend have a good slip and barf."

Of course, I had a problem: no bat. But I had access to plenty of coconut fronds. I found two and stripped them to their stalks. After I pantomimed the particulars of the game, two boys, one of whom was named Harold, stepped up to the line I had drawn in the speck-led white sand. Harold, it turns out, was gifted with plenty of ambi-tion but not much balance. He spun around and around, then bolted straight toward the jungle before falling flat on his face. Harold rose again, this time even more determined, and flailed flamboyantly into the sand.

I laughed, perhaps a little too hard. Moments later someone zinged another coconut at my head, barely missing. I decided it was time to wander back to the men's house.

I took a seat and found two chiefs were in the middle of a debate. The topic: whether Chief Mike knew where to catch marlin. Chief Mike said he didn't want to tell Chief Tony because Chief Tony would go out and catch all the marlin. Chief Tony said that Chief Mike wasn't saying because he didn't know where the marlin were. Chief Paul, back from his nap, proposed a solution to the stalemate. "Chief Mike," he said, "why don't you take Eric fishing, and he can confirm that you know where the marlin are?" All nodded that this was a fine idea.

"Do you know how to fish?" Chief Paul asked.

"Not so much. Do you spearfish for marlin?" I asked. I thought my tone was incredulous, as though I knew one wouldn't use a spear to catch a fourteen-hundred-pound deepwater fish that swims at Mach two. But apparently that didn't come across.

In fact, I feel comfortable saying my question was the funniest thing the people of Pig had ever heard.

"No," Chief Paul tried to say as gently as he could without causing a spleen to shoot out to sea, "we don't catch marlin with spears. We use"—he paused to catch his breath—"spoons!"

"Spoons," the chiefs shouted. "Ha! Ha! Ha! Ha!"

"Very strong spoons," Chief Mike added, as tears ran down his face.

Delirious, Chief Tony added, "And with . . . and with . . . Ha! Ha! Ha! With sugar on top!!!!"

I really didn't get that part of the joke.

"OK, guys," I said in the same defensive tone I had used in junior high every time my clothes were stolen and set on fire in the girls' toilet. "Very funny, but the boat is leaving this afternoon. . . ."

"Ha! Ha! Ha!"

"With sugar on top!"

"Ha! Ha! Ha! Ha! Ha! Ha! Ha! Ha! Ha!"

Not long afterward, the chiefs dispersed one by one—to where I had no idea—until I was alone in the men's house with just one older chief who appeared to be half asleep. The *Microspirit* would be leaving in two hours, so I slipped out and decided to go for a swim, my first in the outer islands. Unsure how my *thu* would stay on underwater, I untied it and, wearing only my boxers, stepped into the turquoise-clear water, the warm sand squishing between my toes. Bright equatorial light reflected off the top of palm trees, off the white sand of the beach, off the surface of the sea. In the distance, a protective reef reduced the big waves of the open ocean to mere ripples. As I went deeper and turned to face the island, those ripples lapped the back of my neck. The tubes being no larger than a quarter, the little waves rolled, almost silently, up the gently sloping beach before sliding back into the lagoon. Perhaps inspired by the pair of frigate birds gliding overhead, I swept my hand through the water, feeling the flow of the warm water between my fingers. Meanwhile, at the opposite end of the beach, four children ran out of the woods, giggling and chasing one another. Farther still, two men slid a dugout canoe into the sparkling water and started preparing their nets for fishing.

In his monologue *Swimming to Cambodia*, Spalding Gray says we travel in search of "the perfect moment," and once attained, we can return home in peace until, in need of another such moment, we head out again. This was my first perfect moment in the Pacific. But I didn't want just a perfect moment; I wanted a perfect life. So I waded out of the lagoon, tied my *thu* back on, and briskly made my way to the men's house. The chiefs had reemerged and were again lounging on their mats, talking quietly among themselves. I sat down next to Chief Paul.

"Chief Paul," I said, "do you think I could stay on Pig?"

"What do you mean?" he said. All other conversation ceased.

"Well, the boat is going to leave soon," I said, "but if possible, I'd like to stay here."

Chief Paul looked at me for a long time, then repeated my inquiry to the others, many of whose faces now wrinkled and frowned.

"What do you mean?" he said again.

"If it's a problem, I can go back on the boat, but I was hoping to stay here for a while. At least till the boat comes back around. Maybe longer."

There was more serious-sounding debate among the chiefs, followed by ponderous looks out to sea. "If you stay here," he said finally, "you will not visit the other islands. The chiefs are upset the other islands may be disappointed that they will not meet you, they will not have gifts."

"I see," I said, pretty sure we were really talking about the Lucky Strikes and not me.

"The chiefs say you will miss Satawal," Chief Paul said, "and Satawal is a very beautiful island. So is Lamotrek."

I thought of Isadore's uncle, the one who made thunder. I'd never get to meet him. And I'd be sad not to visit Satawal too. I'd heard that a Japanese cargo ship carrying three thousand cars had once run aground on its reef. Though they lacked roads, the folks on Satawal stripped the cars of their taillights and batteries and for a month— before the batteries went dead—lit up their island like a Christmas tree.

"I'm sure they are beautiful islands," I said, "but I would like to stay here. I have so many books to read."

As Chief Paul translated, I watched as an older man picked pensively at the frayed edge of his handwoven mat. A fly leapt from the top ridge of a chief's ear to the eyelid of a nearby child. I could hear the name Eric amid the discussion.

"The chiefs have arrived at a consensus," Chief Paul said, and stood. "They said you can stay."

Without much time to think about what had just happened, I went to the ship to collect the rest of my things and told the captain I'd decided to stay on Pig. He only shrugged, as though white people did this kind of thing all the time.

"But you're sure the *Microspirit* is coming back?" I asked.

"We will be back," the captain said.

"On this trip or the next one?"

"Probably this one."

"'Probably'? What do you mean?"

"This one," he said, then added, "You'll be fine." His supposedly reassuring words did anything but reassure me. It was like when someone begins a sentence with "Honestly," and you start to wonder if every sentence not started this way is subject to reevaluation.

"You sure?" I said, but he'd already turned his focus to something other than the nervous tourist with too many questions. I went to my cabin to gather my few things and my bag of books but couldn't find Chief Chuck. I wanted to thank him or at least apologize about the sheets. It didn't seem like it should be hard to find such a big man on such a small boat, but, alas, I left without saying good-bye.

A few minutes later, the dinghy dropped me off again on Pig, but this time for an unknown duration. From the beach, I watched the *Microspirit* drift toward the setting sun, not sure when or if it would return or even if I wanted it to return at all.

For the record, that is a complete load of bullshit. But everyone wants to write something like that once in life. The truth is, I was terrified by the *Far Side* comic strip I was in the process of drawing for myself, and I desperately wanted that boat to return. As the old farmers' line goes: the difference between ham and eggs is that the chicken is involved, but the pig is *committed*. Right then, I felt very much like the pig.

CHAPTER 24

What You Can Expect to Learn in This Chapter:

➤ How do you explain why Communism ended?

➤ Is there anyone left on earth who doesn't have an opinion about Hillary Clinton?

C hief Paul walked me to my house, a thatched hut about twenty feet from his and his wife's. It was delightfully simple: palm timbers connected by panels of handwoven thatch. The panels were made from a thick matting of dried palm leaves and could be easily removed for more light. The roof, also made of dried palm fronds, came to a point over each end of the house, not unlike the bow of a ship. The whole structure was smaller than I would have expected. The roof, for example, was about the height of my shoulder, the door the perfect size for a short goat.

Chief Paul pointed to a silhouetted palm tree that arched over the house. "Usually we like to take coconuts off the trees that grow over houses. Otherwise, the coconuts fall through the roof."

Imagining the sudden thrushing sound of a twenty-pound coconut bursting through dry palm fronds, I asked, "What about the houses no one is currently living in?" (This one belonged to his uncle, who was off-island.)

"You'll be fine," Chief Paul said. I looked around. How many other people were going to tell me I was going to be fine?

"You sure?" I said.

"If you hear one coming, turn on your side."

I crawled on my hands and knees through the door. With the little light that came through the matted walls, it appeared the house was decorated in island chic: palm mats atop a crushed coral floor, a mosquito net, a few old fishing buoys, and three red *thu*s strung over the thin rafters.

"Dinner is in ten minutes," Chief Paul said loudly from outside, but the walls were so thin, he could have whispered.

"Just going to unpack," I said, knowing the statement was more aspirational than anything else. I stacked up my books and a pile of clothes. My last box of Pop-Tarts. I found a pen and my ticket sleeve. Right beside the palm tree, I wrote down my third Life Lesson: "If you hear a coconut crashing through your ceiling, roll to one side." I liked it as useful advice, but also as metaphor: if fate is sending something very heavy and dangerous toward you, try to reduce the odds of getting hit in the face. It is also a handy reminder not to build a thatched-roof home under a coconut tree.

Lying down, I stared up at the fishing buoys. I was glad to have a new Life Lesson under my belt, but what was I actually doing here? I had just pushed my way into this nice family's life on this nice little island. As I listened to the gentle clangs of pots and pans outside, I realized that Pig was just the latest in a series of places I didn't quite belong but had snuck into anyway.

I recalled my junior year in college when I wormed my way into a performance of Mahler's Eighth Symphony at Yale's Woolsey Hall. Tickets to the event in the stately gilded concert hall had long since sold out, but my friend Jessica was in the chorus. It was a big chorus—a few hundred people—so I figured no one would notice if I slid in with them. I rented a tuxedo and xeroxed a copy of her songbook. I even found a binder that looked just like the real thing.

I took a place on stage left next to the other singers—apparently, with the right uniform and a little confidence, you can work your way into almost any room. When everyone else started singing, I did too, albeit tentatively. By the second movement, however, I was not only singing but singing loudly.

Only later did I see how that performance was a metaphor for my whole education. I'd snuck into that performance just as I'd snuck into Yale, feeling unworthy. But at least for Yale I'd filled out an application. To be here, I'd simply mumbled some things to the Council of Chiefs back in Yap and waited for a ride. Which raised the question: assuming this was Paradise—and by all early indications it was—did I deserve to be here? What if everyone who was sick of their jobs in New York similarly washed up on Pig's shores? If nothing else, as Jeb would say, they were gonna wanna poop.

"Eric, dinner is ready," Chief Paul said loudly from outside the wall.

"I'll be right there," I said. Figuring I might as well play the part, I tied my *thu* on and crawled out of my new house and into the fading light of the Yapese sun. Chief Paul, his wife, Johanna, and I squatted together in silence for a meal of rice, fish, and taro.

I was coming to despise taro. It tasted like a starchy potato, but without the flavor. I remembered liking taro chips sold in glossy black bags back in the States. But now I realized if there is real taro in there somewhere, it's what the bag is made out of. As I helped clean the dishes, using a rag and a plastic basin of dirty water, I thanked Chief Paul and Johanna for having me. They both nodded politely.

Back in my house, I draped the mosquito net over myself and listened to the quiet shuffling and muffled coughs of my fellow islanders preparing to sleep. At exactly eight p.m., the island fell into collective silence, the only sound that of breaking waves in the distance.

When I woke up, I found a plate of cold taro sitting in front of my little hut. I managed a few bites, tossing the remainder to a chicken, and made my way to the men's house. As I ducked my head under the thatched roof, Chief Paul asked a question I could tell had been nagging him. "We heard that Communism ended," he said. "Is that something the Americans did?"

"Hi," I said. The chiefs, however, were anxious for an answer and just nodded. "Beats me," I added.

"But you're an American," Chief Paul said. "Tell us." I couldn't believe that more than a decade after the fact, I was really being asked to explain the fall of Communism to a small island in the Pacific. I expected Chief Paul to say, "Ahh, got you! We may be islanders but we're not rubes." But he didn't. More curious than concerned, he and the others simply flicked flies away, propped themselves up on their elbows, and waited for an answer.

"Well, the Americans would like to think it is something that they did, but Communism ended Communism," I said, finding a piece of matting to sit on. "You know how when you go fishing as a group, you do it together and then give the fish to your families." I couldn't help but feel condescending, putting it in these terms, but they seemed genuinely to want to know, so I continued. "With Communism, the government tells you that instead of eating the fish you catch as a group, you have to give your fish to the island next door and tells them they have to give you taro they grow. But you learn that either way they are going to give you taro, so you stop fishing." I wasn't sure I understood myself what I was saying, but several of the chiefs nodded politely.

"Hmm," Chief Paul said. Then, as if to prove a point that things worked differently here, he clapped his big hands three times, and within a minute most of the island—maybe a hundred people—had scampered to the men's house.

"This will be a community day," he announced. "We will clean the church." As soon as Chief Paul said the word *church*, all the assembled walked back to their homes to gather cleaning supplies. They didn't run, nor did they saunter. Just a steady, purposeful walk. Chief Paul turned to me with a grin: though he was a big fish in perhaps the world's smallest pond, it was good to be chief.

The only building on Pig with glass or concrete, the church seemed to be a delicately maintained source of pride. My job was to wipe the louvered panes of glass, of which there were maybe three hundred, without breaking one, as the closest replacement was probably in Singapore. Others were responsible for sweeping; another group, mopping; one team, for repainting the back wall. But like most communist work projects, this one petered out by eleven a.m., when almost everyone found something else they would rather be doing, like getting drunk or invading Poland.

When I went to put my bucket back inside the church, I saw a handwritten note posted on the door:

NEXT FRIDAY–DANCE!
We will be having a dance. You can do the church
dance or any dance that will make people laugh and happy.

After an intense morning, I took a short nap and then returned to the men's house. There, Chief Vincent pulled me aside. Chief Vincent was older than the others, and had bright light brown eyes and was the only man on the island who wore a yellow *thu*. I wondered what a yellow *thu* signified. (Turns out that *thu* colors weren't anything more than an expression of the bearer's preference and mood. Just like, you know, most clothes.)

"Do you have any newsmagazines?" Chief Vincent asked in a hushed voice. "Like *Time* or *Businessweek*?"

"No, sorry, Vincent. I don't." A few steps later I remembered I did have two old issues of *Time* and *Newsweek* at the bottom of my bag. But I hesitated. Like the Coke bottle in *The Gods Must Be Crazy*, a magazine might contribute to the slow erosion of a culture, not something I necessarily wanted to be a part of. On the other hand, they were just newsmagazines, and not *Us Weekly* or something. (Though it was kind of thrilling to imagine the island of Pig turned upside down by "15 Fantastic Makeup Tips from the Stars!")

As I watched the flies buzz in frantic circles, I decided I was being arrogant; it was not up to me. If they were going to preserve their culture, it was going to be an active decision on their part, not an accident of ignorance or geography. Anyway, I figured that global warming and rising seas would destroy their culture long before any magazine could, so why not give it to them? I went back to my hut and returned with the magazines. I noticed Chief Paul was back and was now reclining on a mat. I glanced over at him, holding the magazines up, and he nodded. I handed Vincent the magazines. He said thanks and stepped out of the men's hut to read them under a nearby coconut tree.

I was wondering why he'd chosen to read them outside the men's house when I noticed that a crowd of perhaps thirty had quickly encircled Vincent and the magazines, one of which he held open for all to see. I couldn't make out the specifics, but there was a lot of talking and pointing. I wandered over and, on my tippy toes, saw the object of their awe. It wasn't the Chinese rattling the Taiwanese. It wasn't celebrity gossip. Instead, it was an advertisement for a Chevy Tahoe, a two-page spread featuring a shiny silver SUV on top of a snowcapped mountain. They gawked at the magazine, and I gawked at them gawking at the magazine. Between the sport utility vehicle, the snow, and the jagged peaks, it was hard to imagine anything more foreign to the people of Pig. Nor anything more foreign to me than their wonder.

"Thank you," Chief Vincent said. "Can we keep them?"

"Sure," I said just as a teenage boy grabbed the magazine and ran into the bush.

"Do you think you'll ever see those magazines again?" I said as we walked back inside the men's hut.

"Don't know. At least I have a radio," he said, sitting down and folding his legs beneath him. I noticed he had the sinewy, strong legs of a man who has spent a lifetime in exceptional shape.

"You get reception here?" I asked as I found a spot nearby.

"Very good. It's a transistor radio. Short band," he said.

"What do you listen to?"

"Rush Limbaugh."

"Rush Limbaugh?"

"Yes, Rush. He's great. Have you heard his impression of Hillary Clinton? It's the best."

After a stretch of silence, I asked, "Did you know Rush Limbaugh met his wife on the Internet?"

Vincent scrunched up his face, though whether in confusion or disbelief I couldn't tell. "Do you think unions are making American manufacturing less competitive," he asked, "especially in the car and airline industries?"

"Well, I'm not sure, actually . . ."

"Too many lawyers, don't you think? Did you know the U.S. has one hundred lawyers for every engineer? Japan has one hundred engineers for every lawyer. It's California liberals who are making your country uncompetitive."

"Well, television isn't helping. . . ."

"Vincent is the only Republican on the island," Chief Paul said from across the men's house. "The rest of us are Democrats."

"Oh," I said, chuckling to myself that here, on an isolated atoll barely breaking the surface of the western Pacific, lived the world's last breeding Democrats.

"Do you think we could get your president to come visit?" Chief Paul asked.

"Well, maybe," I said.

"You and Mike could tell him where the marlin are. I bet he doesn't even know where they are," Chief Paul said, watching for a reaction from Vincent.

"Yeah, I'm pretty sure he doesn't know where the marlin are, but the boat will be coming back in a few days," I said.

"Eric," Chief Paul said slowly, "why don't you stay on our island? You can live with my family. Meet my daughters."

"It's Alex."

"Pig is very beautiful. You will like it here."

I searched his face for a smile but didn't see one. Oh, my God, I thought, his incredible offer is sincere. My gut said I should do it. I should stay.

"Chief Paul," I said, "I do like Pig and you have a lovely family. Can I tell you in a few days?"

"Sure," he said. "Just think about it. And don't listen too much to Vincent."

Lying in my thatched hut that night, I knew that this was a rare and special opportunity. After all, how many invitations to move to a small Pacific island and potentially marry the daughter of the chief can you expect in a lifetime? One. Perhaps two. But certainly not more than that.

CHAPTER 25

What You Can Expect to Learn in This Chapter:

- ► How do you know if the hunk of steaming sea turtle you've just been handed is undercooked?

- ► What month is cell phone etiquette month?

The following morning, as I had done for months when unsure what else to do, I decided to read. I found a palm tree and dug *Robinson Crusoe* out of my bag. Then I hesitated. Reading *Robinson Crusoe* in a loincloth on a remote Pacific island felt like a terrible cliché. Nor would it even honor the original story. To name one awkward difference, I hadn't been shipwrecked. To name another, people lived on Pig. And knowing the boat would be coming back soon made me feel phony and lazy, like one might reading *Moby-Dick* while fishing for perch or *Walden* while car camping. Cliché be damned. I decided that reading the progenitor of one of the world's most popular fantasies beneath an actual coconut tree on an actual remote island was simply too appealing. I plopped down under a coconut and started reading.

I quickly noticed that one thing that doesn't come up in Defoe's classic is the flies. On Pig, they are everywhere. They swarm your hair, they nibble on your ankles, and they land on the pages of your book. They don't give you malaria or dengue fever, but they do make you want to do something else, so I walked over to the men's house, where I came across a sight much more disturbing than a swarm of flies. Just outside the house, an enormous leatherback turtle, maybe five feet from beak to tail, lay on its back with a cable threaded through the top of its shell, through the center of its pale green stomach, and then around the trunk of a coconut tree. Nearby, a fire burned.

"We caught this a few days ago," Vincent said. "This evening we will eat it in your honor." While I stared at it, three or four children ran to me and said, "Let's play the dizzy-bat game! Dizzy-bat game!"

I declined but immediately regretted it. The largest of the children paced over to the turtle and started jumping up and down on its stomach. The turtle rocked from side to side in a futile effort to right itself. The other children then formed a tight circle, arguing about whose turn was next.

"Well, um, thank you," I said to Vincent. "But I hope you didn't do it just for me. You would have caught it anyway, right?"

"Depends. We get few visitors." Two adolescent boys ran over. One held the turtle down while the other sawed off the right-front flipper.

"Oh, God," I said. "Can't they kill it first?"

"Bad for the taste," Vincent said. "First, we cut off the arms and legs. Then we cook it."

I looked back at the boys just as they dumped the turtle on top of the fire. It landed with a dull thump, scattering ashes to the side of its cracked shell.

Am I really going to eat this? I thought as I watched it cook. Leatherback turtles are not only endangered but, worse, they're cute. I wouldn't eat panda stir-fry, so why would I eat barbecued turtle? I decided to just play it by ear.

A few hours later Chief Paul handed me a smoking hunk of meat, fat dripping on a plastic blue plate, and said, "Alex, the first piece is for you." The chiefs watched and waited.

Much later, when I told people the story of the turtle, it always seemed to generate the same set of questions:

"What would have happened if you had said no?"

"Aren't turtles endangered?"

One must strike a balance or *When in Rome* . . . , I'd reply, wincing at the clichés. Eating the turtle *did* seem sad, like a betrayal of some kind, yet not doing so would have been rude and insulting. Curious if I did the right thing, I later sent an email to the closest person we have to an expert on such matters:

> Dear Ms. Manners,
> I recently visited a remote tropical island where the local inhabitants insisted on killing and eating a giant sea turtle in my honor. I do eat meat, but not turtle. Should I have eaten it? What would you have done?
>
> Sincerely,
> Alex

I realized it could take months, even years, for Judith Martin, the columnist known as Ms. Manners, to respond. (Assuming she thought it was a question also nagging the minds of many of her readers.) A little searching, however, turned up an even better authority: Jacqueline Whitmore, president and founder of the Protocol School of Palm Beach.

Jacqueline's web site immediately made me trust her. Jacqueline is a blond woman with stunningly white teeth, and her lime green suit ("provided by Escada") perfectly matched the key lime background of the site. Her biography is, in its own way, inspirational. It begins:

> Jacqueline Whitmore is the Cell Phone Etiquette Spokesperson for Sprint and the founder of National Cell Phone

Courtesy Month. Jacqueline is also the Gift-Giving Etiquette Expert for Office Depot.

Ranking as one of the most widely quoted etiquette experts in the United States, Jacqueline has been quoted or written about in numerous publications including *The Wall Street Journal, The New York Times, USA Today.* . . .

I sent Jacqueline an email. She responded less than an hour later:

Alex,
I would have done the same thing. You did the right thing.

Best regards,
Jacqueline

I was smitten by the embedded symmetry of her logic. *I would have done the same thing*; therefore, *you did the right thing*. Because Jacqueline always does the right thing. Jacqueline created National Cell Phone Courtesy Month (July) and, apparently, Jacqueline would have eaten the turtle.

Dear Jacqueline,
Thank you for your prompt response. But I must ask, is it always best to subjugate one's own principles in order to *get along*? What if they had asked me to eat a human they had killed in my honor? There are limits to what it means to be a good guest, aren't there?

Best,
Alex

Jacqueline replied almost instantly:

> Alex,
> Although some local delicacies can be unappetizing (like monkey brains), it is still correct to partake in the dining rituals. We have to be ready for anything when traveling abroad. Believe me, you'll never be asked to eat anything that the locals wouldn't eat. I have learned to chase many foods with a big swig of wine or water! Have a Great Weekend!
>
> ~Jacqueline

There is much to love about her response, but my favorite part was, of course, the squiggle in front of her name, its curvy flamboyance. But what to make of the wine reference? Was it biblical? The washing away of our sins with the blood of Christ? That is, after all, the occasionally too handy calculus of confession: sin + forgiveness = Have a Great Weekend!

I considered responding that "do as the Romans do" is no answer at all—after all, the Romans had people kill one another for sport. But I didn't write anything. It would have been impolite, and Jacqueline was gone for the weekend, perhaps halfway through a bowl of Venezuelan monkey brains.

But, at least according to Jacqueline, I had done the right thing. The turtle meat, however, was still gross. The flipper tasted fishy and oily. Later that night, turtle grease beading in my stomach, I looked up at the buoys hanging from the rafters of my little thatched hut. I was still disturbed by the manner in which the boys had killed the turtle, but maybe I was also sad to see my screen saver view of the remote Pacific island vanish with just a few bites of turtle, a mere brush of the space bar.

I was coming to see some of the flaws with this journey: I'd naively hoped an island would be a place with clear boundaries, a place where questions of responsibility and right and wrong were as clear as the line between sand and sea. I'd envisioned a place where disagreements were short and rare because everyone had what they needed, a place without hostile work environments, or thieving politicians, or, for that matter, any politicians at all. In short, Paradise!

But of course capital P Paradise doesn't exist. Not on Pig or anywhere else. Try as I might, there was no deluding myself—not even way out here on civilization's periphery—that a place or set of rules could fully protect us from ourselves. No island, however small, could ever make a tidy universe out of the one we actually inhabit. Because even in its most idyllic setting, the human capacity to complicate life, to bewilder and enrage, to jump on the stomach of entangled megafauna, would never be diminished. Nor, for that matter, did I really want it to be.

Lying there on my mat, I could feel my understanding of life on the Pacific island slowly getting more realistic—and that seemed a necessary step toward actually making a life in such a place. I fell asleep, thinking happy thoughts about how it was a good thing that Pig was a little bit weird.

Of course, in the way of these things, it was about to get weirder.

CHAPTER 26

What You Can Expect to Learn in This Chapter:

► Classic slumber-party stumper: if you could have just one movie on a remote Pacific island, which would it be? What would it definitely not be?

► If you get sick out there, where do you go?

ust after dawn, I woke to the calls of swaggering roosters and the laughter of girls picking flowers from a tree right outside my hut. I wrapped my *thu* the best I could, but my stomach felt unsettled. Which is a huge understatement. I was about to have three-alarm, fire-hose diarrhea, and there wasn't a toilet for eight hundred miles. So I did as the locals do and squatted in the water on the side of the island with the strongest currents.

"Eric, how are you feeling?" Chief Paul asked when I entered the men's house afterward.

"Alone," I said. He looked askance before remembering his own joke about feeling alone.

"Have a seat, then. Join us."

I jimmied a board against a post. Despite my sun blisters, coral-scraped legs, cut feet, fly bites, and mysterious rash on my lower arms, with this weak impersonation of a chair, I felt I could have been in heaven.

I asked Chief Paul where people on the island went if they had a medical emergency. He looked around. Chief Mike and Chief Tony were lying on their backs, staring at the rafters. Vincent was picking the edge of a fraying mat. "Dunno," he said. "Church?"

He didn't seem to be joking. I nodded solemnly.

It was then that I noticed that none of the chiefs appeared especially old. Chief Vincent, probably the oldest, was maybe sixty. Chiefs Mike and Tony weren't older than fifty. Nor was Chief Paul. Thankfully, Chief Paul intervened before I could ask a follow-up question.

"Time to check the traps," he said.

Together, we dragged a dugout canoe into the water. The canoe was lovely—hand-hewn, elegant, and smooth—and fit two people perfectly. We pushed off and, kneeling, put our wooden paddles into the water. The temperature was somewhere between 72 and 75 degrees; the sun, having just broken through the clouds, warmed our backs, the only sound distant, crashing waves and the nearby dribbling of water falling off our paddles and into the calm lagoon.

As Chief Paul slid overboard to check the traps, I thought, Oh, my God, this, this is the Delta-Dream-Vacation-brochure life I imagined. But then I had a problem. I had to poop again. Chief Paul was right below the boat, so squatting over the side didn't seem all that neighborly. I saw him swimming toward the surface. I was going to ask him about returning to shore, but only his arm and the top of his snorkel broke the surface of the water as he dropped a fish in the canoe and then swam away in search of more.

I then remembered the Peace Corps volunteer who'd jumped out of a palm tree. What did he know that I didn't? If I stayed, how much time would pass before I succumbed to sunstroke, boredom, or a church-based health care system?

Chief Paul popped up again with just one other fish. "Not much luck," he said. "We'll check again this afternoon. Let's get back. I think the video is starting soon."

"There's only one?" I said.

"You'll love it," he said.

Back onshore, I spent some time in the current on the far side of the island and met Chief Paul in the men's house again. He was not alone: the entire island was gathered tightly around a television.

I later learned that the French foreign ministry had donated a bunch of solar panels to Pig about nine months earlier to help "reduce greenhouse emissions," even though their emissions were hardly off the charts. Amazingly, no one had bothered to tell the people of Pig that the panels were on the way.

"Ah," I imagined a chief saying, "someone sent us a gift. Wonder what it is. Oh, and look! There's a card!"

Figuring that electricity is useless without television, the American government donated a TV and an old-school VCR. But the people of Pig had just one video, which immediately evoked the slumber-party stumper: if you lived on a remote Pacific island and could have just one video, which one would it be? Turns out, the folks on Pig have their answer: *Gas-Attack Training Made Simple.*

Grainy and low-budget, this gem of cinematography by the U.S. Army features men in fatigues running into a cinder-block building filled with some sort of smoky-looking gas. The camera follows them inside, where we watch each soldier cough, put on a gas mask, and run out again. For twenty long, long minutes, soldier after soldier runs into the building, coughs, puts on a gas mask, and runs out again while a stern narrator repeats:

> *The poison gas is uncomfortable.*
> *Duty. Honor. Country.*
> *The poison gas is uncomfortable.*
> *Duty. Honor. Country.*
> *The poison gas is uncomfortable.*
> *Duty. Honor. Country.*

The audience was riveted. "Chief Paul," I said, "where did you get this creepy video?"

"Isn't it great? It's from my son," he said without removing his eyes from the screen. "He's in the American army. Stationed in Texas."

"It is great," I said, telling myself I wasn't lying since the word *great* doesn't have to mean something positive.

In some ways Pig seemed so up-to-date, but in other ways so far behind. And what they knew about (Hillary Clinton) and what they didn't (the end of Communism) seemed kind of random—as though they'd picked up whatever the currents happened to have brought to their shores or whatever Rush Limbaugh happened to be talking about when they tuned in.

During a lull in the action, I stumbled through a question to Chief Paul about the cultural future of Pig. "We must work hard," he said, still without turning away, "to balance the old ways with the new ways. Young people who don't like the old ways can leave." In the background:

> *The poison gas is uncomfortable.*
> *Duty. Honor. Country.*

"As long as we have enough people to sustain our population, we will be OK."

I then did the only humane thing I could and asked for his address so that others might forward a few videos along. He swore this address will actually work:

> Chief Paul, Pig Island
> Yap, Federated States of Micronesia

"And you're sure it's OK for people to send them?" I asked.

> *The poison gas is uncomfortable.*
> *Duty. Honor. Country.*

"Yes, Alex," he said, "I think that would be a good thing."

CHAPTER 27

What You Can Expect to Learn in This Chapter:

- ► When on one of the most remote islands in the world, what will you miss more than anything else?

- ► What is the relationship between absurdly expensive cars and happiness?

Before leaving New York, I had known I needed help. The usual sources didn't seem promising: I was too proud to buy self-help books and too cheap to pay a therapist, and I had spent too much time (twelve years) in daily private school chapel services to believe in organized religion. But being a businesslike person, I did have some faith in the power of economics. So, in a particularly low moment late one night at my office, I typed the following into Google: "Will an economist please explain to me why I am unhappy?"

After several articles about unhappy economists, of whom there appear to be plenty, I came across just what I was looking for: a study on happiness written by an economist: "Well-Being over Time in Britain and the U.S.A." by Professor Andrew Oswald from Warwick University in England. I printed out all forty-one pages and slid them into my coat. I didn't have the time—or make the time—to read it, however, until I was on Pig.

I wanted to continue reading *Robinson Crusoe*, but I also needed something to help me make a decision about staying; the boat would be arriving that afternoon. So after watching the gas-attack-training video, I went back to my hut, pulled down a panel of thatch for some light and began reading Professor Oswald's take on happiness.

Unfortunately, "Well-Being over Time in Britain and the U.S.A." wasn't as straightforward as I had hoped. For example, he writes, "There is a negative time trend, −0.0027, with a t-statistic sufficiently large to allow the null hypothesis of zero to be rejected." But as I read, I realized this study provided some context for my problem, and maybe even a prescriptive solution.

The first trick is measuring happiness. There are a number of ways. One is to record the occurrence of Duchenne smiles or what humans consider "genuine smiles." What is the definition of a genuine smile? Apparently, it's when "both the zygomatic major and obicularus orus facial muscles fire." The most reliable method of measuring happiness, however, is simply asking people. Luckily, every year since 1972, the General Social Survey conducted by the University of Chicago has asked fifteen hundred people how happy they are.

Self-reported happiness in America has been declining since the mid-1970s, and probably doing the same in Britain since Roman times. Though black men report being happier over time, all other groups have shown a decline, with the sharpest drop among white women. More than an *explanation*, though, Professor Oswald sought an *equation*. An equation for happiness. Because the University of Chicago also asked people a lot of other questions (marital status, number of kids, income, education levels, and so on), there was a lot of information to work with. After massaging the data, or whatever it is economists do with their data, Professor Oswald was, in fact, able to arrive at a statistically valid equation for happiness:

$$r = h(u(y, z, t)) + e$$

Not too helpful. When translated, however, this equation works out to:

$$happiness = \frac{material\ consumption}{desire\ to\ consume}$$

According to Professor Oswald's research, money *can* buy happiness. Statistically speaking, material consumption, such as buying a Ferrari, makes you happy. Fortunately for most of us, reducing what you want to buy also leads to happiness. For example, you could decide that you really didn't want a Ferrari, that they were cliché and tacky, that driving that fast would be more dangerous than fun, that women aren't smitten by men with Ferraris. None of that is actually true, of course, but if you believe it, your chances of being happy improve.

Professor Oswald also points out that the surest bang for your happiness buck would be if you could *increase* what you buy while simultaneously *decreasing* your desire to buy things. This seemed impossible, or at least counterintuitive, until I remembered Maharaj Ji, the guru who hung out with the Beatles and collected Rolls-Royces he never started. Perhaps he'd understood what Professor Oswald was talking about. Happiness might just well be a garage full of Rolls-Royces you don't want to drive.

Neighbors, it turns out, also play a big role in happiness. Though money makes you happy, it makes you even happier if you have more than the dope next door. In other words, wealth isn't as significant as *relative* wealth. I wondered if this is what had driven me from New York: the (very strong) hunch I would never be richer than all my Manhattan neighbors. Maybe Professor Oswald had uncovered the mathematical logic behind "getting out of the rat race."

I tried to use his study to understand my chances of being happy here, on this sliver of island in the middle of the Pacific. I flipped back to the equation:

$$happiness = \frac{material\ consumption}{desire\ to\ consume}$$

It seemed that Pig, according to Professor Oswald, would offer a statistically reliable environment for the flowering of happiness. Here there was nothing to buy. They didn't have money on Pig, not even stone money. Perhaps enough time here would temper my desire to consume things, or at least reduce them to lower levels than they had been in New York. There I had found myself more and more focused on not only what restaurants I went to, but what table I was seated at. If I stayed here, I could learn to spearfish; I could invest in the lives of my fellow islanders; I could learn to love turtle, cold taro, and military-training videos. But it felt simply too remote. I wanted off the grid, but not this far. Being less than five hundred miles from a hospital, or at least a clinic, wouldn't be bad either.

That night I had another dream from which I woke up laughing. In the dream, I was watching a young man run up a set of stone stairs. He had his hands in his pockets. When he tripped, he fell on his face. This was so funny that I woke up. My stomach hurt again, but this time because I was laughing so hard. It was three a.m. The explanation was clear: I was the boy; the stairs were the island. Once again, I'd fallen. It was probably time to leave.

The next morning, I went down to the beach to watch and wait for the *Microspirit*. Sitting in the sand with little flies biting my ankles and wrists, I realized there was something that Professor Oswald's study hadn't addressed. I didn't miss mirrors, milk shakes, or even friends that much—or not as much as I thought I would. What I really missed was chairs.

Including the week or so spent on the *Microspirit*, I hadn't sat in a chair for seventeen days. People in the outer islands of Yap don't sit on chairs; they squat. They sit on coconut shells. They sit on their heels. But they never sit on chairs. It's not that they don't have the skills or materials to make chairs; they just don't want them, I guess.

My problem was that I'd sat on many chairs in my life and could easily imagine sitting on them in the future. Not to be a materialistic bastard, but seventeen days squatting on a coconut makes you reluctant to spend an eighteenth.

Professor Oswald would, of course, advise that I decrease my desire for chairs. "And what do you really want?" he might ask. "Something to sit on or the fulfillment of the desire for something to sit on?" I supposed I could have made my own chair, but who wants to be the only one on the island grandly sitting on a chair? Especially if you're white and all the islanders are not. That would not just look bad: it might even be bad.

Even if I made something simpler, like a stool, there was another problem: boredom. People in the outer islands of Yap drink, fish, and talk, and they mostly talk about drinking and fishing. I liked fishing and drinking as much as the next guy—probably more—but I also liked the possibility of meeting new people, maybe eating something other than fish and taro. More concerning, how many gas-attack-training videos would I see before I too started looking for my own coconut tree to jump out of?

Just as "you can't go home again," I realized, you also can't return to Eden, a life without microwavable pastry or makeup or that peculiar combination of the two, Ben Affleck. Nor could I pretend that all that has come before has not actually come. Once you have the experience of constant stimulation, convenience, and, most especially, chairs, you also have the expectation. I didn't want to go all the way back—to New York—but I did want to go a little bit back. In the *Far Side* comic strip I was drawing for myself, there'd be a guy and a palm tree but also, somehow, an electrical outlet.

I pulled out my ticket sleeve. Across the back, I scribbled Life Lesson four: "If you ever want to give it all up to live under a palm tree and read, don't do it. It's hot, full of flies, and without a single good place to sit down."

At exactly three thirty-seven p.m., I saw the *Microspirit*'s plume of smoke on the horizon. Within minutes, the island was aflutter with villagers preparing coconuts for the ship's crew, sweeping the men's house, and tightening their *thu*s.

Chief Paul saw me watching the boat and stood beside me on the beach. "So, Alex, are you staying?"

"No, Chief Paul, I can't."

He just nodded. Then I added, "I'll be back before that Korean shark fisherman," but I don't think either of us believed it.

I went to my hut to pack my things and left behind a flashlight, a fishing lure, a pack of cigarettes, and *Traditional Fishing on Yap*. Not much, admittedly, but I was out of Pop-Tarts and wasabi.

Back on the beach, Chief Paul wrapped several thick leis around my head. I knew you could buy these from vending machines at the Honolulu airport, but being given one here, by Chief Paul, felt, well, special.

I walked down to the skiff that would take me to the *Microspirit*. As I turned for a parting wave, about twenty of the good people of Pig gathered together on the beach. With no obvious leader, they simultaneously began singing a melodic hymn, swaying from side to side, as the *Nanospirit* whisked me back to the *Microspirit*.

CHAPTER 28

What You Can Expect to Learn in This Chapter:

► What business opportunity will you be able to pursue directly from your window at the Harmon Loop Motel?

► Where can you expect geography, destiny, and hydrogenated soybean oil to converge in a special, even magical, way?

With few people aboard the *Microspirit* for the return journey, I had a cabin to myself and plenty of time to read. The book that most resonated with me was the autobiography by Henry Adams. Adams too had grown up with good opportunities. Amazing opportunities. His father was the U.S. ambassador to England. His grandfather and uncle had both been president of the United States. "That there should be a doubt of his being President was a new idea," he wrote, oddly, in the third person. Despite his family background, Adams turned away from politics, instead devoting his life to reading. He read everything he could. He learned about the new science of magnetism. He studied phosphorescence, radium, and the kinetic theory of gases. He read almost all of the great literature written until then (1907), putting some time aside to teach himself Ancient Greek. Yet he also knew it wouldn't necessarily add up to much—he simply wanted to see life in "all its 'roundness.'" Fittingly, when he sat down to write his memoir, he called it *The Education of Henry Adams*. Because for him, education was an end—the end—in itself.

A few evenings after leaving Pig, I set down Adams' book and went up to the bow to wait for sunset. A blanket of clouds covered the sky. Either the sunset would be fantastic or a dud. There being no benches or chairs, I sat on the deck and leaned against the white metal gearbox of the ship's crane. As the *Microspirit* struggled up and over swells, rocking forward and backward, I thought about my stack of books mildewing back in my cabin. I'd dragged them out here for the potential wisdom they promised, but now I could see it was also for the cover they offered: go to the Pacific for an indeterminate amount of time and you're an oaf, but go with a stack of books and you're a pilgrim. Or, at least, a curious oaf.

Fine for Henry Adams to devote his life to education, but my education was feeling pretty thin at the moment. I hardly knew a thing about magnetism and my Ancient Greek was rusty at best. In fact, at the age of twenty-eight, halfway between Pig and Yap, I knew only two things for sure: 1) I didn't want to run an Internet company, and 2) chairs are really important to me.

When the sun went down, it simply got dark. If there was a moonrise behind the clouds, I missed it. I went to my cabin, admitting to myself that I simply didn't know what kind of life I wanted to live. Only later did I see how that admission was the first step toward actually knowing.

Meanwhile, I had a pressing problem: where to go next? Most folks would have headed back to the island of Manhattan. And I knew that with a few anecdote-laden conversations, I could slide back into my old life, probably getting a job doing something Internety. But I wasn't ready to go back. Postbubble, big companies were the only ones hiring, so in twenty or thirty years, if I was lucky and didn't offend the wrong people, I might be a senior manager at on online media company. Maybe even a vice president. But I was afraid to fall back into that old life, living in pursuit of things I thought I should want. Only now I'd just be more aware of it. And, therefore, more unhappy. Yap and Pig weren't the paradise I was looking for, but there were 25,993 other islands in the Pacific.

I went down to the galley for a late dinner and found Cargomaster sitting in the booth, reading a newspaper and smoking a hand-rolled cigarette. In front of him was a bowl of Spam and rice. The rice steamed but the Spam looked cold.

I sat down on the opposite side of the booth, appreciating the soft padding of the orange vinyl. He didn't look up. I asked him what he knew about Guam, the island I'd gathered was a bit of a hub out here. Perhaps, I wondered, it offered some of the conveniences I was looking for (i.e., chairs) but without all the stuff I was trying to get away from (i.e., family, an ex-girlfriend, soul-deadening career paths).

"Best of the outer islands and the U.S.," he said, looking at a piece of Spam that he was slicing with a spoon. "Good beaches too."

"Nice people, then, the Guamanians?" I asked.

"Nice enough. If that's what you're looking for." Before I could ask any follow-up questions, he stood and mumbled something about needing to "go weigh the ole coconuts." I hoped that wasn't a euphemism.

I am not one of those ugly Americans who, immediately upon returning from some remote place, heads straight to the Golden Arches. Eating at McDonald's in Guam would be akin to gastronomic imperialism, not something an eco-culture-conscious recovering yuppie indulges in. Unless, of course, that person is trapped. In some bizarre convergence of geography, destiny, and hydrogenated soybean oil, a McDonald's drive-thru happened to be located directly across the alley from my motel window. So near, in fact, that had I wanted to start my own fast-food restaurant, I could have offered a competing product directly to the passenger-side window.

For two months in Yap and its outer islands, I'd eaten mostly Pop-Tarts, Spam, taro, and a few slippery bites of sea turtle. So, as soon as

I set my bag down, I opened my motel window and smiled at the bored Filipina woman working the drive-thru.

"Long night?" I said.

"Yeah," she said.

"Do you think I could place an order?"

She shrugged.

"OK," I said, "I'd like two Big Macs and some fries. And a large Coke, please."

"OK," she said, totaling the order.

"Great. I'm on my way over." I closed the window, and then opened it again.

"Actually," I said, "can you make it a Diet Coke?"

I'd hoped Guam's population of 154,000 would be a perfect, Goldilocks-like fit: not too small—like the sixty or so people on Pig—or too big like, say, Hawaii's population of 1.2 million. What I didn't expect was that Guam's porridge would be so damn hot. When I arrived at the airport at eleven p.m., it was 90 degrees and humid. The smell, a moldy combination of car fumes and grass fertilizer, wasn't quite right either. Most concerning, I had an extraordinarily heavy suitcase and no actual plan. Shelter seemed a good place to start.

I thought it'd be better to stay in a local place, far from the tourist district, so I watched hotel shuttles for the Hyatt, Sheraton, Days Inn, and Best Western drive by. When I saw a battered van for the Harmon Loop Motel, I waved it down on the basis that no focus group would have chosen that name. I brushed some crumpled receipts and used napkins off the passenger seat and climbed in. The driver, who smelled of sour smoke, sped away without waiting for more passengers, probably thinking that there's a sucker on every flight . . . but only one.

"It's my first time in Guam," I said as we passed car-rental agencies, airline-catering offices, self-storage places—the usual scattering of off-airport infrastructure. "You from here?"

"No," he said, turning up the radio. Though he constantly turned the steering wheel 20 degrees in either direction, our heading remained remarkably straight. We didn't speak for the rest of the ten-minute trip, but I bet even today he still thinks of me.

The Harmon Loop Motel was nestled in a quaint shopping strip with that McDonald's on one end and, on the other, the evocatively named Ho Market. Inside, the motel had a well-mirrored lobby with a single green vinyl-and-wood chair. A little corner fountain gurgled almost loudly enough to drown out the sound of the motor that powered the gurgling itself. I asked a woman behind a smudged glass window if any rooms were available. She smiled and handed me a key.

"Do you need me to fill anything out?" I asked. "Pay something?"

"Later," she said, still smiling, "later."

My room had twin beds with matching black comforters printed with an explosion of oversized pink lilies. A small television with a twisted antenna sat on a small table. The dark blue carpet revealed the traffic patterns of previous guests: most walked between the beds and the bathroom and, to a lesser extent, to the air conditioner by the window.

I turned on the air conditioner and stood in front of it, sucking in the cold, dry air. For the first time I fully appreciated why Woody Allen once said, "Between the Pope and air-conditioning, I take air-conditioning." Sufficiently cooled, I opened the motel window and placed my order at McDonald's. I was an American, and apparently I was home.

CHAPTER 29

What You Can Expect to Learn in This Chapter:

► If you happen to find yourself in charge of a radio station that reaches two billion people, what should you broadcast if you want to avoid the competition?

► How much should you expect to spend on electricity a month?

The following morning, I woke up and faced a scenario they don't normally give you when applying for, say, a finance job in New York: it's seven in the morning, you're in Guam, and you have nowhere to be for the rest of your life . . . quick, what do you do? For me, the answer was . . . rent a car and have a look around my new home.

Within eleven minutes of waking up, I was signing for a white Toyota Corolla that an agency was happy to bring over. According to my map, which was illustrated with logos big enough to subsume entire counties, Guam was roughly peanut-shaped. I was near the capital, Agana, which, cartographically speaking, is in the middle of the left side. So I had to pick: north or south. The north end had a U.S. military base. The south had green cartoon hills and smiling Japanese girls on water skis and banana boats. What I found on the way to southern Guam, however, wasn't so much green hills and smiling water-skiers and banana-boat riders but the familiar ribbon of frontage-road America: AAA Car Dealer, Muffler Repair, Mobil Gas, 24-Hour Liquor, and evangelical churches in small metal buildings. And because I was sitting in early-morning traffic, I passed it slowly.

Farther south, development was sparer, with fenced vacant lots separating semigrand entrances to cinder-block hotels, pearl shops with going-out-of-business sales, and rusting warehouses with unmarked trucks parked out front. And everywhere, there was fast food: Winchell's, Denny's, and Dunkin' Donuts; McDonald's, Burger King, and Carl's Jr.; Applebee's, Bennigan's, and TGI Fridays. I'd loved my first Big Mac from the night before and loved the second one only a little bit less, but I was starting to suspect that Guam wasn't a lost canvas of Gauguin; it was Sacramento without the pizzazz.

I figured Guam's sprawl would eventually sprawl out, so I kept driving, farther and farther south. Eventually, the asphalt narrowed as I drove into the lush hills. Up here, the trees grew larger, and the air felt a bit cooler. For another ten minutes, I drove through the hills of southern Guam until, in the distance, I saw an unusual array of metal and wires. As I approached I could make out four giant towers—maybe thirty stories tall—each connected by a net of wires. These were definitely not cell phone related. They looked more like a set of braces belonging to a massive grinning giant.

The road ended at a gate. "Absolutely No Admittance," a sign read. As I turned around, the gate rattled open. Had someone opened it for me or was it just coincidence? Not in a hurry and curious, I drove down the smoothly paved road as it wound its way through a landscape of close-cropped grass and gently waving cypress trees. In the rearview mirror, I noted the gate closing behind me.

A mile or so later, this road also dead-ended, this time at a windowless concrete building squatting at the base of the towers. I parked in an empty parking lot. For some reason, I got out and knocked on the beige metal door. No answer. I knocked again. Still no response. I tried the handle. It turned and, Scooby-Dooishly, the door clicked open.

"Hello?" I said. The entrance lobby was decorated with a wooden chair upholstered in fading blue fabric and a side table. At the far end of the room, a hallway extended both left and right. "Hello," I tried again. "Anyone here?"

There was no response but I did notice, months after Christmas, a Christmas carol wafting out of speakers overhead:

> *Joy to the world, the Lord is come.*

I walked down the hallway and poked my head around the entrance of the first office, where I startled a man sitting at his computer. He appeared to be in his midthirties and had straight blond hair. He was exceptionally skinny.

"Hi," I said nervously, "my name is Alex. I was . . . you know . . . just driving by and saw the towers. I was turning around when that gate opened and then the door opened and . . ."

"My name is Karl. Hello, Alex," he said in a calm, reedy voice as he walked around his desk to shake my hand. He wore a light blue shirt and beige khakis with his shirt buttoned to the very, very top.

"I was just wondering what this was all about." I said.

"S.D.A.," he said. "We're Seventh-Day Adventists. How is your relationship with Jesus?"

"Umm, OK," I said. "It's OK."

"Well, let me show you around. This is a broadcasting facility," he said as once again I heard music overhead:

> *And heaven and nature sing.*
> *And heaven and nature sing.*

"Broadcasting facility?"

"We broadcast religious-oriented programming to Asia."

"All of Asia?" I said.

"Yup. To China, India, Thailand, the Philippines, Japan, and Mongolia. Twenty-six languages to half the world's population. What is it that you said you do again, Alex?"

"I'm kind of between things right now. You don't really broadcast to all of Asia from here."

"Sure do. It's shortwave. The BBC says we have one million daily listeners in urban China alone. Probably twice that in rural areas. We try to reach places that missionaries can't. Let me show you the map."

He stopped in the hallway in front of a world map with little colored flags—red, blue, light blue, yellow—planted in almost every country.

"We think China is a large opportunity," he said, in the same manner you might expect from a technology executive speaking to a room of stock analysts.

"Sure," I said.

"Let me show you the control room."

As we walked the length of another long hallway, I asked about the scary fence outside.

"Oh," he said, "the locals kept sneaking in. They like to plant weed under the towers." He opened the door to a darkened room, releasing a blast of cold air. Inside, I could see only a constellation of red, yellow, and deep blue lights. They sparkled the length of every wall from floor to ceiling, reflecting off the polished black metal of control boards and the glass of dark green digital displays that seemed to control every possible form of audio output. All the buttons were labeled—not just *treble* and *bass* but impressive things like *V-Lock* and *FX Sub Ret*. If God had a control room, I imagined it would look just like this—only without the labels.

Karl took a deep breath, momentarily mesmerized, then took a few steps backward and closed the door.

Joy to the world, the Lord is come!

"Umm, if you don't mind me asking, who pays for all of this?" I think I physically winced at the crassness of my question.

"SDA headquarters. They're in Silver Spring, Maryland. Let me tell you about how spectrum works. . . ."

While Karl explained something about radio waves and reception analysis studies, I was thinking, Silver Spring, Maryland? Couldn't they have chosen a city more suitable for a world religion? Some place where people throw rocks at one other like Damascus or Constantinople or Detroit?

Karl led me outside through a side door. The brightness of the light briefly blinded us. "These are the curtain antennae," he said, spreading his arms up and forward, like Moses on a very wired mount. "The reception is best at night when sunspots are less of a problem," he said.

"Karl, are all these radio waves, you know, good for you?" I imagined church groups for seniors coming here and pacemakers suddenly broadcasting the book of Genesis.

"Not sure," he said. "But I do know all of the buildings are lined with metal." He then directed me back inside. I gladly followed.

Repeat the sounding joy.
Repeat the sounding joy.

"No one has ever reported a problem at any of the other facilities," Karl said.

"There are others?"

"This is one of six. We have exact replicas of this in Russia, Europe, Africa, Central America, and South America. But this one reaches by far the most people." He next led me to a warehouse-sized room with what he said was a generator in the middle. It was green and larger than an industrial tractor.

"We got tired of power outages. In the event of a disruption this eight-hundred-thousand-watt beast will get us back up. You'd think if you spent thirty thousand dollars a month on electricity, they'd try to keep the juice flowing. But with this, we can be on air again in four seconds."

"That's fast," I said in a way that suggested I had a sense about such things. I asked Karl what they broadcast. I was floored by his answer.

"I have no idea," he said. "It's all sent from Silver Spring. There are fourteen of us working here, but not one of us understands any of the languages we broadcast in."

"So let me get this," I said. "Fourteen of you sit at the end of this island broadcasting programming you don't understand to two billion people, most of whom, I presume, you don't know?"

"That's about right," he said with a chuckle.

"Are you ever worried that they'll slip in some content that's—I dunno—naughty?" I regretted this question almost immediately, but since leaving New York, I'd decided to only ask questions I actually cared about the answers to.

"No," he said sincerely, patting, almost caressing, the generator. "Not really worried about that."

As we walked back to the front entrance, passing Karl's office and a poster of Jesus standing in a field of purple flowers, he stopped and turned to me. "Alex," he said, "are you a Christian?"

Well, I was until I found out how tasty they were, I thought about saying, until I remembered that in under four seconds Karl could fill my body with eight hundred thousand watts of Psalm 13 in Farsi. "Umm. Sort of." That was accurate enough. About once a week in chapel at St. Andrew's Elementary School, then later at St. Stephen's High School, I'd sung "Onward, Christian Soldiers." In case we didn't get that message, our football team was named the Crusaders. In an ideal world, we would have played against the Jihadists.

As I thanked him for the tour and his time, Karl handed me a Bible and an inch-thick stack of identical brochures. "Good stuff in there," he said, looking into my eyes. The cover was an illustration of a beach at sunset. In the sand were two sets of footprints that blurred into just one, above which was printed in elaborate cursive, "When you see only one set of footprints, it was then that I carried you."

I drove back up Guam's western coast, passing a sleazy assortment of adult-video parlors, liquor stores, and businesses with confusing names like Suzy Kim's Midnight Massage—"Open 24 Hours." And, I now noticed, a lot of churches. An *extraordinary* number of churches. (On this—and probably only this—I was right. As I'd later learn, on a per capita basis, Guam has twice the number of churches as the United States.) Driving past the Wild West Gun Club—not far from the Calvary Baptist Church—I wondered if way out here on civilization's edge, one could see the front lines of America's culture wars: Team Tulsa versus Team Vegas. I probably leaned more toward one than the other, but mostly I just didn't want them to mate.

CHAPTER 30

What You Can Expect to Learn in This Chapter:

► What questions should you ask before starting a solo guerrilla war against the world's most powerful country?

► What will David Sklansky's *The Theory of Poker* have to do with your search for paradise?

I was almost ready to give up on Guam, but there was one place I wanted to see first.

I'd long heard stories about Japanese soldiers who kept fighting long after World War II ended, but had considered them urban legends, or at least exaggerations. Now I read in a brochure that tucked into the hills of southern Guam is Yokoi Cave, named in honor of Sergeant Shōichi Yokoi, the Japanese soldier who fought World War II here until 1972.

Before I left New York, a former colleague had given me a book called *No Surrender*, I presumed half as a joke and half as a cautionary tale about what happens if you find yourself on one of these island paradises for too long. It's the autobiography of a Japanese soldier, Lieutenant Hiroo Onada, who fought World War II in the mountains of the Philippines until 1974. In addition to providing my fifth Life Lesson and revealing a little of what Sergeant Yokoi's experience in Guam must have been like, Lieutenant Onada had an amazing story to tell.

In 1945, a young Lieutenant Onada was sent to the island of Lubang and told to remain at his post until instructed otherwise by a superior. Not too long after Lieutenant Onada arrived, the Americans invaded the island. In the chaos, Lieutenant Onada and a few others retreated to the mountains, where they prepared to fight a guerrilla campaign to retake the island. Vastly outnumbered, however, they decided they'd be better off waiting for the Americans to remove their troops or let down their guard. So they waited, polished their guns, and searched for food—mostly rats, bugs, lizards, and a little rice stolen from local farms. Eventually the war ended, but the Americans weren't quite sure how to communicate with the few Japanese soldiers still holding on in the hills.

First, they tried loudspeakers. "Come down," they said through translators. "The war is over." That didn't work, so they dropped leaflets and newspapers from a plane. That kind of worked. A few of Lieutenant Onada's companions believed them and walked out. Lieutenant Onada, however, decided it must have been a trick, so he decided to keep fighting . . . alone.

With the help of those who left, the Americans learned Lieutenant Onada's name and dropped more letters into the jungle, but none was sufficiently convincing. One item, however, did make a particular impression: a package containing letters from Lieutenant Onada's family, including personal photographs. Lieutenant Onada's canny take? "The Yankees had outdone themselves this time. It's supposed to be a photograph of my immediate family but that man on the left is not in my immediate family. He's only a relative. I think this is just another enemy hoax."

More "poisoned candy" continued to arrive. Two-foot stacks of bundled newspapers. Interview requests from Manila- and Tokyo-based reporters. Transistor radios with extra batteries. Lieutenant Onada's own brother even showed up and called to Lieutenant Onada by loudspeaker. "That's really something," Lieutenant Onada thought to himself. "They've found a prisoner who looks at a distance like my brother, and he's learned to imitate my brother's voice perfectly."

Eventually, the world moved on: the leaflets stopped falling, and the local farmers grew accustomed to their eccentric, if well-armed neighbor. Lieutenant Onada passed the time—decades—gathering water, plucking bananas, setting up rodent traps, and, of course, preparing for the Japanese reinvasion.

Then, in late February 1974, a young Japanese hiker on a camping trip happened upon Lieutenant Onada. After what was no doubt a very long conversation, Onada said he'd consider coming out, but only if he received in-person orders from his immediate superior. Incredibly, his commanding officer was still alive, and a few weeks later, he arrived in Lubang and relieved Lieutenant Hiroo Onada of his official duties. The date was March 9, 1974—twenty-nine years after Lieutenant Onada first headed to the hills. Amazingly, Lieutenant Onada's calendar was off by only six days. After almost three decades, he'd caught only two fevers. And not once had he seen his own face in a mirror. Lieutenant Onada emerged from the jungle a hero. He met with President Ferdinand Marcos of the Philippines, appeared on television in Tokyo, and received high honors from countless other officials.

Right now, you're probably saying to yourself, "Um . . . this guy and those other straggler soldiers must have been loons." But Lieutenant Onada's sanity is proven by the way he concludes his autobiography with this tragically endearing assessment of his solo war:

> Not until I returned to Japan and looked out the window
> of my hotel at the streets of Tokyo did I understand that
> my world was no more than a figment of my imagination.
> I cursed myself. For thirty years on Lubang I polished my
> rifle every day. For what? For thirty years I had thought I
> was doing something for my country, but now it looked as
> though I had just caused a lot of people a lot of trouble.

At Sergeant Yokoi's cave in Guam, however, I could find little that was endearing, tragic, or otherwise. I'm not sure what I was expecting—reenactments?—but to get to his cave, you have to pass through a ticket booth and walk around a rusted roller coaster and under a broken tram ride. Then, up a short hill, you find not so much a cave as a little hole in the ground. I looked inside and found just a dusty patch of earth barely large enough for one small person to lie down in. A nearby sign said it was a replica since the real cave had long since eroded away. I followed the exit path, which took me to a little museum. As I read the diorama labels and between the lines of a history pamphlet, it was clear that Sergeant Yokoi had had an experience similar to Lieutenant Onada's. Unlike his colleague in Lubang, however, Sergeant Yokoi had actually gone insane, which was easy enough to understand.

I realized that this cave really didn't have much of a story to tell. Whereas Lieutenant Onada's experience speaks to the remarkable (and dangerous) ability of the human mind to see what it expects to see, this place showed only what happens when that mind becomes lost and disoriented. That and the optimism of a few Guamanian tourism developers—it costs twenty bucks to see a fake hole in the ground, a musty museum, and a broken roller coaster.

Saddened by the whole experience, I got into my car, dug around in my backpack for my old ticket sleeve, and wrote down Life Lesson five: "When considering sneaking into the jungle to single-handedly fight a guerrilla campaign, give yourself a minute, maybe two, to make sure that it's something you really want to do."

On the way back to my motel, I stopped at a Mobil station and bought myself a hunger-buster deal: corn dog, large soda, and ice-cream sandwich (total price: $1.19). As I sat in the car, air conditioner running, and chewed my corn dog, I wondered why I was still in Guam. Was it to honor some sort of commitment either to myself or others? If so, would I too return home in thirty years, look out a hotel window at a country I no longer recognized, and ask why I had caused so much trouble for so many people, including myself?

But I realized that unlike Onada and Yokoi, or even Karl, I could fly away from this island without too much shame or fear of retribution. Besides, I wasn't staying because of a promise. I was staying because of a premise: I still hoped to create an ideal life for myself in the paradise I still hoped existed on one of these islands. Granted, at that point, I wasn't sure exactly what "paradise" meant, but I was starting to see some of its contours: a community of friendly people, enough time to read (though not too much), plenty of sitting options, and not too many Dunkin' Donuts.

Before moving to the Pacific in search of paradise, I had actually thought about escaping from my old life by becoming a professional poker player. I'd always loved how poker forces you to understand people as well as odds, with the best players able to take both into account, though not always in equal measure. I enjoyed the way the game was all about risk management, about knowing when to go for it and when to lie low. I also loved how so many of the lessons of poker applied to real life. For example, in poker it sometimes makes sense to make a risky bet (but only if the *pot odds* are right—in other words, if the potential upside is large enough relative to the cost of the bet).

But playing professionally? A lifetime spent in a dark Las Vegas casino gorging on chicken wings while filching antes from drunken tourists didn't seem promising for the soul. Or the physique. So the Pacific it was. Yet the appeal of poker still lingered, and I had brought with me a book called *The Theory of Poker*, just in case.

The two divergent tracks, however, seemed to merge when I happened upon a brochure in my motel for the Dynasty, a huge casino on an island just north of Guam called Tinian. Besides being a small footnote in history—the *Enola Gay* took off toward Hiroshima from a large airfield there—Tinian seemed to be a pretty place with three thousand or so English-speaking folks. And, of course, one very large casino. Finding paradise on the island of Tinian felt like a long shot, but, as I'd learned in poker, sometimes long shots were, in fact, rational bets.

So I took a bet and bought a ticket. According to my itinerary, the flight was just thirty minutes. The proximity sounded perfect: I could live on a small, palm-tree-intensive island while Guam, with all of its myriad chairs and other conveniences, wouldn't be far. In other words, I could have my South Pacific cake and eat it too.

CHAPTER 31

What You Can Expect to Learn in This Chapter:

► Why did the Chinese Red Army spend $200 million to build a casino on a nearly empty island in the western Pacific? (Hint: not to make money.)

► If you write a book about searching for paradise that refers, however obliquely, to the potentially treasonous activities of a large American aerospace company, can you expect that large American aerospace company to sue you and your publisher or just have a good laugh about it before buying up all of your books so no one else can find one?

After landing at Tinian's tiny airport, I hopped in a taxi, the only one waiting, and asked to be taken downtown. "The casino, you mean?" said the driver, a Filipina woman in her midfifties.

I was indeed curious about the casino, but that was a place for tourists. I wanted to at least start off life here as a local. "Oh, no, just downtown," I said.

"OK," she said before placing a call on her cell phone.

At first appearance, Tinian didn't exactly fit the paradise screen saver I'd expected. Waves of heat shimmered off the wide cement road before being blown into the desiccated shrubs that seemed to cover most of the broad, flat island. In the distance, I could see the tops of only a handful of coconut trees—no doubt planted near the entrance to the casino. San Jose, the capital and only town on Tinian, wasn't exactly bustling. About half of the dozen or so concrete houses I passed were boarded up, though it wasn't clear the occupants of the other half were dying to get in. In fact, every man-made thing—from the cars without wheels to the leaning chain-link fence to the pier without any boats—appeared prematurely ruined, unable to stand up against a sun so bright or wind so saturated in salt. A few stray dogs lay asleep on the road or panted in the fleeting shade. Neglect didn't seem the right word since it implies a once better time. As far as I could tell, San Jose had never had it so good.

The taxi stopped in front of a motel, which, from its peeling paint and Art Deco style, I assumed to have been built in the thirties. "This is fine," I said politely, but the driver only nodded, as though to convey *Of course it's fine, you rube. This is your only choice.*

I dropped off my bag in a simple room and returned to the lobby. For the first—and only—time I missed Chief Chuck. How could I decide to live in a place where I'd never been before and knew no one? Perhaps I should just ask around, I thought. And who better to ask than the mayor? Fortunately, city hall was a short walk away, in what looked like a mobile home. It had a dirt parking lot with five spaces, though only one was occupied. Not sure what else to do, I just walked in.

The mayor's assistant was sitting behind a Formica desk. "I know this is a strange question," I said, "but I was thinking about moving here. Do you think I might ask the mayor a few questions?"

"Please have a seat," she said in a matter-of-fact way that suggested she'd heard this question five times that morning. She picked up the phone. "Hi, Mayor. It's Melanie. There is a gentleman here who is thinking of moving to Tinian and wanted to speak with you." I noticed she sat in a metal chair, a lovely specimen with four legs that dropped straight to the floor. It looked like the back might even be adjustable.

She turned to me. "He said to go on in."

Mayor Ignacio K. Quichocho was in his early forties and had thick, short forearms, puffy cheeks, and dark brown eyes. "Call me Ike," he said, handing me a card. I knew that people who give you a business card before shaking your hand should be approached with caution, but I kind of liked his friendly, have-a-seat way.

"Call me Ike," he repeated.

"I was just passing through," I said.

"Here, take a few more cards," he said, handing me a thick stack. He sat behind a desk cluttered with papers faded by the sunlight, which slid through the office's unusually high window. "Now, how can I help you?"

"I was just wondering what it'd be like to stay longer, perhaps someday live in Tinian."

"Tinian is a wonderful place," he said. "Palm trees, great weather, a close relationship with the United States. Just look around." He made a circular motion with his arms, taking in the entire sweep of the trailer's fake-wood walls. "Are you thinking about starting a business here?"

"Umm . . . maybe."

"Well, we have a great casino, don't you think?"

"I haven't been there yet," I said.

"Really? Well, are you interested in the garment industry? Tinian soon will be home to a model garment industry."

"You mean sweatshops?"

"Oh," he said, "maybe they're sweatshops—if the air-conditioning is down!" His body jiggled up and down at what I guessed was a joke. "Do you have one of my business cards?"

"Yup, got one." I smiled, flashing the full deck of cards.

"Good," he said.

As if to illustrate how far they'd come, he said that Tinian's last cattle-rustling conviction was in 1986. The coincidence struck me: 1986 was the same year the captain of the *Microspirit* stopped using a sextant for navigation—must have been quite a year out here.

"Cattle rustling?" I said.

"Stealing someone's cow," he said, adding, "We've been working on a zoning bill."

I'd never thought of cattle rustling as a zoning problem, but I was happy to defer to the mayor. He then went back to the tax advantages available to Tinian's future textile industry. I put down my pen. Being a small-town mayor on a small island couldn't be a fun job. Then again, being a big-town mayor on a big island can't be much better; either way, you're sitting through a lot of meetings about pension plans.

"This has been very helpful," I said at no point in particular.

"We are very business-friendly here. If you do decide to invest, let me know how I can help. In the meantime, be sure to check out the casino. It's terrific."

I thanked Ike for his time and stepped out of the building, temporarily blinded by the bright tropical light. While walking back to my motel, I noticed that the streets had familiar names: Eighth Avenue . . . Riverside . . . Broadway. They'd been named by U.S. marines who felt Tinian's shape resembled Manhattan's. As I looked at this salty, windswept place, more potato- than Manhattan-shaped, the idea now seemed an especially large stretch, not unlike those lonesome sailors who once confused manatees for mermaids.

The presidential suite in the Tinian Dynasty Hotel and Casino has a designated mistress bedroom. "How is it different from any other bedroom?" I asked Justin Roberts, the mustachioed American safety manager recruited to give me a tour of the best room in Tinian's $200 million casino hotel.

"No drawers," he said without a pause. "All the other bedrooms have dressers."

Apparently, mistresses have only one outfit: naked.

The three-thousand-square-foot suite felt like a P. F. Chang's decorated by Donald Trump. Door handles and faucets, side tables and canopy beds, picture frames, phones, and the oversized chandelier—all were covered in gold or, more likely, gold-colored paint. Most everything else was made out of porcelain or cotton. A good quarter acre of red carpet connected the mistress' suite to the two other bedrooms, the living room, the sitting area, the full-sized kitchen, and the office. And I couldn't help but notice the abundance of chairs. There were chairs in places you would never use them: in the kitchen, for example, and in the bathroom. Wandering over to the living room window, I thought about Graham Greene's *Journey Without Maps*. "If the hotel were silly," Greene wrote, "it is only because magnificence is almost always a little silly. The magnificent gesture seldom quite comes off."

I opened the curtain. Outside . . . an overcast sky, a broken fountain, and a vast empty parking lot. I could also see the other wings of the five-story hotel. By the standards of Tinian, the Dynasty Hotel and Casino was huge. Not Bellagio or Mirage huge; more big-city Marriott huge, but here, on this sleepy little island, the Dynasty felt like it might as well have been a spaceship.

Justin was saying something about showerheads when I interrupted to ask him if the Dynasty had poker.

"Not sure," he said. "Let's go find out." Justin had been assigned to give me a tour only because he was the only staff member who spoke English. Apparently, he didn't give many tours.

On the way to the casino, we had to pass through the lobby again. Accustomed to Las Vegas style, I tried to identify the Dynasty's theme. After all, you can't spend $200 million on a casino and not have a theme, whether that be pirate, Egyptian, or flamingo. I asked Justin for his opinion. He thought a moment and then said, "Shiny."

And no doubt it would have been, had the lights been on. The lobby—a huge, vaulted marble room—was lit only by the swinging glass doors at the entrance. As a result, the white marble floors, the white marble walls, and the white marble ceiling took on a sickly gray tone. Another theme could have been *smooth*. Every surface was polished so smoothly and furnished so sparsely, they could have cleaned the place simply by opening up a giant hose. Justin directed me to a large door marked, simply, CASINO. The room was cavernous yet silent. Completely silent. No music played. No coins clink-clanked into metal bins. Not even the dull thump of plastic *spin* buttons on slot machines filled the air. Instead, I was met by the sullen stares of two dozen blackjack dealers, none of whom moved in even the slightest way as we passed. Perhaps I'd figured out the theme here: shiny, smooth, silent, and sullen. The casino developers probably referred to it as S4 in meetings.

"They'll turn on the slot machines if you ask," Justin offered helpfully.

"I'm OK. Thanks," I said.

This casino was just . . . depressing. It certainly didn't lend itself to the ideal life I wanted to create for myself from scratch. On the other hand, should I judge all of Tinian by its casino? I wouldn't reject the United States simply because I found the lobby of Caesars Palace to be a bit tacky. (Though if I were to judge the United States based solely on the lobby of Caesars Palace, I wouldn't be too far off the mark either.)

Back near the front elevators of the Dynasty, three young women were squeezed onto a small couch in the corner. I hadn't seen them before. No wonder. All three wore matching beige miniskirts and matching blouses with a pattern of red flowers; and their clothes not only matched one another's but also the pattern on the couch.

"Are they customers?" I asked Justin.

"No," he said. "Officially, masseuses. But they're really prostitutes." If Justin had been given any talking points, he clearly had ditched them.

"Doesn't seem like there's much business," I said. They didn't look sad as much as very, very bored.

"Well, there's nowhere else for them to go," he said, directing me to an elevator. "They're brought in from China and the hotel takes their passports. They can't go back until they repay their airfare and agency fees. I want to show you the vice presidential suite." We stepped inside and Justin pushed a button for the top floor.

"But without customers..."

"Yup," Justin said matter-of-factly, "hard to be a prostitute without customers."

I was thinking about whether it's worse to be a prostitute with or without customers when I noticed the doors weren't closing and we weren't actually moving. Justin pushed another button. This time we heard a loud bang, then a crunch of metal grinding against metal.

Justin looked up at the ceiling. "I could show you enough safety violations to have this place closed in fifteen minutes," he said.

"Maybe we should take the stairs," I said.

"We can't. The doors are locked. Let me show you the barracks instead."

We left the elevator and passed through an unmarked door and down a linoleum-lined beige hallway. Out the back door, he showed me a collection of squat cinder-block buildings, where the hotel's workers lived. We walked around their peeling-paint walls, stepping over piles of trash and shallow pools of water giving off a peculiar smell. A skinny tabby cat dove into some dying bushes. A few men in white overalls squatted together, sharing the tail end of a cigarette. Overhead, a few sheets hung out a window, struggling to dry in the humid air.

"The hotel is being sued for not paying its workers," he said, adding, "It's a bad feeling when you don't have civil rights."

I later heard that the Dynasty was built with money from Hong Kong that had, in turn, come from the Chinese Red Army. Apparently, the Chinese government, unable to expand politically in the Pacific, was extending its influence economically. This would certainly explain why no one seemed especially concerned that this $200 million casino had no customers. Some years later, 287 employees won a brave lawsuit over back wages.

He walked me back to the lobby, where our tour would end. "And the women on the couch over there," I said, "don't they have any recourse . . . ?"

"Tinian's ex–police chief has them all living in his house."

"Is that legal?" I said.

"It is if you are the chief of police and they are Chinese masseuses." His circular answer, like Tinian and its giant, empty casino, felt as absurd as it did sad.

That evening I wandered into my motel's restaurant/karaoke bar to find something to eat and consider my options. The only other customer was a paunchy, bald man with a finely trimmed mustache. He wore a blue button-down shirt and sat alone at a booth, eating French fries one at a time, sweeping each one slowly through a puddle of ketchup. I asked to join him.

Turns out, Robert was from St. Louis, living in Tinian while working as a contractor for Boeing. I asked what that mom-and-pop commercial aircraft conglomerate was doing sending people out here.

"Installing radio towers," he said.

"Who for?"

"The U.S. government," he said. "For broadcasting Voice of America."

I looked around, curious to see who was tuning in. Our waitress was reading a paperback by the cash register. "Not here," he said, "but to China."

I ordered us both a beer. "Out of curiosity, how big is their electricity bill?"

"You ready? Three hundred and eighty thousand dollars a month," he said, shaking some salt over his fries. "You've heard about the Pentagon buying four-thousand-dollar hammers? This is where they send 'em."

"Good, if you're in the hammer business . . ."

"The hammers? They're peanuts. Boeing has a real thing going on here," he said. "After building the towers on Tinian, Boeing went to China to build towers for them. Blocking towers."

"Oh, yeah?"

"Yeah, they block the signals coming from . . ."

"Tinian?" I said.

"You got it."

"You're shitting me."

"I'm not," he said, sliding another fry through his ketchup.

"How do you know?"

"I was just there. I installed the jamming equipment." I noticed that Robert had paced his fry-and-ketchup consumption perfectly, finishing his last fry at the same time as his last dab of ketchup. Meanwhile, on the other side of the room, a drunk Japanese man stumbled in, went straight to a karaoke machine in the corner, and started fiddling with the buttons. I heard the first few notes of a familiar synthesizer-intensive song and the revving of a motorcycle engine, but I couldn't quite place it.

"What are you doing back in Tinian?" I said.

"Upgrading the towers so they'll overcome the Chinese blocking equipment," he said without smiling.

"Which you just installed?"

"Makes the four-thousand-dollar hammer look like a pretty good deal, doesn't it?"

I considered that he might be lying, perhaps making it all up. But then I remembered I'd approached him, and he didn't seem to have much of a motive to lie. I was about to change the subject to other Pacific islands he might recommend, but Robert excused himself politely, insisting on taking both of our bills to the cashier. I finished the rest of my beer alone while listening to a slurred, if fairly groovy rendition of the Eddy Grant classic, "Electric Avenue."

STEP 4

STOP BEING SO PICKY AND JUST PICK A DAMN ISLAND

CHAPTER 32

What You Can Expect to Learn in This Chapter:

► How will the spreadsheet program Excel help in your search for paradise?

► Should a high concentration of radiation in an island's soil be a deal breaker?

The following morning, I called my mother from the phone in the lobby. Texas was ten time zones ahead. She answered on the fourth ring. "You're alive!"

"Yes," I said, "I'm in Tinian."

"Oh, thank God. When I became a mother, I thought I'd never be relieved to hear my son is in some place called Tinian. Ha! Ha! Ha!"

"I went to Guam too. But now I'm on this little island—"

"When are you coming home?" she said.

"Not sure."

"Not sure?"

"Maybe you should move out here. To Tinian. They have a restaurant and a—"

"Fuck no, I'm not moving to Tinian. When are you coming home?"

"Well, I have a lot more books to read and—"

"You can read them here too. Lots of people read books here—"

The phone connection went dead. I considered calling back, but at $3.50 a minute, the upside eluded me. Instead, I took a cab to the airport, rented another white Corolla, and headed toward Tinian's only tourist attraction: North Field. It's the massive airfield known, if at all, as the last place the atom bomb Little Boy touched the ground before being dropped on Hiroshima. Having recently read Richard Rhodes' *The Making of the Atomic Bomb* back in Yap, I was interested in having a look around. I wasn't sure what to expect, but it seemed important to Tinian's past and, perhaps, its present. So before giving up on Tinian, I decided I should at least take a look.

Not surprisingly, I was the only visitor that day. Unfenced and abandoned, the vast network of runways and taxiways is open to the public, or at least not closed: you can simply drive wherever you like. I turned off the air-conditioning, rolled down the window, and passed by Bomb Pit #1, a simple concrete hole where Little Boy had been loaded into the plane. I then turned and started up Runway 16, the yellow paint still visible on the runway from which the *Enola Gay* had taken off fifty-five years earlier. I accelerated, imaging how the view compared to that of Colonel Paul Tibbets', the *Enola Gay*'s thirty-year-old pilot.

At fifteen mph, the support buildings passed by like a celluloid Möbius strip: row upon row of bomb shelters with doors hanging by a hinge; small sheds leaning at preposterous angles; abandoned buildings with faded gray walls falling inward, exposing an inner, twisted rebar. Sprigs of weed poked through seams of crumbling concrete.

Building this complex in the middle of a war had been a huge achievement, requiring seven thousand people to construct its six runways and eleven miles of taxiways. At its peak, a B-29 took off every fifteen seconds here. (Only one airport in the United States now approaches that capacity: Denver International's three runways allow one plane to take off every thirty seconds.)

At twenty-five mph, I considered taking a picture. But what would I do with it? I felt like one of those guys who dresses up in Civil War garb and spends his Saturdays firing blanks into the woods.

At thirty-five mph, a crosswind buffeted my car slightly. I compensated by steering into the wind. I wondered if Colonel Tibbets would have made a similar adjustment.

At forty-five mph, I passed the frame of a two-story building. Its outer walls had fallen away, its offices reduced to crumbling concrete cubbyholes. Maybe it had been the local command headquarters.

I thought of my father's father, Victor, and his role in the U.S. atomic program. His research at Columbia had focused on the dissipation of heat through steel and other metals. And in the 1940s, the government of the United States happened to be interested in dissipating a lot of heat.

At fifty-five mph, the sweep of buildings began to blur. For some reason, my mind went to the Holocaust Museum in Washington, DC, specifically the famous pile of shoes—thirty-five hundred in all—belonging to the victims of a Nazi prison camp. Of course, they represented only a tiny fraction of those killed, but it was a start toward understanding. Which was plenty. The idea of finishing, of actually understanding, was too terrifying.

At sixty-five mph, I could see the end of the heat-soaked runway. My car started to wobble in the deeper and deeper potholes. I knew my grandfather's involvement was a point of contact that could conceivably connect me to this airfield and whatever it represented. But it didn't. He'd had no idea what he was working on.

At seventy-five mph, I reached half the takeoff speed for the *Enola Gay*. This was one of the last places where things could have worked out differently. Here Colonel Tibbets could have made up an excuse—say, a warning light on the dashboard—and come down for a landing on what little runway he had left. In the time it took to dismiss the problem, the clouds would have continued to gather over southern Japan. That could have delayed the flight, since the forecast predicted a week of bad weather. In the meantime, maybe the Japanese would have surrendered. Or Truman might have had second thoughts and gone with Einstein's plea to drop a demonstration bomb over some ships in the ocean, just to show the Japanese what might happen to one or more of their cities. Or perhaps the wind would have blown the clouds over Japan out to sea, delaying the flight by a single day. In that case, sixty-six thousand people still would have been killed, just those who happened to be in Hiroshima on August 14 instead of August 13.

Finally out of runway, I stopped and turned around. I had no idea what this place meant. Nor, for that matter, did the U.S. government: more than half a century after the war, the Department of the Interior and the Pentagon still can't decide whether to bulldoze it or memorialize it. So it just sits, a sad slab of concrete slowly yielding to the salt air of the Western Carolines.

My motel's screen door slammed behind me as I walked down the nearly dark hall to my room. To reduce the heat, I closed the curtains, which immediately cast the room in a weird red-hued light. I stretched out on my bed and watched the blades of the ceiling fan twist above. I wanted to give Tinian a chance, but Tinian didn't feel like paradise. It just felt creepy.

All I'd learned so far from Tinian is that my perfect place wouldn't have mistress bedrooms without drawers—in my paradise, there'd be plenty of wardrobe space for the mistresses. But I could spend the rest of my life picking up such kernels of wisdom from each of the Pacific's twenty-six thousand islands.

Clearly, I needed a new approach. For months, I'd been searching for paradise as a tourist might choose between beach loungers: too much sun here, too far from the bathroom there. Those weren't bad ways to pick a beach lounger, but I'd never stayed long enough to get a real sense of the place. When the tide came in, I simply moved on. If I was going to create a life in paradise, I had to slow down and actually invest, even if it meant pretending for a while that I had a tidy reason to be there, that I belonged. Without the excuse of family nearby or a job, I'd feel a bit phony just moving to an island and settling in, but sometimes, to mix metaphors, like any good wedding crasher, you just have to pick a seat near the back and start chatting up the aunt.

But I still needed an island closer to the paradise I was seeking. After Pig, I'd given up on capital P Paradise, but Guam and Tinian weren't even paradise-*ish*. I knew rationally that only a fool thinks the ice in the mai tais on the Delta Dream Vacation brochure is actually ice and not just clear cubes of plastic used for the photo shoot. Yet there was a part of me that still longed for the ice to be real. Perhaps somewhere there was a magical island or just a hidden beach with its own microclimate where there are plenty of chairs and the ice never melts. When I went back to the Dynasty's business center and opened an Internet connection, however, I didn't quite know where to start.

I wondered if perhaps population size wasn't the problem as much as population density. After all, that was part of what made the island of Manhattan so stifling; with sixty thousand people per square mile, it had twice the density of Mumbai. So what I needed was a Pacific island with a low population density. Arbitrary, sure, but I wasn't sure how else to choose.

I pulled up an Excel spreadsheet and started cutting and pasting. In about an hour, I'd nerded it up and calculated the relative densities of every country, if not every island, in the Pacific. The lowest population density was Pitcairn, with forty-seven people on just 1.9 square miles. Forty-seven people felt like a concerningly small number, especially since you can get there only by ship every six months. Next up was Niue, with a population of two thousand. I thought that might work until I read that Niue is also nearly impossible to reach, and its soil is the most naturally radioactive in the world. If I had only those two choices, I might have been able to look beyond a little radiation, but I thought it better to keep going down the list. Third was Palau, the archipelago where the Yapese used to quarry the stone for their stone money. It had 19,300 people spread over 177 square miles. That meant Palau had about the same area as Guam but one-eighth the population. A little more searching revealed Palau had a protected wilderness area covering three hundred small islands, and that, having been a U.S. territory until 1994, the residents spoke English and would allow me, as an American, to stay at least a year without a visa. That could be extended to up to four years, unless, of course, I did something stupid. In that case, I'd be given twelve hours to leave.

By choosing Palau, I worried that I was being naively optimistic but after I read that Palauans were known for their habit of waving at strangers, I decided it simply had to be the place. I went to a travel site and bought a one-way ticket—the last, I hoped, I'd ever have to buy in the Pacific.

CHAPTER 33

What You Can Expect to Learn in This Chapter:

▶ Just because Palau and Ponape have similar names and are geographically close to each other, does it mean that the residents of both are famous for waving at strangers?

▶ Are maps, you know, all that?

With its three stories of concrete, peeling paint, and tinted glass, Palau's Waterfront Villa, my hotel, was villalike in the same way the U.S. embassy in Saigon circa 1975 was villalike: both could have used a little more water in the swimming pool, if you know what I mean. But unlike the embassy, Waterfront Villa at least had access to the ocean—provided you had some initiative and a machete sharp enough to hack through the thick barrier of mangrove that separated the hotel from the sea.

Anxious to see what the paradise of Palau looked like—I'd arrived the night before at two a.m. and taken a hotel shuttle—I went to the front desk and asked which way to town. The Filipina woman who seemed to be the hotel's only employee simply pointed to the door.

"Oh, do you have a map?" I said.

"You can find one in Koror," she said, referring to Palau's capital.

"Is that walking distance from here?"

"Not sure," she said.

"Not sure because it's kind of far, or not sure because . . ." But I didn't finish. She'd already started filing something, clearly uninterested in clarifying.

The hotel was at the end of a jungle-lined dirt road, and I gamely started walking. I only needed to take a dozen steps, however, to realize it wasn't the distance that gave her pause but the humidity. It had just rained—I'd learn it has always just rained in Palau—and I was so quickly soaked in sweat that I worried something might be medically wrong with me. I went back inside and asked the receptionist for a water bottle. She reached under the counter and, without a word, handed me a warm bottle with a ripped label. "Thank you," I said as she made a note of my purchase in a little pad.

Back outside, I began walking again, but the sun was already bright and hot enough to make everything, including me, move in slow motion. Though only nine a.m., even the chickens pecked around with a certain sulkiness, as if resigned to the weather as much as their eventual fate. I passed abandoned cars, then a dog lying on her side, a belly full of nipples. Her ear twitched in the dirt, briefly suspending a hot puff of dust into the thick, wet air.

As I continued walking, passing small houses with rusted tin roofs held down by discarded tires and houses built on tidy grass lots cut out of the dense vegetation, I thought there must be no greater barrier to prosperity than humidity. This place was so fertile—people "planted" fences just by putting live branches into the ground—but how could innovation flourish where movement itself was so difficult, where cuts festered and concrete crumbled? Yet, from first impressions, at least some Palauans appeared to be doing better than those of the other places I'd seen in the western Pacific. The houses were concrete and occupied, instead of empty and made of thatch. Even if through sun-faded drapes, I often could see large televisions glowing in many of the living rooms.

As the new guy in town, I decided I'd be the one to initiate the waving I'd read about. So when I passed women hanging laundry, young boys sitting near a basketball court with netless hoops, and two heavyset men drinking beer and working on a truck, I made a point of smiling and waving first. All smiled and waved back. I'd somehow expected that these waves would help me meet someone right away. I'd wave, we'd start up a conversation, and perhaps I'd be invited over for lunch. Or at least a snack. Yet the closer to the center of town I got, the lower my chances seemed to become. There were neither pedestrians nor sidewalks for them to walk on. As I approached the outskirts of Koror, I passed a modern-looking gas station, a Japanese restaurant, and a pink two-story motel. Traffic picked up too. So much traffic, in fact, that I was walking faster than the cars, most of which seemed well traveled: Toyotas without hubcaps, muddy Mitsubishis, dented minivans, and comically small pickups with Tonka-sized wheels. Though cars drove on the right side of the road, their steering wheels were evenly divided, with half on the left side of the car, half on the right. The only streetlight I passed was flashing yellow.

The downtown area, which wasn't more than a mile long and a few streets wide, had a scruffy, frontier feel that I imagined was similar to that of towns tossed up on the edge of the Brazilian Amazon. Lumber trucks splashing through potholes and puddles, dump trucks trundling by with loads of men holding shovels and wearing bandannas, doors of unmarked warehouses sliding open and closed, revealing little of their darkened interiors.

Most of the storefronts were home to an eclectic mix of goods and services, as evidenced by the church with a bank in its lobby. Or the Art Deco–style movie theater with the words *Palau Supreme Court* on the marquee. Almost every building had sprigs of metal rebar optimistically poking out the roof, as though further floors were shortly on the way. But where was the money coming from? Not tourists. I didn't see a one. Yet there seemed to be at least enough cash in circulation to keep afloat the store that sold only children's purses and dusty blender lids.

I asked inside a few places if they sold maps. The attendants—almost all of whom appeared to be from the Philippines—only shook their heads. I then wandered into a three-story place called the Western Carolines Trading Company. Downstairs were groceries. The second floor was general merchandise. (According to a sign, the third floor housed the German consulate.) I walked inside the grocery store, hoping for a peek inside the Palauan pantry; turns out, though, WCTC offered just about what you'd expect to find in a very small-town American grocery store: frozen steak and frozen chicken, lots of soda, some bruised lettuce and a few apples. There also were a few things you wouldn't expect: dried fish flakes, canned lychee fruit, fifty-pound bags of rice, wasabi mayonnaise. Upstairs: big couches and twinkling stereo systems, fishing rods and inflatable pools, backpacks for kids and nonstick pans. Just about everything, except a map. I asked a woman getting into her car where I might find a map and she pointed just down the street. "Try the Palau Map Office," she said sensibly enough.

The Palau Map Office was a squat concrete building with a simple wooden sign out front. No one seemed to be at the reception area, so I proceeded through a few doors and into a windowless room that was less the bureaucratic office I was expecting and more like a James Bond villain's lair. Only, instead of Russians sitting in front of brand-new computers, I found forty or so Palauan men sitting in front of brand-new computers. All were in their fifties and wore caps with different logos—Bud Light, New York Mets, Ducks Unlimited. Some gazed outside; a few squinted at their Apple screens, typing with one finger. While I was wondering if their screen savers were of a Manhattan street scene, a Palauan woman asked if I needed help. I noticed her hair was pulled into an extraordinarily tight bun.

"I was looking for a map," I said, a bit startled. "But I have a question too. What are all these guys doing?"

"Making maps," she said matter-of-factly. "What kind of map were you looking for?"

"Just a map of Palau."

"Not sure if we have that," she said, "but let's go look." She didn't appear to be joking; there was a chance I'd leave the Palau Map Office without a map of Palau.

She directed me to another room lined with oversized flat metal drawers. She opened and closed a few, shaking her head.

"So," I said, "what are those guys making maps of?"

"Palau," she said. "Mostly for development. Marinas. Hotels. Ahh, what's this?" she said, reaching under some sewer-line surveys, and pulled out a piece of paper about the size of a folded newspaper. "I knew we had a map here."

Map was a generous characterization. Dusty, torn, and written in pencil, it was closer to a sketch. Or maybe just a hunch. There was only the general outline of the archipelago of Palau. Babeldaob, the largest and most Seussily named island, was blank except for a few hash lines indicating footpaths. The date at the bottom said 1965.

"I'll make a copy," she said.

Thinking of all those men staring at their computers, or just beyond them, I said, "Umm, do you have anything, you know, more recent?"

"This is the best we have," she said. "But the copy is free."

I asked if she had anything with a little more detail.

"Hmm," she said, looking at her feet. "How much detail were you looking for?"

"Oh, quite a bit," I said.

She informed me that there might be a charge and that it would take a few minutes.

I went back to the reception area and looked at a world map hanging on the wall. Most islands in the Pacific are part of a loosely scattered constellation stretching from Tahiti on the far right of the Pacific to Fiji, closer to the middle. But Palau was separate, its cluster of islands tighter and more isolated. Guam was about a thousand miles, or half an index finger, to the north. Same with Irian Jaya, Indonesia, to the south and the Philippines to the west.

Like most world maps, this one had Palau twice. These islands are so isolated from the mainland that they must be a convenient place for the mapmaker to cut the world in half. As a result, Palau appeared once on the far left and again on the far right. Thinking of the cars with left- and right-hand steering wheels, I wondered if the map reflected Palau's bifurcated place in the world, not so much stuck between East and West as existing in both. But, as I had been in the country for all of fifteen minutes, this slim profundity might have existed only in my mind—a cartographic coincidence, as they say, signifying nothing.

The woman returned. "Here you go," she said, handing me a five-foot-long cardboard tube. I thanked her, paid the twenty-dollar printing fee, and started to walk home. On the way back, I decided to conduct a test: Instead of initiating the friendly wave, I would pause to see what people did. I soon found that they didn't wave if I didn't wave first. In fact, they just stared. Flipping through my guidebook at the hotel, I made an awkward discovery: it's the island of Ponape—not Palau—that is famous for waving. At this very moment, I suspect at least a dozen Palauans are sitting on their stoops, sipping Bud Lights, and swapping tales about that peculiar visitor who not only walked places, but also waved as he did.

After a long shower, I opened my hard-earned cardboard tube. Inside were ten color maps representing different areas of the country. Each one, and I am not exaggerating, was five feet wide by seven feet long—thirty-five square feet. Altogether, I'd managed to procure a 350-square-foot map of Palau—about the size of my old studio in New York—reminding me of that Steven Wright line: "I bought a map of the United States. Each foot represented one foot. It took me all summer to fold it up."

The detail, not surprisingly, was phenomenal. Every path and patch of coral was marked, every inch of elevation indicated—so much detail, in fact, that it led to a different sort of blankness. Was no middle ground possible—not just in the maps but in understanding? Some middle ground between the local and the tourist, between the thick tube of giant maps and the long-dated sketch?

CHAPTER 34

What You Can Expect to Learn in This Chapter:

► After a successful military coup, what's the best drink with which to raise a toast?

► According to the Palauan roadside sign, *Running and Chewing* equals what?

According to my local natural history book, Palau is home to a long, skinny fish called the Pacific cornetfish. *Fistularia corneta* is roughly the shape and size of the wind instrument with which it shares its name and has a remarkable behavior. Cornetfish eat the stomach lining of moray eels by swooping into an eel's mouth, down its throat, and into its stomach. This is an especially impressive trait when one considers that moray eels have two rows of sharp teeth and live in holes. And moray eels are green—a scary color in any animal except parrots.

So why would the moray eel permit such an indignity? For one simple reason: the eel doesn't have any choice. Moray eels leave their mouths agape in order to snatch passing fish, and cornetfish discovered (God knows how) that if they twist their snouts in a certain way, they can touch a spot at the back of the eels' mouths that temporarily debilitates the eels, allowing them to pass on down to the stomach. For humans, this would be like sticking a fork into a wall socket to get some electricity out: it works, but comes with considerable risks.

As I'd soon learn from some American expats, it was also the perfect metaphor for Palau's relationship with the United States.

"No problem," the driver said late that night when I asked to be taken to a bar, any bar. "But bars close at midnight." That gave me about an hour, which felt like plenty. I already felt a bit uneasy about spending so much time in bars, but I didn't know how else to meet people and start getting my mind around the place—two necessary, if not sufficient steps for making a life here.

I'd expected the taxi to drop me off somewhere in downtown Koror, but instead we passed through town and crossed a causeway, maybe half a mile long, built over the ocean. It didn't have guardrails— or even a curb. The lagoon itself was the shoulder.

"Many people drive off that?" I asked him once we reached the other side.

"Every Friday night," he said. "People come in the morning to see who slid off the night before." I imagined people taking photographs of half a dozen cars, their noses in the mud, their bumpers in the air as a kind of Pacific perversion of Cadillac Ranch.

A song called "Hey Uncle Sam, Leave Us Pot Smokers Alone" played on the radio. I'd already heard it and its strong reggae beat many times in Palau.

We turned down a potholed street and into a dark industrial area, passing fuel storage silos, a few run-down motels, and a karaoke bar decorated with red lanterns many months after Christmas. The side of the road was lined with hand-painted billboards:

RUNNING AND CHEWING = DEATH

and . . .

PALAU: IS IT A DREAM OR IS IT A REALITY?

and my favorite . . .

NO SPITTING A.S.A.P.

Finally, we pulled in front of a two-story cinder-block building with a sign out front that read *Pirates Cove Bar & Grill*. A Budweiser sign glowed through a smoky second-floor window. A bit reluctantly, I walked up the concrete stairs at the edge of the building and shook open the sticky door. Unoccupied tables, some without chairs, filled the large space between the bar and the bathrooms. The musty yellow walls were covered with mirrors and beer posters. It would have had a lovely view of the harbor and its small islands, but besides being dark, the windows were covered in condensation. A large Palauan man sat in a white plastic chair in the corner, watching a television on a white plastic table in front of him. He was wearing a very snug and very old Spuds MacKenzie tank top.

I approached the bar. Four middle-aged white men were each sipping Bud Lights. They'd left at least one stool between each of them in the same way men discreetly space themselves along a wall of urinals. I sat down on one at the end and reached for a basket of greasy popcorn. Another television hung from the ceiling behind the bar. The Discovery Channel was showing a documentary about handmade canoes.

"Is that the Solomon Islands?" one of the men said.

"No, it's Hawaii," said a bald man in a tank top. He had thick arms and thin legs, suggesting he lifted a lot of weights but neglected his lower body in favor of puffing up his chest. The result: a human who appeared always on the verge of tipping over.

"No, I think it's Guam," said another.

"There's the dock. It's Palau," said the first man definitively. The other men agreed.

"Yup."

"Yup."

"Yup."

The camera zoomed in on one of the paddlers. "That's the receptionist from the hospital," the tippy one said. "I should know."

"Yup."

"Yup."

"Yup."

Though the segment continued for several minutes, no one asked the Filipina bartender to unmute the television. Everyone knew what they already wanted to know about Palau, canoeing, and, apparently, the receptionist at the hospital. After the bartender switched the channel to CNN, the tippy man turned to me and said, "Where you from?"

"Well, I was living in the States," I said, "but I'm here now. I don't have a ticket back." All four nodded at what I supposed was a familiar story. One, a man in his late sixties with frazzled gray hair, held up a beer as if in a toast.

"That's John," the tippy one said, "the most important person in Palau. He's the local Budweiser distributor. Because of John, you can buy a Budweiser in Palau for about the same cost as you can in Guam."

John, the first celebrity I'd met in Palau, nodded slightly but with genuine pride.

"And you," I said, "you from here?" I had a hunch, but thought I'd better be polite.

"Oklahoma. My name is Jim. I'm Palau's public defender."

I asked if he had much work.

"Sure," he said, "plenty of crime, but Palauans, they're too damn honest. It's hell on a public defender." He explained how just that morning a prosecutor had asked his client on the stand whether he had sold the drugs in question.

"Yes," the defendant had said before Jim could object. His client was sentenced to twenty-five years.

"The dumb thing is," Jim continued, "pot used to be legal here. But the American war on drugs changed that." The bartender announced last call and went to lock the front door. I gave a concerned glance.

"Bars close at midnight," Jim said. I nodded knowingly. "But those already inside can stay."

"That midnight rule, an American thing also?" I said.

"Probably," Jim said. "They make the big calls around here. Four hundred forty-seven million dollars goes a long way on an island with twenty thousand people."

"That's four times what the Federated States of Micronesia got," I said, pleased to have remembered how much the U.S. paid Palau's neighbor after independence.

"Yeah, but Palauans are cagier. They used to be part of FSM but separated, figuring they could negotiate a better deal on their own. They did. They got more cash and got it in a lump sum instead of a little every year."

"Why would the U.S. give them anything at all?" I said.

"Good question," Jim said. "It's supposedly to help with their transition from U.S. territory to independent country, but no one really buys that. Anyway, most of the money goes to John." John smiled and held up his beer again. "Bruce here thinks the Americans are shitty colonizers."

"The worst," Bruce said. Bruce looked about forty and wore flip-flops, an extra-large blue Hawaiian shirt, and tan shorts that fit tightly around his thick pale thighs. "You get the British in here and you'd be able to drink the water."

"Oh, yeah," I thought about saying, "the Brits did a bang-up job, especially in Bangladesh, Iraq, and Sudan. And have you been to New Jersey lately?" Instead I just asked what brought him to Palau. (Since leaving New York, I'd tried not to ask people what they did for a living. But I was too curious not to ask Bruce.)

"Ahh, a lot of things," he said, his jowls flapping at such an open-ended question. "But first, the little man who lives in my pants needs to throw up."

"Excuse me?"

"Gotta take a whiz," he said. He took the last slurp from his beer and slid off the barstool.

"Anyway," Jim said, "the U.S. gave them all that money so we could have a military presence here. It's a huge installation—seven Navy guys. The Seabees."

"The Seabees?"

"Actually C.B. Stands for 'Construction Battalion.' Mostly they just drink beer and watch movies."

"But why so much money for that?" I said.

"Well, they did drop off sand on the beach the other day," John said, his tone genuinely appreciative.

"But it took them six months," Jim said, then took a sip of his beer.

"So where was I?" Bruce asked himself as he waddled back from the bathroom. Before anyone could answer, he spun his nearly empty bottle once in the air and caught it. Spitty light-beer foam splattered onto my shirt and on the linoleum floor.

He then explained that, like Jim, he'd also grown up in Oklahoma and worked as a lawyer there until, unlike Jim, he got in a fight with the Oklahoma Bar Association. Something to do with "inside baseball," so he moved to Saipan, an island north of Guam, where for sixteen years he "dabbled in various things, various women." These days, he said, he spent most of his time suing the estate of Larry Hillblom. "You know," he said, "the 'H' in DHL, the shipping company."

I had a hundred follow-up questions, but Bruce's cell phone rang. He looked at the caller ID and muted the phone.

"Bruce's wife is pregnant," Jim said. "Due soon. Right, Bruce?"

"Gonna calve one any moment now," he said.

"Well, if you need to take that call . . . ," I said.

"She's fine. She's Palauan. If she was actually in labor, I wouldn't get a call until afterward. And then I'm out of the picture for at least a year. That's the way they do it here." I wondered if that's the way they did it here or that was the way Bruce *hoped* they did it here.

"Another coup in the Philippines," John said, reading a ticker across the bottom of the screen.

"Let's do what we did last time," Bruce said, his voice rising and his gut beginning to jiggle, "and have a bar-be-coup!"

"I'll bring the mar-coup-ritas," Jim, the tippy public defender, said. I sat in silence, my coup puns not nearly as at the ready.

"That's good news for Alex!" Bruce said as if remembering something. He then explained that Gibson, the owner of the bar we were in, rented the upstairs of a house he owned to the Philippines' ambassador to Palau. Every time there was a coup in the Philippines, Gibson had to find a new tenant.

I told him I'd just moved to a new hotel room. "I even have my own phone line," I added, but Bruce wasn't interested.

"Hey, Gibson," Bruce said loudly to the man sitting alone in the corner, "why doesn't Alex here move into your place?" Without turning around, Gibson waved his arm as if telling Bruce to go away. "If you're going to be here awhile, you should meet Gibson."

"Best boat mechanic in Palau," Jim offered. No doubt, a significant accolade on an island full of boats.

"Almost was governor of Ngardmau too," said John.

Bruce and I slid off our stools and walked across the room. Even by Palauan standards, Gibson was a large man—perhaps six foot three and oil-drum thick. His black tank top exposed thick wedges of fat that prevented his arms from actually touching the sides of his body. He held a big bowl of spaghetti in his lap. He seemed to be sitting close enough to the television that he could change channels without a remote.

"Hey, Gibson," Bruce said, "I want you to meet someone." I wasn't sure Gibson could hear us—both the air conditioner and the television he was sitting in front of were on full blast.

"Gibson," Bruce said louder.

Without turning toward us, Gibson slowly spit something into a Diet Coke can. The lid had been shorn off, as if in a struggle, leaving a sharp and jagged rim. I then noticed what was playing on the television: *The Good, the Bad, and the Ugly*.

In a way, it's a wonder Palau had television at all. I'd recently read that the remote island group was one of the last places on earth to get television, in 1986. An American ethnologist, Michael Ogden, was there to study its effects and found that, in addition to increasing obesity, television reversed the generational flow of information: for the first time in Palau's three-thousand-year history, Palauan kids started explaining the ways of the world to their parents, instead of the other way around.

Finally, someone in the movie pulled a trigger, and the station broke for a commercial. Only then did Gibson turn and look at Bruce. "Gibson, this is Alex," Bruce said. "He's new."

Gibson rose slowly from his chair and held out a fleshy hand. His hair was black, curled, and short, but his most notable feature was his cheeks—enormous dark brown disks that appeared to be taking over his entire face and nearly obscured his alert brown eyes. He was the first Palauan man I'd seen in shorts.

"Be horse you are ew here an a fraid of bruthe, ill go itching neh wee," he said. I blinked.

"I'm sorry?" I said.

"Hurray. Itching," he said, and turned back to the television.

"Ungil tutau," I said, putting to use my only Palauan. My only Palauan, however, was *good morning,* and it was well past midnight. Gibson looked back at me and then again at the television. I gave a helpless look to Bruce.

"Gibson," Bruce said, "your betel nut."

With his index finger, Gibson extracted a large wad of spitty red fiber from his mouth. He dropped it into the Diet Coke can, where it landed with a dull, moist thud. "Because you are new here and a friend of Bruce's," Gibson repeated, "we'll go fishing next week."

"Great. Thanks, Gibson," Bruce said, then gestured that it was time to go.

Back at the bar, I asked Bruce, "Fishing, right?"

"Next week," he said. "Gibson looks tough, but he's a softy. He's the youngest of ten children. He has nine older sisters."

Just then, we heard banging at the door.

"That's the old lady," Bruce said. "I should go." He then stood and set some bills down on the counter. "New guy's beer is on me."

"Thank you," Jim said with a smile, but Bruce didn't respond.

As we finished our beers, Jim and I watched the muted TV together in silence. I didn't belong here, I thought, but I didn't not belong here either. I'd just arrived but had already been invited to go fishing with a local and been bought a beer by a stranger—two things that rarely happened in New York. Perhaps Palau had been a good choice after all.

STEP 5

SETTLE IN

CHAPTER 35

What You Can Expect to Learn in This Chapter:

► Which of the following stamps from Palau's "Disaster Series" is the best choice for mailing a box home:
a) the *Challenger* space shuttle explosion?
b) the Union Carbide tragedy in Bhopal?
c) Ronald Reagan?

► If that box arrives with a stowaway—a package for, say, a complete stranger in Germany—what should you do?

I began to make long-term arrangements to stay and, for the first time since embarking on my search for paradise, time started to stretch out and feel less harried, less precious. At least, each load of laundry no longer required a journal entry. Pretending like I belonged here *did* feel a bit phony. Fortunately, I'd recently read a Friedrich Nietzsche quote in one of my books that helped guide me: "All great art," he wrote, "begins as imitation." In other words . . . fake it till you make it. I certainly didn't have a better idea about how to go about creating my own Gauguin-like paradise, unless it was to start painting.

Accordingly, over the next few days, I switched from a rented car to a leased car (another dented Corolla), bought a Palauan-English dictionary, arranged a monthly rate at my motel for a room with a kitchenette, and stuffed as many groceries into my little fridge as it would hold. I even bought a toaster and an answering machine. In light of my upcoming social commitments, the latter seemed especially important: not only did I have plans to meet someone . . . I had plans to meet two people! In short, morale was high.

Until, of course, I went to the post office. It looked like any small-town post office you'd find in the United States, which wasn't surprising: in perhaps the worst form of in-kind foreign aid, the U.S. Postal Service handles all of Palau's postal needs. I'd gone to mail home some things I'd be unlikely to need in Palau (jeans, long-sleeve shirts, a sweater), so I asked for a box and a sheet of stamps. I was pretty excited about the stamps. I'd read that in order to raise money, Palau had retained the right to issue its own stamps, and cleverly, they were the first country to issue an Elvis stamp.

The clerk sold me an unremarkable box, but the stamps were unique. The sheet was titled "The Twentieth Century: 1980–1989" and featured stamps commemorating Chernobyl, the Union Carbide Bhopal disaster, the space shuttle explosion, and, to round out the series, Ronald Reagan. Each had a photo and a tiny explanation: a picture of a mushroom cloud, for example, with a little label that read, "The Chernobyl Nuclear Explosion Kills an Estimated 7,000." And next to the iconic image of the exploding space shuttle, "The Space Shuttle *Challenger* Explodes, Killing the Entire Crew." The Bhopal stamp I found especially unsettling. It showed two women with bandaged faces and the caption, "A Deadly Gas Discharged at Chemical Plant in India. Palau 20¢."

I later called my mom to make sure she'd received the box. "What should I do with all of this?" she said. I guess she hadn't noticed the stamps.

"My jeans and stuff?" I said. "Just put 'em in my old closet."

"But what about this box to Germany?"

Apparently, my box had arrived with two stowaways. The first was a small, stamped box addressed to a Yan Shoenfeld of Hamburg, Germany. The second—and this took me about fifteen dollars of long-distance charges to figure out—was a plastic eye shield designed for an American football helmet. The box to Germany I could kind of understand: someone at the Palauan post office must have slipped it in my box, assuming all white people must know one another and that we'd just forward it along—which, in fact, my mother did. Yet the eye shield still baffled. They don't even play football in Palau.

I asked her to send me the rest of my books. When the box showed up a few weeks later, there was a bonus gift inside. No, not cookies or even a card. Rather, religious propaganda. Twenty brochures with an illustration of Jesus on the cover. They were written in Palauan and, therefore, unlikely to have originated from my mother.

I started pondering the cosmic significance of religious propaganda smuggled in my inbound mail and athletic eyewear in my outbound, but realized that could take a lifetime to understand.

CHAPTER 36

What You Can Expect to Learn in This Chapter:

- ➤ Which dive guide should you not hire in the Philippines?

- ➤ What is, arguably, the coolest place on earth?

I knew Palau was famous, if at all, for only one thing: a scuba-diving site called Blue Corner. It usually ranks as the best or second-best dive site in the world. It was touristy, but living in Palau without going to Blue Corner would be like living in New York without ever passing through Times Square—you could do it, but you'd be missing a lot of the action. A huge density of sea life congregates at Blue Corner, not because of the coral but because of the current. Two thousand feet down, a river of nutrient-rich water slams into a sheer wall and shoots up before cresting over a ledge submerged only sixty feet below the surface. The flow of water coming over this ledge is so strong that divers must *hook in* by jamming a metal hook with a rope attached into the rock. (If they miss the rock, the dive is over—the currents simply wash them to calm and comparatively lifeless water.) If they do manage to hook in, the three-foot-long rope snaps taut, stopping the divers with a jerk. Even then, the currents must be reckoned with. Turning a mask perpendicular to the flow can rip it off. Sometimes the rope snaps or the rock that forms the ledge breaks. It was, therefore, with some trepidation that I signed up to get certified.

The only other student in my course was a nice Filipino man, also named Alex, who failed the swim test three times. Apparently, two hundred yards was simply too far. Our instructor passed him on the basis that Alex had swum two hundred yards *cumulatively* in his three attempts. When asked why he wanted to be certified, the other Alex said he wanted to return to the Philippines to lead dive trips. Perhaps needless to say, I didn't get a lot of personalized attention, but I dutifully memorized—and quickly forgot—all my charts and tables, safety procedures, and nitrogen ratios. As far as the Sam Dive Shop and the self-governing certification people were concerned, I was ready.

When the morning came to actually go to Blue Corner, I boarded a small boat with eight tourists, mostly American and Japanese. When a friendly doctor from Denver asked where I was from, I hesitated.

"I grew up in Texas," I said.

"Oh, yeah? And where do you live now?"

I wasn't sure how to answer. Even though I was living in a hotel, I didn't feel like a tourist. But I certainly wasn't a local—I was on a dive boat to Blue Corner, after all. But even native New Yorkers have to pass through Times Square on occasion. "Well, I'm just kinda here," I said cryptically. We both smiled awkwardly at each other for a moment. "Yup . . . just kinda here."

Before he could ask to be transferred to another boat, however, the engines started, making further talking impossible. Which was just as well—the scenery was too spectacular for small talk. For ninety minutes—as exotic white birds with absurdly long tails soared overhead—we threaded our way through the Rock Islands, an archipelago of three hundred or so protected islands stretching south from Koror.

Most of the deserted islands were a few hundred feet high, and ranged in length from a couple hundred feet to over a mile. For eons, little waves have lapped against their bases, eroding the islands into strange mushroom shapes with gray limestone stems supporting densely jungled green caps. Occasionally, however, larger slabs of limestone have slid into the water, creating protected little coves ringed with white-sand beaches and at least one palm tree arching out over the turquoise water. We passed a few small boats with Palauans heading out or returning from fishing. They'd hold on to their hats as they zipped past, expertly avoiding coral heads teeming with fish.

After we finally crossed through a break in the reef, the captain slowed the boat to absorb the waves of the open ocean. It was too rough to tie up to a buoy, so the captain tried to keep the boat steady while we struggled with our equipment and a seemingly endless array of buckles and clips. More or less prepared, we jumped overboard. The water was probably warm, but the swells rising and falling and the tangle of hoses made it hard to notice such details.

Not wanting to linger on the surface, our guide signaled and we descended in a blur of bubbles. Still far from the ledge or anything else to orient us, we dropped to eighty feet and, with hooks at the ready, followed our guide toward the wall. To have the best chance at hooking in, we had to come in low so the currents could push us up and over the top of the ledge. Swimming hard through the deep blue, I didn't think it was going to be that tricky, but just as the wall came into view, the currents picked up fast. I approached the top of the wall at what felt like twenty mph. Just over the lip, I happened to see a small hole and jammed my hook in. It held. Two other divers missed the ledge, however, and floated up and, effectively, out. Although the other end of the rope was tied to my equipment, I gripped it tightly out of simple fear.

At first, all I could focus on was the current. I felt like I was sky-diving. The hose connecting my mouthpiece to my tank shook like a cord on a flagpole in a strong wind. It was hard to believe it wasn't going to be torn loose. I could barely get my mind around being so far below the surface. Humans simply aren't supposed to be here, I thought. (And, in fact, until Jacques Cousteau coinvented the Aqua-Lung in 1942, they never were. In other words, only the last two generations in all of human history have been able to even glimpse wild places like this.) I looked up. High, high above me, the sun shimmered on the surface of the water. Finally calm, I released my grip on the rope, relying instead on the little knot connecting it to a buckle in the center of my chest. Now I wasn't skydiving. I was flying.

Seeing that I was still alive, and actually breathing quite normally, I finally looked out over the ledge and into the dark blue water. Dozens of gray reef sharks, maybe five feet long, darted into and out of giant shoals of silver jacks. A huge school of barracuda—a scary, toothy fish on its own, but much more so in a school of thousands—floated by, passing within a few feet. Meanwhile, a spotted eagle ray hovered nearby, just watching me watching it. Then a school of perhaps a thousand fusiliers, small blue fish with fluorescent yellow stripes, cruised by, mouths agape. Something caught my eye below me. A hawksbill turtle was munching algae on some nearby rocks amid a swarm of gaudy tropical fish.

Just being underwater this far down in the open ocean was a thrill, but doing so amid this swirl of life and color nearly brought tears to my eyes. Only our guide clanging his tank with a knife snapped me out of my little moment. It was time to go up. After a dreamy boat ride back, we pulled into Sam's dock just as the sun was setting, concluding what I thought was my first perfect day in the Pacific.

What I didn't know, however, was the day was about to get much better.

STEP 6

MEET SOMEONE

CHAPTER 37

What You Can Expect to Learn in This Chapter:

- ► Are confession booths a good place to meet someone? Why or why not?

- ► While on a first date, should you make a joke about your future divorce?

As we pulled into Sam's and started unloading, I noticed eight or nine folks were carrying beer and dry bags down the dock, in the opposite direction from my dive group. All appeared to be expats in their late twenties and all were in a chirpy mood. I hadn't heard this many American voices together since arriving in the Pacific.

"What are you guys doing?" I said to a woman dragging paddles and gear behind her. It was dark enough that I couldn't tell if her hair was brown or blond.

"Going kayaking," she said. "It will be a full moon tonight." Her voice was high, not helium-balloon high, but sixteen-year-old-girl-on-the-phone high.

"Great," I said without thinking. "Can I come?"

She looked around. The others were loading their boats.

"Sure," she said. "I think we're an odd number and we have only double kayaks. You can go in mine."

As I lowered myself in a few minutes later, the kayak rolled unsteadily from side to side. I'd heard once that the difficulty of maneuvering double kayaks had prompted the nickname "Divorce-eye-aks" so I said, "I bet we get married and divorced by the time this night is over."

"Good thing I'm steering, then," she said.

For the first few minutes, we paddled in silence as Sam's slid away behind us, and we started threading between the northernmost of Palau's semifamous Rock Islands. During the day, these spectacular islands are almost impossible not to photograph; at night, however, they're mostly just large, dark shapes to be navigated around.

"Are we going straight?" I said.

"Anyone can kayak straight," she said. I could hear the kayak's plastic pedals alternating back and forth, trying to find center. "Besides, we get to see more this way."

We continued in silence, the only sound that of the water dribbling off the ends of our paddles and the muffled voices of our fellow kayakers, now distant. Each stroke in the otherwise pure black water ignited an explosion of sparkling, then dimming phosphorescence. The penumbra of the moon was just visible above a jungle-lined island ridge.

"Beats being excited that the subway is on time," I said finally.

"Personally, I could use some cable TV right now," she said. "Or an Applebee's. Maybe there's one around the bend?" I turned to look back, to see if she was joking, but even that slight twisting caused the boat to lean steeply. So she remained only a voice. And to her I was just the back of a head. I'd later learn she'd forgotten her glasses, so I wasn't even the back of a head: more a fuzzy patch of hair with a voice. The result was a bit like meeting someone in a Catholic confessional (not that I have a lot of experience meeting people in those).

"So what's your story?" I asked, immediately regretting such a dud of a question.

"Well, the morning of September the 29th, 1973, the dawn broke bright and clear. Historians would later note . . . Just kidding. What about you? You just visiting?"

"No. I bought a one-way ticket. So I'm here for the duration. You?"

"Well," she said, "I've lived and worked here about a year. So, are you running from a woman, the law, or both?"

"Maybe both. But for the record, I was acquitted."

"They all say that," she said, shuffling the plastic pedals again. "So . . . what are you reading these days?"

"Really?"

"You don't move to the Pacific without bringing books."

"I brought some. A big box of 'em, actually," I said. "And you? What are you reading?"

"*War and Peace.* Kind of. It's about the Russian Revolution, and it's long." Given most of my conversations so far in the Pacific, I felt like I was sharing a double kayak with Tolstoy himself.

"Started but didn't finish it. You sure it's about the *Russian* Revolution?"

"Pretty sure," she said.

While talking, we'd paddled around the corner of an island and stopped at the entrance of what appeared to be a large and empty cove. The rim of the moon crested the top of the island in front of us, shining through the higher branches of the canopy. Giant fruit bats twirled in lazy arcs. We watched one land in a tree amid awkward, frenetic flapping.

"Have you read *The Hedgehog and the Fox*, by chance?" I said. "It's a book about *War and Peace.*"

"I haven't. Quick question. Do you usually read books about books you've only started?"

"Sometimes, I guess. It's more of an essay. Isaiah Berlin, the guy who wrote it, says there are two kinds of people—"

"Men and women?"

"He says there are hedgehogs and there are foxes. Hedgehogs are people who know one thing really well whereas foxes are easily distracted and find just about everything interesting. Hedgehogs run the world, but foxes enjoy it more."

"I'm definitely a fox," she said, "and so are you."

"How do you know?"

"Because hedgehogs don't buy one-way tickets to Palau and go on full-moon kayak rides at the last minute." I was thinking that she had a reasonable point when we heard a distant voice call out to us on the far side of the cove.

"I forgot about those guys," I said.

"Let's play a joke on them," she said.

"Great. Any ideas?"

"Well," she said, "we could sneak up on one of their kayaks . . ."

". . . and tip them over."

Without another word, we slowly lowered ourselves into the shockingly warm water, leaving our kayak to float around the surface. We started swimming the few hundred yards that separated us from the other boats. I tried to follow her—she was an excellent swimmer—but I couldn't keep up, so I simply swam toward the swirl of phosphorescence that appeared and disappeared behind her.

As we swam, I thought about how unusual it was that neither of us had asked the other what we did for a living. In New York, it is the very first question, coming out in virtually the first exhale in the conversation. But here that question seemed unimportant. Every long-term foreigner in the Pacific has conjured up some pretext for being there. The specifics were as relevant as the name of the travel agent who sold us the tickets.

About ten yards away from the closest kayak we both poked our heads out of the water, and made eye contact. She had a cute face with a small nose and pretty lips. Her wet hair appeared to be blond, maybe a little wavy. I couldn't quite tell. We took a deep breath and went under again. I swam hard but with only one arm, keeping the other outstretched as I waited to feel the hard plastic edge of a kayak. Though I'd known her about fifteen minutes, I already felt we were somehow coconspirators, like two actors backstage.

Finally, I felt something, but it was coarser than I expected. I moved my fingertips quickly, trying to find the lower edge of the kayak in order to push it over, but couldn't find it. Nearly out of air, I burst out of the water at about the same time as she did, both of us yelling, "ARGHHHHHH!" No one was surprised. We'd snuck up on a rock.

"Are you guys OK?" said a voice still some distance away.

We couldn't stop laughing.

"Are you guys OK?"

"Ha, ha, ha!"

"Yup. We're OK!"

"Ha, ha, ha, ha, ha, ha, ha!"

"Ha, ha, ha, ha, ha, ha, ha!"

She then lifted her hand out of the water, about parallel with my head and said, "Hi. My name is Sarah. Good to meet you."

CHAPTER 38

What You Can Expect to Learn in This Chapter:

► What rodents, other than rats, carry the bubonic plague? And why is it important to know?

► When starting an Internet company which is more important: the idea behind the business or free food?

For the next few days, I didn't *stalk* Sarah. Stalking, after all, implies that you are following someone, perhaps hiding in the bushes. More than stalking, I considered what I was doing a kind of *strategic positioning.* The day after we met, I went to Palau's only coffee shop, where I assumed Sarah would stop by. I found a square table near the front door but had to consider which direction to face—after all, she'd be more likely to recognize me by the back of my head than by the front of my head (an area more commonly known as *the face*). Yet, for obvious reasons, that seemed risky. So instead I chose a position where she'd see me in profile.

While drinking my third cup of coffee, I thought back to all of my reasons for rejecting various islands—Yap, Pig, Guam, and Tinian—and wondered if the problem wasn't the place but the lack of a companion, a partner in crime. Or at least a friend? Sarah could be all of those, I thought. Or none. But I wouldn't know unless I found her.

About lunchtime, I made my first of two trips to the grocery store. I bought some toothpaste. At five ten p.m., about the time I assumed she'd be getting off work, I went back for a new toothbrush since, technically, you're supposed to replace those every three months. But still no Sarah. When the hell does this woman buy groceries, I thought as I wandered down aisles of mostly frozen, mostly expired food, if not after work on a Tuesday?

I repeated, more or less, the same routine the following day, but varied it slightly: I went to the doughnut shop instead of the coffee shop, for instance. As I drove around, I noticed the music always remained the same. It didn't matter if I was in the coffee shop, the grocery store, or my car: the same song always played. I pressed the scan button on my car radio only to loop back around to the same station where I started. From what I could tell, Palau had only one FM radio station: 88.9. Everyone, it seemed, was listening to the same station.

In other words, the country had, in effect, a national sound track, in this case a lively mix of country music, Filipino covers of American rap songs, eighties love ballads, and a few remixed classics. Best of all, on 88.9 the music never stops—not even for commercials. But that didn't prevent 88.9 from promoting itself—and not just between songs but during songs. Thus you could be singing along to a Billie Holiday song at the grocery store when you heard the whisper of a male voice, as if from the next aisle over:

> *The way you wear your hat*
> *88.9 . . . The Sound of Palau*
> *The way you sip your tea*
> *The memory of all that*
> *88.9 . . . The Sound of Palau*
> *No, no, they can't take that away . . . from me.*

In search of lunch, I pulled into Yokohama, a small Japanese diner near downtown and, presumably, near where Sarah worked. Perhaps it would have been better to know where she worked, I thought as I found a table near the front and sat down in a small metal chair with the plastic wrapping still on. The same song I'd been listening to in my car now played overhead. I felt a bit of sympathy for the station. Their business model was certainly one I could relate to. My former company, E-The People, had the same three-pronged strategy: 1) give away the product, 2) promote the brand endlessly, and 3) hope it all works out somehow.

During the Internet boom, that was enough. Back then, venture capital investors had a high tolerance for expensive schemes, especially for the promotional side, which for us came down to painting a forty-foot bus like a giant mailbox and driving around the country talking to whoever would listen.

At first we'd pull up in front of a town hall in, say, Lubbock, crank up the dance music, and spill out of the bus in matching blue polo shirts, handing out pens with *www.e-thepeople.com* printed on the sides. We'd then lure anyone passing by onto the bus for a *free demonstration* of the web site. At eleven a.m., though, there weren't many people lurking around town halls in the hope of finding free pens and a new e-government web site. If we were lucky, we'd snag a few women walking together who'd sit through a few minutes of our presentation and nod politely before nervously looking at their watches.

The problem, we decided, was the bus. Its leather seats and wet bar belonged more to a Las Vegas bachelor party than to the rolling headquarters of a scrappy political movement. So we ditched the matching shirts, scattered some newspapers and funny bumper stickers around, and switched the music to Willie Nelson. We even bought a copy of Alexis de Tocqueville's *Democracy in America*, ruffled the pages, and threw it on the couch, as though we'd just been catching up on the Frenchman's observations on early-nineteenth-century America between stops at Dairy Queen. To get better crowds, we started calling government offices and local nonprofits in advance, promising free food as well as a short product demonstration. This helped. Soon, we had a few dozen people at each stop.

Reporters, especially, liked the idea of a new technology that could help hold government accountable. Soon *The New York Times*, *USA Today*, the *Wall Street Journal*, *Businessweek*, *Forbes*, and *Time* ran stories. Even Germany's *Der Spiegel* did a story under the headline *"Die Demokratie Maschina."* (*The Austin American-Statesman*, however, had my favorite headline: "New web site Offers Free Bar-Be-Que, Access to Government.") After we made a video of the bus driving along back roads flanked by waving wheat fields, old barns, and American flags, we started getting television coverage as well. CBS and CNN broadcast stories, as did ninety local stations. The Associated Press sent a reporter to travel with us for four days. His story was, in turn, picked up by another two hundred newspapers. Its first line read: "Like a modern-day Alexis de Tocqueville..."

Being on the evening news on four television stations in El Paso, however, wasn't as thrilling as I imagined it would be. It felt—because it very much was—contrived. Worse, the publicity was just leading to more publicity, not to actual users. Turns out, we'd tapped an idealistic vein in journalists and not the American people. The few users we tended to attract were drawn mostly to our political-discussion sections. And there weren't many companies keen to advertise in abortion-debate chat rooms. By the time the bubble burst, we didn't have a viable business model. Or even an idea that resonated.

A year after the last stop of the bus and an ocean away from the country I once tried so grandly to save, I found myself sitting in a tiny Japanese restaurant, alternately reading *Huck Finn* and a week-old newspaper from the Philippines. The lead news story was about their two ongoing civil wars (one in the north against Communists, one in the south against Muslim extremists). The poor Philippines, I thought. As much as Americans like to complain, at least things basically work in the United States. Laws are written and usually enforced. Coups are rare. And though not everyone bothers to vote, at least we have the right to if things get really bad. The fact that everyone hadn't raced to E-The People's newfangled microphone now seemed, in a very small way, testimony to the strength of the Republic, not its weakness.

Then, just as my food arrived, I heard Sarah's voice. She was placing a take-out order. It was the first time I'd seen her in the daylight. She was about average height and had dirty blond hair made slightly blonder by frequent exposure to the sun. It fell down both sides of her face, framing delicate eyebrows, a small nose, and, behind a pair of brown plastic glasses, light blue eyes. Though she was only in her twenties, her faint laugh lines suggested someone who'd been smiling a lot. I thought I saw a dimple.

"Hi," I said from my plastic-covered table. "It's Alex. We were on that kayak the other night."

"Right," she said. "Good to see you." I noticed her yellow sundress had a pattern of small white flowers. She glanced down at *Huck Finn*.

"Did you not go to high school? I thought you were reading . . . What was it? 'The Gopher and The Groundhog'?"

"I'm rereading it," I said. "And I think you're thinking of *The Hedgehog and the Fox*."

"Not groundhog?" she said. "I always get my burrowing rodentia mixed up." I looked for a smile, but she didn't give me one. Either she had perfect delivery, or she really did get her burrowing rodentia mixed up.

The woman behind the counter handed Sarah her lunch order, knotted in a plastic bag. "OK. Good running into you," she said.

"It was," I said as she stepped toward the door.

"OK, bye," she said. The bell on the metal-frame door dinged lightly. I didn't want the conversation to end, but I also didn't know what to say.

"Hey, did you know prairie dogs can carry the plague?" I said.

"No," she said, quickly rummaging through her purse for keys as one might in a dark parking lot.

"It's true," I continued. "If you get breathed on by one, you can get the bubonic plague."

"Well, this will mean some different life choices . . ."

"I'm just saying, be careful."

Her to-go order swinging in her hand, she paused just long enough to look at my book again.

"Huck Finn had his raft," she said. "Seems like if we're going to live on this little island, we should have a raft too. Or at least know how to make one. Want to make one together?"

"Of course," I said.

"We could make it at the old stone pier. At the end of the week, maybe Friday at five thirty p.m.?"

"Great," I said. "I'm free."

"I think we'll need some twine."

"No problem," I said. "I go to the grocery store all the time."

CHAPTER 39

What You Can Expect to Learn in This Chapter:

► In what ways will your handmade raft differ from one built by a deranged beaver?

► According to *The National Enquirer*, who has the best job in the world?

W hen the afternoon came to meet Sarah to build our raft, I arrived twenty minutes early, twine in hand. The old pier was just a slightly elevated stone path that started in a parking lot and meandered through a mangrove swamp. The broad waxy leaves encroached on both sides, dimming the light and making the late afternoon seem much later. I followed the path for a maybe a quarter of a mile before it crumbled into the lagoon beyond the mangroves. In theory, one could paddle across the dark murky water to the open ocean beyond. Closer to shore, a thick blanket of humid heat had muffled even the crickets, enlivening only the gnats, which quickly found their way into my eyes, my nostrils, and the corners of my mouth.

Was this a date? I wondered. It felt like a date. But what if it went badly? What if we didn't leave friends, much less boyfriend and girlfriend? What if the raft didn't work and, along with our relationship, promptly sank? Worse, what if the raft *did* work—for a while, at least, until we ended up several miles off shore, only to be swept out to the Philippine Sea and a long salty death?

Sarah arrived right on time, pulling up in a puff of dust in a white

Toyota station wagon. Dents ran the length of both sides; a side mirror had been knocked off. "I brought us each a paddle," she said with a smile, gesturing to the backseat. She stepped out and gave me a kiss on the cheek. She was wearing light blue shorts and a white tank top.

"Paddles will be good," I said. "I brought us masks and snorkels. Got them both at the grocery store."

"Seems we have different expectations," she said, tossing her keys through the window onto the seat. "It'll be dark soon. Let's find branches. Did you bring twine?"

"Of course," I said.

We walked along the path in search of sticks. "So what are you doing in Palau again?" she said, seemingly oblivious to the heat. We were both oozing sweat, like giant sponges being squeezed.

"Not much," I said. "Sometimes I go on walks. You?"

"Oh, you're an omphaloskeptic."

"Pardon?"

"Omphaloskepsis," she said. "The contemplation of one's navel in search of a mystic experience."

"Well, my navel and other people's, I suppose. I brought a lot of books. A hundred actually." I reached down for another stick, but all were limp from the humidity or from soaking in the sea. It seemed we were trying to build a raft out of the structural equivalent of overcooked linguine.

"And you?" I said. "What are you doing here?"

"I've been working for the Supreme Court," she said, "but not for much longer. My contract is up in a few months." Just a few months? Oh, shit.

"Then what?"

"Not sure. Maybe go back to California."

This was not welcome news. So far, I'd learned Sarah was leaving soon and thought I was a self-absorbed navel-gazer.

In search of safe ground, I said, "So you're an attorney?"

"Technically," she said, "but I don't really think of myself that way. My boss is a judge. According to the *National Enquirer*, he has the second-best job in the world."

"Who has the first?" I said.

"Any guesses?"

"Saudi Arabian prince? Male prostitute to the stars?"

"Bob Barker—the *Price Is Right* guy."

"No way."

"Yup. I guess he gives away cars all day while surrounded by beautiful women. So tell me," she said, switching subjects, "where do your handlers at the DEA tell you to say you're from?"

"Umm . . . Texas," I said. I was sweating so much that the back of my heels slid off the slippery rubber of my flip-flops with every step.

"Really? Where's your accent?"

"I don't really have one. My father's from small-town Arkansas, but my mother's Canadian. I wish I had an accent, though. At first, I think people with accents are kind of slow, but then I trust them. Usually more than I should."

"Well, do you own boots?" she said, handing me a few sticks.

"No," I said. "My feet are too narrow."

"So you're from Texas, but you don't have an accent and you don't wear boots because your feet are too narrow?"

"Well, that's about right. And you?" I said.

"I grew up in San Diego but went to school in the Bay Area. Hey, let's split up. I think we'll find more wood that way."

I stepped off the path and walked into the mangroves. Mud sucked between my toes and flip-flops. If this was a date, it didn't seem to be going well. She thought I was either a drug agent or an unemployed liar. The only thing she knew for certain was that I had unusually narrow feet.

We met up again a few minutes later. "Is that what you found?" she said, looking at my handful of rubbery sticks. Most were about a foot and a half long—a good three feet short for a proper two-person raft. Sarah, however, had gathered a good bundle of sticks, even a couple of thick, dry ones. "Do you have the twine?" she said. I proudly pulled a small roll out of my pocket. She knelt and began cutting it with a rock from the path. It looked like hard work. I offered to help, but she declined.

"If you could have just one movie on a remote tropical island," she said, as I watched awkwardly, "which one would it be?"

"Well, the first half of *Raising Arizona* and the second half of . . ."

"*Xanadu?*"

"Hmm," I said, "I do love roller-skating movies but . . ."

"You seemed the type."

"I was going to say *Airplane.*"

"Oh, miss, I speak jive," she said, then held up a short length of twine. "Shiiiiit . . ."

"And you?" I said.

"Well, I did bring one . . . *Casablanca.*"

"Nice choice."

"It's not a hot item around here, though. A month ago someone broke into my apartment. They stole my DVD player but left the movie on the coffee table. They actually bothered to eject it before stealing the machine."

"Pretty insulting."

"It still stings. Can you hold the twine more taut?" she said, wiping the sweat away with the side of her hand.

"Sure," I said. "So before you came here, you were where?"

"Alaska, working for a judge," she said,

"And you're not married?" I said, kneeling down to help. "I thought a woman couldn't leave Alaska single."

"What is it they say about dating in Alaska . . . ? The odds are good, but the goods are odd."

"Ha!"

"And you? Did you come here from Texas?"

"New York City. I worked for the same Internet company for five years. But at least I learned a lot."

"What did you learn after year five that you hadn't picked up after year four?" she said.

I stopped and looked at her.

"Keep cutting," she said, smiling.

"I guess I learned I didn't want to spend a sixth," I said.

"Well, I suppose that's something," she said, adding, "Hold the sticks. I'll tie them."

I held the sticks as she tangled them together. The result looked less like a raft than a housewarming gift you'd be given by a deranged beaver.

"And is it still going?" she asked.

"Not really. That's the problem with these Internet things. They're kind of ephemeral. Vaporware, they called it. But anything online, it just doesn't feel real or lasting. You put all this time into something that just kind of disappears. Someday, I'd like to do something more permanent." Just as I said those words, we both paused and looked at the raft.

"Like a shelf for all your books," she offered.

"Yeah," I said, "or even a house."

"Maybe start with this raft—which I think is ready, by the way."

"How far do you think we're going to get?" If you saw our raft on the road, you'd drive right over it rather than swerve. You probably wouldn't even feel the bump.

"Not sure," she said. "Let's find out." We gathered our paddles, slid our masks and snorkels to our foreheads, and began walking to the end of the pier.

"Remind me," she said, sounding genuinely puzzled. "What are you doing here again?"

"Well, the answer is complicated. Either it takes a long time or I sound like Tony Robbins."

"The big-jawed infomercial man?" she said.

"Yup. The short answer is, I came here to read and find paradise."

"You mean find yourself in the shadow of the palms?" she said, sweeping an arm around at the muddy, dark mangrove forest around us.

"Something like that," I said.

"One thing I've always wondered about people doing that: what if you find yourself and don't like what you find?" she said. I stopped and turned to face her again. Again, she smiled.

"Well, I'm about halfway through my books," I said.

"And when you're done?"

"Well, maybe I'll know myself better and what's important. At least, to me."

Arriving at the end of the pier, I set down the paddles as Sarah gently slipped the raft into the water. It bobbed awkwardly for a moment before settling into a steep tilt.

"Suppose we could have just bought a raft at the store, blown it up," I said, "but that's not very rewarding."

"This is definitely not store bought," she said.

"It's not awesome," I said, "but we made it with our own hands."

Sarah leaned back to admire it. "Yeah, though it looks like we just used our feet and elbows."

Before I could respond, she took her shorts off, revealing a red one-piece bathing suit underneath. We both stepped into the water, careful not to slip on the algae-covered rocks.

"You can go in front this time," I said.

"Seems to be working," Sarah said as she boarded the raft, hesitantly, as one might the last, unchosen horse at a dude ranch.

We were, in fact, floating, but barely; the body-temperature water was up to our armpits. We started paddling. A few tentative strokes later, we started moving forward, albeit slowly. A few minutes later, I looked back toward shore. We were thirty yards out . . . but our raft was slowly going down. "I think we need to paddle faster!" Sarah said with a laugh.

"A lot faster!"

When the water reached our chins, Sarah suggested we pull our masks down. Through the murky water, I could barely make out her hair, just inches in front of me. But then something happened. Perhaps the water farther out was saltier and denser, or perhaps we just got better at paddling, but we stopped sinking. And the water cleared up, becoming a nearly clear turquoise.

"It's working," I thought I heard Sarah say through her snorkel.

I looked down. Twenty feet below us, I could just make out the fleeting dark shapes of fish scattering into purple coral. The sun was out. The water was warm. I was sharing a homemade raft with a funny and beautiful woman. For the first time since arriving in the Pacific, I was very happy with all the choices, big and small, that had brought me here.

Then our ship started sinking. Fast. Yet we kept paddling. And laughing. Had someone been watching from land, all they would have seen were two plastic tubes—one green, one blue—wiggling toward the horizon, the tops of two hands barely breaking the surface together.

CHAPTER 40

What You Can Expect to Learn in This Chapter:

► Does the U.S. government actually employ someone with the title *chargé d'affaires*?

► How do you complete this popular saying in Palau, "The Spanish came to Palau for God, the Germans for glory, the Japanese for gold, the Americans for ____."

I figured if I was going to spend the rest of my days here, I needed to understand the place a bit better. Unsure where to start, I began reading several books about Palauan history. Apparently, little is actually known of Palau's early history. The islands were settled sometime between 2500 BC and 1000 BC, most likely by people from Java in Indonesia, though some say Polynesia. The language that they developed, Palauan, is an Austronesian language, which I'm pretty sure means that many of their words end in a sneezing sound. In any case, the Palauan language was rarely written, and through the 1970s, there was disagreement about the spelling of even common words. Even today, some spell the country's name *Palau* while others refer to it as *Belau*.

The first foreigners to stay for a while were a few luckless Spanish priests. They were vaguely tolerated before either being killed by the locals or swept away by typhoons. Those who clung on were forced out by German traders, who themselves were booted out by the Japanese during World War I. To relieve crowding at home during the

Great Depression, the Japanese government sent lots of emigrants to Palau. The new arrivals imposed their own education and legal systems and language on Palau and brought back to Japan fish and bird crap, the latter of which they turned into fertilizer and bombs. Their reign here too was relatively short. During World War II, the United States attacked the islands as part of the Pacific campaign. More than eighteen hundred American troops and eleven thousand Japanese soldiers died in this island group, which some later argued was of questionable strategic value. (Unlike other islands captured by the Americans, Palau was never used as a staging ground for future attacks.) But having captured Palau, the U.S. hasn't been keen to let it go. A popular saying in Palau: "The Spanish came to Palau for God, the Germans for glory, the Japanese for gold, the Americans for good."

After World War II, much of Micronesia—including Palau, Guam, and Yap—was placed under the authority of the U.S. Department of the Interior, just as Native Americans had been a century earlier. Perhaps someone in DC liked the irony of declaring some remote islands in the Western Pacific part of the *interior* of the United States? Regardless, the Western Pacific was pretty much forgotten as *the rust territory* until President Kennedy, in one of his wackier moments, decided to send more than eight hundred Peace Corps volunteers to Micronesia. This worked out to be one volunteer for every twenty-three locals.

"Here you go," you can imagine the State Department saying in the letter of introduction. "Maybe this will help." According to P. F. Kluge, a former Peace Corps volunteer who wrote a lovely insider's account of Palau's independence movement, on a per-capita basis this would be the equivalent of sending five million liberal arts graduates to India.

By the time I showed up on Palau, seven years after its official independence, the U.S. Peace Corps contingent had been reduced to twelve. Yet the money still flowed—most recently, I read in the local paper, $150 million for a road through the almost uninhabited island of Babeldaob and $40 million for a new capitol building. This was on top of the $447 million they negotiated as part of their severance package. Later, President Obama would pay Palau $200 million to take seventeen prisoners from Guantánamo.

But still mysterious to me was why the United States had given so much money to such a small country. The expats I met at the bar and who'd been here who knows how long had no idea. Did we send that money out of guilt or moral obligation, a kind of divorce settlement agreement between two unequal partners? And what would happen when it was all spent? This last question seemed especially relevant if I was going to live here, well, forever.

Fortunately, I had an excuse to go by the U.S. embassy: to renew my passport. Maybe, I thought, I could just pop into the ambassador's office and ask him or her directly?

"There is no U.S. ambassador to Palau," a male clerk in his twenties informed me, "but we do have a chargé d'affaires. What is your question regarding?"

"Oh, just a quick geostrategic thing that's been nagging me."

"Umm . . . let me see if he's available." He stepped around the corner and, returning, said, "OK, go on in."

The chargé's office overlooked a beautiful bay sprinkled with little green islands. The American flag towered behind him, ruffled just so, at the ready for a photo opportunity. The chargé was a sandy-blond-haired man with a surprisingly bushy mustache. He looked busy signing papers.

After some quick pleasantries, I said, "Oh, I was just curious. Do you know why the U.S. government gave Palau so much money in the Compact Agreement?"

"Strategically," he said, looking at me severely, "Palau is very important to the United States."

"But all that money, all at once?"

"Palau is very important to the United States," he said.

"I saw that the Japanese just gave forty million dollars for a new bridge and twenty million dollars for a coral research center," I said. "But then we agreed to a hundred-fifty-million-dollar road. Is there competition for influence here?"

"Look," he said, "Palau is important to the United States. It's not just money we send, but Seabees and Peace Corps workers as well. It is very important for us to contribute to the community."

That didn't explain much, but as I left his office, the guy at the front desk gave me a lead to follow.

"Hey," he said, "are you going to be here on Friday? The USS *Frederick* will be at the harbor. We've having a party on board. Come by. There will be food."

The USS *Frederick*, I'd later find out, is a Navy landing ship that sails around the world, serving as a very big carrot and stick of U.S. foreign policy: it carries about a thousand tons of deveined shrimp and, just in case, about thirty tanks, ready to deploy either—or both—at a moment's notice.

CHAPTER 41

What You Can Expect to Learn in This Chapter:

► Is a musician who wrote songs titled "Mean Mr. Mustard" and "I Am the Walrus" a good source of wisdom when it comes to relationships?

► What about a friend who painted the Sistine Chapel on his dorm room ceiling?

Returning from the embassy, I checked my answering machine as soon as I walked into my little studio. This was part of my usual routine. I'd glance over at that machine even before I took my key out of the door. Until that day, its red display always had flashed the same number: 00. I'd begun to hate everything about that answering machine and its digital display of insensitivity. Why did it have to flash and why red? And why did the readout have two units? Who received calls numbering in the double digits anyway? You'd have to be a pretty superficial person to have that many friends.

So I was thrilled when I arrived home that day and found it flashing 01. Immediately, I pressed play.

"Hey," a woman's voice said. It sounded like Sarah's. That's interesting, I thought, she must have tracked my number down through the motel.

Some of us are going camping next weekend. *Great!* I wanted to know if you wanted to come? *I'm in!* We're going on outrigger canoes and will leave from T-dock about ten a.m. on that Saturday. *That works for me.* We'll get back sometime Sunday, probably late afternoon. *Oh, no, I don't have a sleeping bag. Maybe I can borrow one?* So anyway, Jason (*Jason?*), if you're interested just let me or Carol know. *Who's Carol? Who's Jason?*

I called the front desk. My studio's previous occupant happened to be named Jason. And when I replayed the message, the voice didn't actually sound like Sarah's. I could do nothing but conclude that, as they had done to Sergeant Yokoi, the Americans had found someone to impersonate her voice in order to lure me out of the jungle. Either that or it had been the wrong number.

I lay down on the bed, my shoes still on, and watched the fan wobble overhead. I knew only one person in the entire Eastern hemisphere, and she didn't know my phone number. Or even my last name.

The following afternoon, and not entirely by coincidence, I ran into Sarah again at Yokohama. I told her about the message on my answering machine. She nodded, as though she was familiar with the trip, then gave me a pitying look—the same kind of pitying look you might give a puppy trying to scramble up onto a couch before you give it a nudge.

"Hey," she offered, "I heard the U.S. military is having a party on a big boat or something on Friday. You should come."

I considered saying something smug about how I'd already been invited, by someone at the ambassador's office even, but he wasn't an ambassador, and I didn't remember how to pronounce *chargé d'affaires.*

"I'd love to," I said. We then exchanged email addresses—a choice, I suspect, she quickly came to regret.

Back at my motel room, I tried reading *The Size of Thoughts*, a collection of essays by Nicholson Baker, but every other page I stopped to think how much Sarah would love it, especially the quirkier bits. I finally put the book down, bought a card from the front desk enabling me to get dial-up Internet access, and started an email to her:

> Dear Sarah,
>
> Have you read anything by Nicholson Baker? He has an entire essay devoted to the books that appear in the photographs of mail-order catalogs—like *The Adventures of Augie March* placed discreetly on a Pottery Barn bedside table. Or *Jane Eyre* near a new line of linens. He says he's reviewed a mountain of catalogs but never seen a self-help book or even a bestseller. He writes that those "who live in the rooms of the mail-order catalogs" never read those things. In fact, "they never read paperbacks." Isn't that a funny idea!
>
> But it also makes me wonder about my own books. Did I bring them here as window dressing as well? Am I just trying to live the life of some make-believe person in a make-believe brochure?
>
> Best,
> Alex

I hesitated before sending. Maybe she'd already noticed the bedside books in mail-order catalogs. And would she find these little musings more endearing or creepy? Impulsively, I clicked send. While waiting for a reply, I went back to reading, but a few minutes later I couldn't help drafting another email:

> Hi Sarah
> You really need to take a break from work right now. On the way to my motel I saw three different thunderstorms on the horizon. Also, I have some things I want to read aloud to you . . .
>
> Alex

When I showed up to the Pacific, I had no desire to be in a relationship. Nor did I expect to meet someone like Sarah either. I clicked send. A few minutes later, she still hadn't written back. That's weird, I thought, so I wrote her again:

> Dear Sarah,
> Like Nicholson Baker, have you ever wondered why velvet, despite having a bristled surface, feels smoother than chrome?
>
> Best,
> Alex

And, again, I clicked send. I looked out to sea or, rather, toward the sea just beyond the mangroves outside my window. I realized Sarah and I had spoken to each other, essentially, twice. And I'd just gotten out of a long-term relationship. Perhaps I wasn't thinking clearly? Perhaps it was time to check in with my friend Gordon for advice.

I trusted Gordon's judgment. During college, he had painted the Sistine Chapel on his dorm room ceiling. Now he's an architect who designs high-end prefabricated houses. "Dear Gordon," I wrote:

> I met a woman from California. We seem to share a similar sense of the absurd. Do you think that alone can form the basis of a relationship?
>
> Alex
>
> p.s. I think she may be a lawyer.

Five minutes later, he sent a response:

A woman aboard the *Microspirit* walks away after looking over a tarp where a woman is delivering a baby. That baby, like almost every baby born aboard the *Microspirit*, will be named Microspirit—not a great name for a baby, but better than, say, the *Titanic* or Ship for Brains. *(All photos courtesy of the author unless otherwise noted.)*

Though still in use, Yap stone money isn't moved around—people just remember to whom each one belongs. More photos from Yap and Pig can be seen at www.abeginnersguidetoparadise.com. *(©iStock.com/Tammy616)*

Some of Palau's three hundred Rock Islands as seen from the air. The television show *Survivor* filmed among this island group but needed two helicopters, a crew of five hundred, and every single nail in Palau to create the illusion of a dozen foolish but attractive castaways on a remote island. We needed only a plane ticket. *(Geoff M. Cook)*

Me and Palauan president Tommy Remengesau in a photo taken by a member of his security detail. One word: twinseys!

Part of a pod of dolphins that regularly circles Angaur. Despite hundreds of attempts, they never seemed as keen to swim with us as we did with them.

Every piece of wood, human being, and ambitiously bad idea comes to Angaur via this little ferry—assuming the weather is calm, the ship isn't chartered for a funeral, and someone remembers a pair of scissors to fix the steering. In other words, almost never.

A parrotfish that Steve caught off the rocks at the site. I wish I could say Steve would never eat such a beautiful fish, but he is British, and the Brits are a bloodthirsty people who will eat anything: tripe, Marmite, and pretty reef fish.

Part of the eight-mile path that circles Angaur. The island is home to a few cars, but almost no one drives beyond the quarter mile separating the harbor from the village. Except for monkeys throwing sticks and the occasional saltwater crocodile en route to a nest, this is a great path for a morning jog.

Looking down the coast from the site. The currents on Angaur are so strong that if you snorkel without paying attention, you'll be swept to the next island—West Papua, New Guinea, eight hundred miles south.

Cabot with a miter saw. Bikes were our primary transportation from the harbor to the site for everything from groceries to generators. It wasn't nearly as convenient as it sounds.

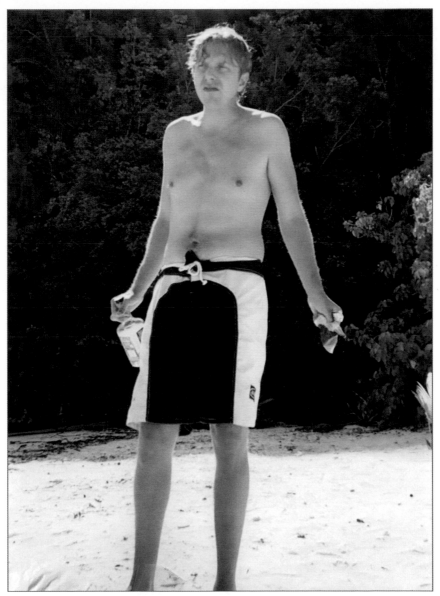
Alex looking as dashing as one does after waking up on a beach with an empty bottle of Jack Daniel's and a granola bar wrapper.

Were this photo not blurry, you could see the incredible precision of our craftsmanship, bodies.

A boy named Cortez picks a papaya, one of the few fruit grown on Angaur and, arguably, the only thing that tastes worse than Marmite. *(Josh Bearman)*

Looking over a healthy coral reef from the north shore of Angaur. Just barely visible, six miles to the north is Peleliu, the site of a really nasty WWII battle.

A WWII-era American plane that crash-landed after a mechanical problem in the jungle where, sixty years later, a bunch of fortunate but underskilled Americans would build a porch with a roof.

Nature, we learned, doesn't really do straight lines. Nor, in fact, did we—this might be the world's first rectangular house without a single right angle.

A young boy on Angaur demonstrating the use of an exotic tool we never, technically speaking, used. *(Josh Bearman)*

Sarah and short-termer Justin Roberts asleep on the four-hour ferry ride to Angaur. When the waves at the harbor were too rough, the ferry had to turn around to reattempt the journey the following day.

Some of the local men who occasionally wandered by the site during construction.

One of forty-four holes dug during construction. The holes alone took us a month.

There isn't much that's heroic about building a house on a remote Pacific island, but Darren and Butch installing this ladder was pretty close. Keen observers will note the foot at the top right. It belonged—and still belongs—to Sarah, who was standing helpfully at the top. Even keener observers will note how I helped by taking the photograph. Shockingly, the ladder was swept to sea a few days later.

Though we captured rainwater from the roof, we made the mistake of building the shower platform so close to the ocean and the spray of waves that our showers were more brackish than fresh.

The house as seen from the bathroom. Note the tent inside—that's how good our finished house was.

A man named Thomas visiting the site. As might be supposed, Thomas had a story to tell—or, more likely, a lot to keep. *(Josh Bearman)*

Palauan tradition says that housewarming parties, like the one pictured here, should happen on the full moon. Fortunately, Palaun tradition says nothing about houses needing "walls." Those are children, by the way, below the deck—not small adults.

The finished house with zip-up canvas walls. In retrospect, we could have chosen a more child-friendly site.

Turns out, baby monkeys are not that good at poker: They overplay their hand, they're terrible bluffers, and they poop their pants a lot.

Rather than trying to write a funny caption about this photo of Sarah *(top)* and Gomez *(bottom)*, I encourage readers to submit their own caption and vote for their favorite at www.abeginnersguidetoparadise.com.

Dear Al,

Have you heard how John Lennon met and fell in love with Yoko Ono? Sometime in November, 1966, Lennon wandered into an art gallery in SoHo. He found a room devoid of color. White walls. White floor. White ceiling. The only thing in the room was a ladder. He climbed the ladder. Halfway up he could see something on the ceiling. It looked like a smudge. He got closer. It was something printed. He got closer still. Squinting, he could barely make out tiny text. It was just one word. The word? "Yes." The artist? Yoko Ono.

—Gordon

I replied right away:

Gordon,

What are you talking about?

Alex

p.s. Should I start listening to more songs about walruses?

His response:

For John and Yoko a shared optimism in turbulent times was the most important thing for them. Maybe for you and Sarah, a shared sense of the absurd in these serious times is the most important thing.

Gordon

p.s. Yes.
p.p.s. Just try to spend some more time with her.

I liked his last advice especially. So I sent her another message.

> Hey Sarah,
> Sorry to bother you, but you want to go on a hike sometime?
> There's so much of this place I want to see.
>
> With warm regards,
> Alex

Finally, a message from Sarah arrived in my inbox. It was a response to my first email.

> Alex,
> A bit busy here, so will keep it short. No need to get all tangled up in your own underpants. You're lucky to be doing what you're doing. Just enjoy the books and time you've set aside.
>
> See you soonish . . .
> Sarah

A moment later a message from Gordon appeared. The subject line, "One last thing . . ." In its entirety, the email read:

> Male lawyers are boring. Women lawyers are sexy.

Three days later, however, Sarah still hadn't responded to my thoughts about hiking, thunderstorms or even the one comparing velvet and chrome. In fact, she still hasn't.

Feeling a bit pensive, I drove to a small park near the water. My intention was just to go for an afternoon walk by myself, but instead I met a smartly dressed woman from the Philippines. She had dark hair, poor teeth, and soft brown eyes. She was carrying a baby. We chatted about her baby for a while, then the weather. She said she'd come to Palau with her two children to work as a waitress in a restaurant.

"They showed me pictures of Palau," she said. "The Rock Islands looked so pretty." But she said the restaurant turned out to be a karaoke bar whose owner had "different expectations."

"You've seen those places, right?" she said. "The ones with the red lanterns."

"I guess so," I said, even though I hadn't.

Effectively stuck, she said she had two kids to care for and no way to pay back the agent's fees, much less the airfare. She asked what I was doing in Palau. I briefly explained the best I could.

"We live in the barracks. Where are you living?" she said abruptly. I told her.

"Are the rooms big?" she asked.

"Normal sized, I suppose."

"Can we move in with you?"

"Well, not, not that big," I stammered. "Probably not much room."

She looked down at her feet. I could only imagine the desperation it takes for a woman to ask a stranger if she and her two children could move in. We chatted awkwardly for a few more minutes, before I said I needed to get going. She knew I didn't.

As I drove back to my hotel, I noticed that Koror had a lot of bars with names like Crystal Palace and Carnival Karaoke. And they all had red lanterns hanging out front. In fact, the city was aglow in red lanterns—even in the middle of the day. I felt guilty for feeling anything but appreciative for my circumstances. I'd come to Palau, by choice, in a search. Not in desperation for survival. And I could leave whenever I wanted. No more feeling sorry for myself.

CHAPTER 42

What You Can Expect to Learn in This Chapter:

► While fishing in Palau, when can you start drinking:
  a) after someone catches a fish?
  b) after a half hour has passed?
  c) whichever comes first?

► How do you ask a man about the size of his engine without sending, you know, the wrong message?

When I met Gibson at Pirates Cove's dock to go fishing, he was standing in his small boat, looming over its tiny steering wheel as a child might a toy. I was happy to be heading out on my second fishing trip in the Pacific. And while fishing on a Thursday morning felt indulgent, it was also in keeping with Sarah's advice to just enjoy the time I'd set aside without getting too tied up in my own underpants. As jauntily as I could, I again said *ungil tutau*—good morning in Palauan.

Instead of acknowledging my earnest, if flawed, second foray into Palauan, Gibson just said, "Do you have your boarding pass?"

"Nope, no boarding pass," I chuckled and started looking for a nonbloodstained place on the floor of the boat to put my little backpack, but Gibson's face was serious.

"This time you have an excuse," he said. He then looked up to his restaurant and yelled, "Anwar!"

Immediately, a very skinny young man of maybe sixteen popped out the door and flew down the concrete stairs. He seemed to be from India or Bangladesh. Gibson grunted. Anwar turned and ran back upstairs, reappearing a minute later with a twelve pack of Bud Light, which he handed to Gibson.

"Always bring your boarding pass," Gibson said to me, before once again grunting at Anwar, who then ran back upstairs. At the top, Anwar held up a pair of flip-flops for Gibson to see. "Of course," Gibson yelled. Anwar ran downstairs, shoes in hand.

"Gibson," I said, newly aware of the issue, "is Anwar, you know, your slave?"

Gibson looked at me like I'd just asked him if pork is a kind of chicken.

"Anwar," Gibson called, "do you want to quit?"

Anwar seemed as confused as he was out of breath. "No," he said. "No, sir."

Apparently, that settled the question for Gibson. "Then fix the generator while we're gone," he said before turning to me. "And, Alex, get in." As we pulled away from the pier, Anwar waved good-bye. He was smiling, apparently delighted to spend the morning fixing the generator rather than fetching Gibson's shoes and beer.

From the water, Palau's capital, Koror, looked even more neglected than it did on land. We puttered past a sketchy warehouse, a hotel abandoned midconstruction, and a basketball court without nets, then more rusting, sketchy warehouses. But as we turned north and away from town, concrete gave way to jungle and the water cleared up too, eventually becoming light turquoise, like a big bucket of water with a single drop of blue food coloring. The water was shallow too— not more than five or six feet deep—allowing us to see fish of various sizes and dark hues before they scattered from the boat.

We passed under a half-constructed bridge connecting the island of Koror to a much larger island. A sign proclaimed the span *The Japan-Palau Friendship Bridge*. We increased our speed, and the temperature seemed to drop about twenty degrees as we turned to run up the coast of Babeldaob. Fifty miles long but only ten or so miles wide, Babeldaob makes up 90 percent of Palau's land area but is home to only 10 percent of its population. I'd read that it was still a wild place; new species of lizards and frogs are discovered in its jungles almost every year.

We then passed a tiny island—an island off the coast of an island—with a single palm tree growing at its center. Around another bend, we surprised a solitary fisherman tossing his net. He waved as we passed. Must be from Ponape, I thought, recalling my initial mis-understanding. We sped up even more, traveling fast for the next forty minutes. During that time, we didn't see one other person or man-made thing, only the steep green hills of Babeldaob rising and falling to our right, the deep blue Philippine Sea crashing over the reef to our left, and the shallow turquoise-tinted lagoon in between.

I'd never really understood the appeal of boating for boating's sake. But now I felt how everything seems to slip away when you're on the water, especially things like the swirling closeness of a small island, where I presumed constant heat and limited space make the Venn diagrams of everyone's lives overlap a little too tightly.

We rounded another bend. On a cleared hillside, a tangle of wires connected half a dozen steel towers. I turned to Gibson.

"Missionary radio station," he yelled.

"I thought Palau only had one channel."

"They broadcast to China."

I nodded knowingly.

Twenty minutes later, we slowed, slipping through a small break in the reef. Slow-moving ocean swells rolled toward the barely sub-merged reef in confused splashes. We continued another mile north, until Gibson stopped the engine and told me to drop the anchor.

"Here?" I said. This looked like an extraordinarily ordinary bit of ocean.

"Here," he said.

I tossed the anchor and asked if he would like a beer.

"On this boat," he said, "no beer until someone catches a fish."

He handed me a rod and flung his line and lure far into the water near the reef, reeling it back in with little jerks. My reel had a little button on top—the trick seemed to be knowing when to release it. I flicked the rod forward while pressing the button. The lure and its three barbed hooks ricocheted scarily around the inside of the boat.

"The thing is, Gibson," I said, "I usually fish with a spear." He looked at me from the corners of his eyes but didn't respond.

The second time, I let go of the button earlier and whipped the rod forward, not noticing the extravagant loops of line that must have magically appeared around my feet. To say that my line developed a knot is a vast understatement: with just the touch of a button, I'd turned chaos theory into chaos practice. I slowly started to pick my way through it. At first I tried making a plan—a methodical let's-start-from-the-beginning approach—but I only seemed to make things worse. I then gave one promising loop a good yank. This did not produce the outcome I was expecting. My line was now to a simple knot what the Internet is to a can-and-string telephone.

I sat down, wanting to get a little comfortable. I knew I should have found the Zen of knot untying while enjoying the quiet of a calm sea under a hot sun, but as I worked the knot, my mind kept returning to a nonfiction book I'd just been reading about the American rat race.

"Can I ask you a question?"

Gibson raised an eyebrow.

"Do you ever, you know, get jealous about other people's boats or engines?"

"Alex," he said, "what are you talking about? I like my engine. I can fix it when it breaks."

"Yeah," I ventured, "but do you ever look at someone else's engine and wish you had an engine like theirs?" Gibson's look suggested he thought I might be trying to flirt with him.

"Guess not," I said as he made another cast, and I returned to my knot. I knew that thinking about a book called *The Overworked American* while floating in a small boat in the Pacific was a bit like reading a cookbook in a restaurant—both relevant and irrelevant—but for five years I'd ceded my life to work. Five years of fourteen-hour days without a vacation, yet I didn't have much to show for it. Where had I gone wrong?

According to the book's author, Juliet Schor, an economist at Harvard, American housing is mostly to blame for our crazy work habits. Apparently, each year, homes have increased in size. In the 1970s, the average house was 750 square feet. Today it's more than two thousand square feet, despite our smaller family size. To pay for that extra space and to pay for filling it up with stuff, people have to work harder and harder.

That pretty much reflected my own experience in New York. There, I'd moved into a succession of apartments, justifying each move by telling myself I'd worked hard, that housing costs were going up, that a little less noise and a little more light would be nice. Yet no matter how many boxes remained unpacked from my last move, I always paused to look at the storefront real estate listings, their perfect pictures and one-paragraph descriptions beckoning like glossy cupcakes in the window of a boutique bakery.

Gibson glanced at the bird's nest of fishing line on my lap and handed me a beer.

"Don't we have to catch a fish first?" I said.

"No beer until someone catches a fish or a half hour, whichever comes first."

The bigger houses we keep moving into apparently aren't making us any happier. Fifty-seven percent of American adults in families say they want more time to spend with their children and spouses, many of whom, I suspect, are in the room when the surveyor calls.

"There must be a rat race here in Palau," I said. "Do you and your wife ever want to move into a better house?"

"Nah," Gibson said with a cast. "We just built a better one, in Meyungs in Koror, but we rent it out to help pay for our daughter's school."

"You built it yourself?" I said, giving a tug to one loop of line in my tangle.

"I hauled the ironwood trees out of the jungle alone," he said.

I paused to look up at him. Gibson was big enough that I imagined he just leaned against trees to push them down, then dragged 'em out two at a time.

"And building it yourself, that was better than buying it?" I had no skills, but I'd always romanticized the idea of building my own house. To me, it seemed fundamental and satisfying to create your own shelter rather than sitting at a desk long enough so you could pay someone else to build it for you. In that sense, it was the opposite of building an Internet site. Gibson seemed to agree, at least on the former point.

"Of course," he said. "I did it myself. I know how it's built."

"I'd love to see it someday," I said. He ignored my transparent hint and kept fishing.

"How did you know how to build a house?" I asked.

"Just had to learn," he said.

I told him again I'd love to see it, but Gibson just grunted. He then walked to the front of the boat and pulled up the anchor so we could drift with the current.

As Gibson fished and I worked on my knot, I thought again about that magazine that ranked me ninety-sixth out of the one hundred most influential technology people in New York. The better metaphor, I realized, wasn't a rat race (whatever that would be) but a car race. In the car race that had been my life, I had worried mostly about who was in front, who was behind, and how to advance my position. For five years I had watched as others passed me (by cashing in their stock options) or fell behind (through bankruptcy or fraud). Crashes were relatively rare but always fun to watch. Occasionally, there were pauses for pit stops (health problems), but mostly we just went around and around.

Seeing I'd made little progress, Gibson took my rod and its accompanying knot and handed me his fishing rod.

Now on my own extended pit stop, I could see that the race wasn't all bad. It had enabled me to live a comfortable, if overextended life. And the track itself prevented me from driving all over the place. The problem, however, was that the race never ended. No winner was ever declared at, say, five hundred laps or fifty years, whichever came first. Instead, drivers simply pulled out, either by retiring to the bleachers (i.e., Phoenix) or the skyboxes (i.e., Palm Beach). Or by dying. Hopefully not in the Atlanta airport as my father always feared.

"Gibson," I said. "Do you . . . ?"

"Alex," he said, handing me my reel back. He'd untangled it in about a minute. "Stop talking."

That seemed a reasonable suggestion. For most of the rest of the day, we just fished in near silence, except for the zip of the line, the little plop of plastic hitting the water, and the muted, methodical whirl of the reel as we pulled the lures back. Reel, reel, reel, cast, plop, reel, reel, reel, cast, plop, reel, reel, reel. Though fishless, Gibson didn't seem upset, and neither was I.

"It will be dark in an hour," he said finally. "Time to go home."

We pulled anchor and slipped back through the same break in the reef before turning south toward home. It had just rained over Babeldaob, making the jungle leaves shimmer in the late-afternoon sun. Flying fish leapt away from the boat, skimming the surface like aquatic hummingbirds before diving back into the sea.

Arriving back in Koror, Gibson cut the engine, and we drifted the final few feet to the dock, arriving at the same moment and just as silently as the sun slid below the horizon.

CHAPTER 43

What You Can Expect to Learn in This Chapter:

➤ Is it a good idea to sneak into the officer's wood-paneled dining room on a very large U.S. military ship?

➤ And, if you do, what should you steal while there?

A U.S. Navy sailor greeted me with a crisp salute before ushering me up a set of metal stairs to the oversized deck of the USS *Frederick*. "Welcome aboard!" he said. "And help yourself to the shrimp."

Up on deck, I didn't see Sarah, but every other U.S. expat appeared to be in attendance. People I'd later identify as anthropologists, Peace Corps volunteers, dive guides, engineers, lawyers, and judges mingled with drinks in hand, their deep tans and chirpy Hawaiian shirts a resplendent contrast to the matte gray of the tank-transport ship. A slight breeze blew most of the heat and humidity away, the half-moon casting a flattering light on the twinkling harbor. A military band played "Celebration" by Kool & the Gang.

"Asparagus?" a waiter asked me.

"Sure," I said.

I looked around at the men sipping their drinks, the women laughing gaily. The U.S. had had a good run, I thought. Rome had puttered on after the Vandals took Carthage, as did the Brits after World War II; America too would putter along just fine long after the gas stops flowing to the nation's oversized barbecue grill. I headed for the bar, eager to get a drink and my share of the crustaceans before they too ran out.

While I was waiting in a good-sized line, a middle-aged man behind me said, "What would Palau be without the U.S.?" He had a mustache and puffy, graying hair and wore an orange-flowered shirt tucked tightly into a pair of uncomfortably snug white shorts, giving him the appearance of an aging Tom Selleck—without the dimples.

"Not sure where Palau would be," I said, "but I'm sure they're thrilled to have our Navy anchored in their harbor."

"Sure they are," he said. "You bet they are." I wondered why he was waiting in line at all: he held a full mai tai in each hand. He took a long sip, his bushy mustache bristling the maraschino cherries floating on the edge of each cup.

"I mean, look at this," he said with a sweep of his arm and drink around the ship's deck. "The United States is great, a great, powerful country." His nodded to the beat, perfectly in sync with "Cel-e-brate good times, come on!"

"It is," I said, "but, I dunno. If we were so strong, would we really have to send in the Navy to such a small place?" From a class in college, I vaguely remembered something about how countries usually acquire foreign territories out of weakness, not strength. Like sports cars for middle-aged men, empires are status symbols for countries in decline: when things are going well, more subtle power is sufficient. You don't have to actually send in the gunboats; the threat is enough.

"What's that?" he said, only half-struggling to hear over the music.

"I was just wondering—" I started to repeat myself, then reconsidered. "Yup, a pretty nice night."

"Too fucking hot here," he said, just as the band stopped for a break. "We stopped in Hawaii on the way, before moving here. Now, that's a sweet spot. And the boats in Pearl Harbor were a lot bigger than this one." I was trying to understand where he was going.

"It was great," he continued. "We rented a white convertible and drove all around the island."

"No kidding?" I said.

"We went to the Dole Pineapple Factory. Have you been there? They keep that goddamn floor so clean you could eat off it. . . ." He trailed off, then stared into his drink, no doubt lost in remembrance of that floor. Just as it was my turn to order, Sarah walked up the steps. She was wearing a yellow sundress. I asked for two Bud Lights.

"Well, good talking to you," I said. "My name is Alex, by the way."

"My name is Randall."

"See you around sometime," I said.

"Oh, I'm sure about that," he said.

I smiled nervously and handed Sarah her drink.

"Did you see the crab cakes?" she said as we stepped away.

"We live in a special time."

She nodded, then pointed toward an open metal door that led belowdecks. "Wanna snoop around?"

"Of course."

Beers in hand, we discreetly walked behind the bar and through a door that had been propped open, then scrambled down a steep set of stairs. As we walked the ship's narrow halls, we could see inside a few fluorescent-lit cabins. Each was a classic picture of navy life: a sailor reading a magazine on a tidy bunk, say, or someone writing a letter on a little desk that folded against the wall. Down another set of stairs and a long corridor, we came upon a wood-paneled dining room. It had a mahogany table at the center, old-fashioned portholes, crystal lighting, and carved antique cabinets. The door clicked closed as we stepped inside.

As Sarah casually opened a drawer, I thought about kissing her. I knew I wasn't ready for a new relationship—having just gotten out of a doozy in New York—but as the relationship cliché goes, when you drop everything to move to a small island in the Pacific, don't be surprised when you meet an amazing girl on a full-moon kayak ride. Or something like that. I leaned a bit closer.

"Look," she said. "Spoons!"

"What does the engraving say?" I said, pointing at the cutlery.

I was really attracted to her, but if she rebuffed me, could we go back to being friends, especially on such a small island?

"*Life, liberty, and the pursuit of all who threaten it.* Weird."

"It says *weird*?"

"No, I said *weird*," she said, handing me the spoon. "It just ends with *all who threaten it*. What happened to *happiness*?"

"Good question," I said lamely. I was distracted. If we were going to have a relationship with kissing, didn't it make sense to start sooner rather than later? I started to turn toward her.

"These drawers," she said, opening a few more. "They don't have knives or forks. Just spoons. That's weird. Do they only eat soup at sea?" She'd said the word *weird* twice in thirty seconds, and I felt whatever moment we could have had slip away. We heard someone walking toward us. "Let's get going," she said.

As she opened the door and stepped into the hallway, I slid the spoon into my pocket. I'm not sure why. Perhaps I wanted a way to remember the night my life almost changed forever. Even if I didn't kiss this incredible woman, at least I got a souvenir spoon.

As we walked the hallways on our way back up to the party, I thought about the only other thing I'd ever stolen: a Twix candy bar when I was about eight. For reasons still unclear, I'd shown it to my parents right after taking it. Their response was entirely consistent with their approach to parenting. Without a lot of fuss, they simply drove me back to the grocery store, took me to the same checkout person, and told me to return it. I was embarrassed, but there was no reprimand, no punishment.

My parents raised my brother and me the same way most people raise dogs: run 'em twice a day, hug 'em on occasion, don't let them poop on the floor. Whereas other children had curfews, chores, and limits, I had none. Take television, for example. I had one in my room, and I could watch it as late or as early as I wanted to. There was a certain genius, albeit a risky genius, to this approach. Like a kid caught smoking and forced to smoke an entire pack in one sitting, I became so tired of television that by fourteen I'd given it up. I didn't rebel because there was so little to rebel against. Compared to the other kids' parents, mine seemed reasonable—enlightened, even. That I didn't end up in prison is greater proof of the existence of a divine creator than anything I've yet to come across.

When Sarah and I reached the top deck, we found Randall and a few others dancing. Randall made eye contact with me and, over the song "Y.M.C.A.," yelled, "Eric, let me buy you another drink." That the drinks were free and my name wasn't Eric clearly didn't matter to Randall.

"Sure," I said as Sarah and I stepped forward. The dance floor was large—maybe two hundred square feet of modular parquet. I presumed they stored it belowdecks, between the tanks and the artillery shells. And it worked well enough. Sarah, Randall, and I spent the rest of the evening dancing to wedding standards while uniformed waiters walked past with yet more barbecued shrimp, courtesy of the U.S. government. Across the water, the shadowed silhouettes of palms shimmered in the light of the moon. Not exactly paradise, but not not paradise either.

If Sarah noticed or cared that this was our second lovely evening at sea together, she did a very good job of hiding it. In the dirt parking lot, she gave me a friendly good-bye hug before hopping into her little station wagon and driving away in another swirl of dust.

CHAPTER 44

What You Can Expect to Learn in This Chapter:

▶ Imagine you're a Palauan prostitute with a meth addiction. Now imagine you happen to get pregnant by a client who also happens to be the cofounder of a global shipping business. The *H* in DHL, for example. When it comes time to file your $90 million paternity suit, do you ask around for a lawyer or just wait for one to call?

▶ What is the only thing worse than having the first name Bruce?

Gibson and Bruce were both finishing their beers when I walked into an otherwise empty Pirates Cove Bar & Grill. They were watching a FOX story about a woman who killed her husband, a dentist. The TV, as always, was on mute.

"Gibson," Bruce said, "have you decided to rent your place to Alex yet?" Gibson arched his eyebrows slightly.

"He built it himself," Bruce said, turning to me. "It's beautiful. And huge—three separate apartments. But the neighbors are a handful." He then made an awkwardly aggressive karate chop in the air.

"Why? Who are the neighbors?" I said.

"Oh, you'll be fine," he said.

"Fine?"

"Anyway, Gibson, at least let him see it."

Gibson raised his right index finger. I thought he was acknowl-edging the suggestion. Instead, a waitress brought me a beer.

I then asked Bruce about his suit against Larry Hillblom, the founder of DHL. "Why you suing him again? Didn't get your pack-age on time?"

"The estate," he said. "I'm suing his estate." Bruce went on to explain that before his death in a seaplane crash, Mr. Hillblom had had a habit of visiting girlfriends all over the Pacific. Bruce said he thought some of those girlfriends must have had kids.

"If I can prove paternity," he said, "then they'll have a claim on his estate. It's worth a few billion. If I win, I get a share."

"And if you lose?"

"All that money goes to some fucking hospital or university or something."

"Well, sounds like you're doing God's work," I said.

"You bet it is," he said, taking the last sip of his beer. "The prob-lem," he continued, "is the DNA. His body was never recovered, and someone scrubbed his entire house with alcohol. Even the tooth-brushes."

Bruce seemed to be particularly irritated about the toothbrushes, as though he somehow had the right to a stranger's DNA. He said his plan was to round up a lot of the kids and get enough of their DNA to prove they all had the same father. "But first you have to find the women he screwed and get them to sign on. I know one of them is here in Palau. I just called her. She's a crack whore named Lolita."

"Bruce, stop talking," Gibson said. "Alex—come by here tomor-row. I'll take you up to Gibson's complex." He then spit into a sheared-off can of Diet Coke, a different one, I hoped, from the one I'd seen him spit into days earlier.

"Okeydokey," Bruce said, standing to leave. He then signed his tab and, turning to me, said, "Give me a call sometime. We'll go to the Officer's Pube." A pun on pub, I assumed. "Just look me up. I'm in the phone book."

"Umm . . . what's your last name?"

He told me. I couldn't believe it. It's horrendous. I hesitate to even mention it. But here goes. . . . I swear I am not making this up: it was Lee.

"Never wear shoes in a home in Palau," Gibson said, opening the front door. It was the upstairs unit of a two-story concrete building perched high on a hill.

To get here, I'd followed Gibson in his truck to Ngerkebesang, an island connected to the main island of Koror by another narrow causeway without guardrails. After the causeway, we'd passed an auto-repair shop made from discarded shipping containers, a few houses with metal roofs and chickens out front, and a restaurant with the evocative name Sarah's Yum Yum. A few more curves and we ascended a steep driveway cut through a canopy of jungle, passing along the way a concrete pillbox from World War II. Finally, at the top, he parked beside a bright red Honda Accord and stepped inside the yellow concrete house that Gibson had built with his own hands.

Stepping around an unplugged lamp and some cardboard boxes, I walked over to the floor-to-ceiling windows that ran the entire length of the room. They framed one of the loveliest views I'd ever seen. To the right, the entire length of the green west coast of Babeldaob stretched off for miles to the horizon. To the left, the vast dark blue of the Philippine Sea appeared empty except for a couple of distant tropical thunderheads releasing rain in windblown slants. And below the window: a sun-glistened canopy of banana plants and pink flowering trees cascading to the ocean, maybe a thousand feet below.

"This wood took a lot of work," Gibson said, drawing my attention inside. I believed him. The living room was huge—maybe sixty feet long and nearly as wide—and all its floors were made of the same rich dark wood. As I untied my shoes, he said, "Cut down the trees myself. Have you ever cut down an ironwood tree?"

Before I could answer, a well-dressed Filipina woman in her fifties walked into the living room from what I presumed was a bedroom; she was carrying a cardboard box. Startled to find anyone else there, I mumbled an apology for intruding, but she didn't respond. She set the box in the middle of the floor, returned to the same room she'd come from, and closed the door.

"Tenant?" I said. Gibson just raised his eyebrows—a distinctly Palauan gesture I was coming to learn that meant yes, but to most any foreigner, it would just be a look of mild surprise.

"Two chain saw blades for each tree," Gibson said in reference to the floors—and most every other surface: the window trim, the support pillars, the counters and the cabinets of the open kitchen in the corner. "Fifty dollars a blade."

In response, I raised my eyebrows. In response to my response, Gibson raised his eyebrows. I raised my eyebrows back and looked carefully at his face for a smile. But he was completely serious. I couldn't help but laugh aloud. Instead of laughing, Gibson tilted his head, confused. As far as he was concerned, we were just having a conversation in eyebrow.

Recalling what I thought had been a warning from Bruce (and eager to change the subject—though from what exactly I wasn't sure), I said, "So, the neighbors? Where are they?"

"Downstairs," he said. "One unit upstairs, two downstairs. They have their own entrances." He then gestured to the side of the building. This all seemed potentially important, but I was too distracted again by the view to ask any of the follow-ups I should have asked.

"What are we looking at?" I said.

"Babeldaob."

"Babeldaob," I said.

Before leaving New York, I'd managed to sublet my apartment for more than I'd been paying. I now wondered if the difference might cover a lot of the rent here—or even all of it. "If you don't mind me asking," I said, "what is the rent?"

But he did seem to mind me asking. Instead of responding, he just walked over to another window and stared into the distance. Having already moved into a hotel room with its own refrigerator (granted, a mini refrigerator, but still an upgrade), I knew I might be repeating my mistake from New York—namely, always searching for a better nest—but I couldn't imagine a nicer nest than the one that Gibson had built.

"Gibson," I blurted out, "I'd really like to rent this place. Depending on the price of course . . ."

But again, no response. For a full minute, in fact, he didn't say anything. That is a long time when waiting for an answer to a question. Count it out . . . 1 . . . 2 . . . 3. . . .

Finally, he spoke. "Alex, there's a chief's swearing-in ceremony at my village in Babeldaob a week from Sunday. Bring a hat."

CHAPTER 45

What You Can Expect to Learn in This Chapter:

► How do you not come across as a stuck-up skink when talking about the interesting things you've recently learned from a book about group psychology? (Hint: you can't.)

► If you grab the trunk of a poisonous tree, how long can you expect the welt to last?

S arah and I had our first fight at a place called Jellyfish Lake, a brackish, tea-colored lake in the middle of one of Palau's Rock Islands. The lake is not much larger than a typical Best Buy parking lot, but unlike a typical Best Buy parking lot, it's home to six million jellyfish. As explained in countless documentaries, these jellyfish are unique in that they've been isolated from predators for millennia and lost their ability to sting. Every day, all six million *Mastigias papua*, or golden medusa jellyfish, migrate across the lake, following the sun and returning overnight. Visitors are advised to be gentle when swimming with them; their fragile flesh is easily shredded by a careless fin, even a fingernail.

To reach the lake, we found a guy with a tiny boat and a tiny engine and threaded our way through the lovely Rock Islands. Upon landing, we walked a few hundred yards up a short but steep hill and down its back side, grabbing vines and tree trunks to avoid sliding on the narrow, muddy path. Arriving at the lake a few minutes later, we saw that we weren't the first. In addition to the six million jellyfish, seventy or so Taiwanese tourists were in the water, forming a sort of human raft by linking arms. A few jellyfish lay tilted at awkward angles on the surface behind them.

"Why do you think they link arms?" I said as we sat down on the little wooden dock to wait for the tourists to leave. These were among the first tourists I'd encountered in the Pacific. Palau receives only sixty thousand visitors a year (compared to Oahu's five million annual visitors). Other than a smattering of American and Australian tourists, most of Palau's come in groups from Taiwan and Japan for long weekends and stay and eat all their meals in one of two large hotels. And almost all visit Jellyfish Lake.

"Hard to imagine American tourists, especially strangers, linking arms like that," I said.

"The last time I was here, it was the same," Sarah said. "Maybe it's cultural?"

"Well, not sure I buy *it's just culture*," I said. "I was just reading a book that says there are six social factors influencing individual behavior—"

"Oh, God," she said.

"This seems to be an example of social proof. Everyone in the lake is wearing a life jacket because everyone else is wearing a life jacket."

"Maybe they're just helping each other out, you asshole. Maybe they're not all comfortable in the water. Is fear of death one of those motivating factors?"

"Commitment and consistency are two others. Then there's obedience to authority. . . ."

"Have you ever considered the supply and demand of your own words?" Sarah said. "You could auction them on eBay one by one and see exactly what they're worth."

"I'd worry about people's credit card limits," I said.

"I'm serious," she said. "Are these books actually giving you a better understanding of the world or just the perception of under-standing?"

"Well, they probably aren't hurting."

"They do if they make you smug. Take psychology. It's a huge field. Did you bring any other books on the subject? Or just that one?"

"I have something by Dave Barry, if that's what you're asking."

"The problem is that you get good at cocktail party conversation. But there's no context. Before you know it, you're reducing human behavior to four bullet points."

"Six, actually," I said.

"Sarcasm is the weapon of the weak," she said.

"Well, humility is the weapon of the month," I said, despite having no idea what that meant.

For a few moments, we watched in silence as the Taiwanese tourists made their way back. I did like my books, but I could see her point. Kind of. I supposed in an ideal world, I would have brought a thousand books.

"I get what you're saying," I said, "but what's the phrase? We shouldn't let the perfect be the enemy of the good."

"You think making snarky comments about people who are afraid of the water is good? Anyway, they're almost here. I think we should go in now."

We slid into the warm water and started swimming toward the jellyfish swarm. I wasn't quite sure where things had gone off track. Perhaps I'd been alone with my own thoughts for too long with no one to keep me in check.

I certainly didn't feel alone here. Within moments, I saw my first jellyfish: a baby about the size of a pea, looking more peach than gold. Then I saw another and another and another. They had round tops, a circular ruffle of gelatinous tissue, and short, dangling tentacles. Two strokes later I was completely surrounded by pulsating orbs, the largest about the size of a cantaloupe. I stopped swimming and cupped the smooth, waxy dome of one golden jellyfish in the palm of my hand. It fluttered forward. Hundreds of others gently thumped against my arms, my legs, and the side of my head as they tried to go around me, intent only on following the slow arc of the sun.

"Amazing," Sarah said.

"Amazing," I agreed.

I made a mental note: if I ever felt that all was not quite right in the universe, I'd just think that at this very moment, six million friendly cantaloupes in pink tutus were slowly pulsing their way across a small, tea-colored lake in the middle of a remote island in the western Pacific.

We played among the jellyfish for an hour, occasionally diving down to the colder water, where the moon jellyfish lived. These classically shaped white jellyfish were larger than the ones above. Though also stingless, they live in deeper water low in oxygen and high in ammonia and phosphate—both of which leach through human skin and are potentially lethal. But it was irresistible nonetheless to swim to the border of this anoxic layer to catch a glimpse of this world within a world.

"Going to get dark soon," Sarah said. "We should go."

As we swam to shore and walked back up the hill, I thought again about Sarah's comments on the dock. I deserved her criticism. Mostly, however, I was surprised how much her comments stung. Before then I hadn't known that she could hurt my feelings, that I cared so much about what she thought. Along the way, I grabbed the trunk of a tree to steady myself on the slippery slope. Its sap must have been poisonous. The welt lasted a week.

CHAPTER 46

What You Can Expect to Learn in This Chapter:

➤ What kind of unexpected items can you find while scuba diving in a flooded Pennsylvania quarry?

➤ Under what circumstances might it be necessary to self-induce an allergic reaction?

I didn't know it at the time, but I must have been feeling unsettled after my fight with Sarah. I had, at most, two friends in the Pacific, and I might have been losing one. Figuring a nice place to live with a long-term lease would make me feel less adrift, the following afternoon I drove back up to Gibson's triplex just to have a look around. Out front, I found a man in his early thirties washing the hubcaps of his Honda Accord. His brown hair was cropped tightly, except the front, which ramped skyward.

"You my new neighbor?" he said, hardly looking up.

"Umm, I hope so. Hi. My name is Alex."

"I'm Michael," he said, giving another pass at an already sparkling rim. "Hot enough for you here? Never gets this hot back home in Philadelphia."

"Not terrible," I said. "It gets pretty hot in Texas."

"Texas, huh?" he said suspiciously. "Where's your accent then?"

"Not sure. My mother's Canadian—that might have something—"

"Before coming here, my wife and I had never left the good ole U-S-of-A," he said, making a gentle, circular wipe on the back door.

"I hear you," I said, not knowing what else to say.

"This place is kind of a dump, don't you think? You'd think with all the money we give them . . ." He then trailed off.

"It has some rougher parts, I guess. So, you're here with your wife?"

"Yes," he said, "but you'll love her."

One of my pet peeves is when people I don't know tell me I'll *love* something. How did he know I would love his wife? And why would he want me to? Furthermore, why use the word *but*? Was he telling me I shouldn't worry about our nice rapport being ruined by another person, i.e., his wife?

"Look forward to meeting her," I said.

"I guess you came for the diving?"

"Not really—"

"Best in the world here," he said, "bar none."

"Oh, you're a keen diver, are you?" I said.

"Well, we've dived every quarry in Pennsylvania if that's what you mean."

It wasn't, but I let it pass. "What do you find down there?" I said. "Mostly old tires and stuff?"

"Oh yeah, everything . . . old tires . . . old cars . . . and"—he paused to admire his spiffy hatchback's clean windows before finishing—"I found a lawn mower once."

"A lawn mower? No kidding, way down there?"

"Oh, yeah. Pretty amazing, huh? God works in pretty mysterious ways."

He could be right, I thought. Perhaps, after creating light and the oceans, the Almighty dropped a lawn mower in that quarry outside Scranton?

Before I could say anything, however, Michael's wife pulled up and stepped out of a beige Chrysler Sebring convertible. She wore a black suit and had her black hair pulled back tightly.

"Hi, honey," Michael said. "You're home early. It's only three thirty-seven p.m. How was work today?'

"Same ole, same ole," she said, holding out a cheek for him to kiss. "I see you're washing the Accord again." Turning to me, she said, "He's got nothing else to do." I thought Michael might be offended, but he nodded in agreement.

"Elise is a lawyer," Michael said, returning to another hubcap. "But you could probably tell by the suit." They both laughed at this one. A lot. "You could probably tell by the suit," they repeated together.

I introduced myself and, figuring that it was a small island and they were both lawyers, asked Elise if she happened to know Sarah. "We have mutual friends," she said. She seemed surprised she hadn't heard of me. Searching, she said, "Do you see her a lot?"

"Not really. Kind of."

"Why don't you two come over to our place for dinner?" Michael said. "I'll cook."

Elise smiled at me and said, "That would be great." I felt stuck. Yet also optimistic. I hadn't been invited over to someone's place for dinner since I was on Pig. And besides, I really wanted to see Sarah again.

"That would be great," I said, hoping Sarah would be available.

Elise went downstairs to her apartment, presumably to call Sarah in private.

"So," Michael said, still cleaning his car, "if you're not a diver, why are you here?"

I tried to explain, mumbling something about books and choices and paradise.

"If you like books, you'll love *The Book of Virtues* by Bill Bennett. But that's probably already on your list."

"Actually, it's not," I said. I was about to add, sounds like a hoot, though, when Elise returned.

"We're on," she said. "See you at five thirty p.m. Two hours should give us time to get ready."

"Actually," Michael corrected, "it's only an hour and fifty-one minutes."

Elise looked at her watch and said, "Actually, only an hour and fifty minutes now! Better get going! Ha! Ha!"

Get it? Time passes. Even when you're talking about time. Ha. Ha.

Exactly an hour and fifty-five minutes later, just as darkness was approaching, I drove back to Gibson's complex. Sarah arrived just behind me.

"Why did you do this?" Sarah said in a low voice as she stepped out.

"Do what?"

"Make plans with them. They're terrible."

"I didn't know," I said, adding, "I wanted to make some friends."

We walked down the side stairs and knocked on Elise and Michael's apartment door. "They're fun suckers," Sarah whispered. "You owe me."

"Besides, how could I know?" I said as Elise swung the door open. She was still wearing her business suit.

"Come in," Elise said, locking the door behind us. Michael was in the kitchen wearing a white apron printed with a few small flowers and the words *Kiss the Cook*.

Their apartment, located just below what, potentially, would be mine, was exceedingly spare. There were no rugs to cover the white tile floor. The furniture included only a beige couch (with a beige cat sprawled in the middle) and an extra-large television with the volume turned up. A long white wall ran the entire back length of the apartment. Except for a single five-by-seven-inch photograph hanging in the middle, the wall was entirely bare. I stepped forward to look closer at the picture. Michael was wearing a tuxedo, Elise a white wedding dress. The two of them were smiling, but their smiles looked determined, almost angry. Stepping back, I noticed how the placement of the little photo on that huge wall made the two of them seem like a pair of penguins—two lonely penguins lost on a vast sheet of ice.

"So, Alex, where again in Connecticut are you from?" Elise said, walking toward the open kitchen. Was that a trick question to try to trip me up? I wondered. The geographical equivalent to *Have you stopped beating your wife yet?* to which the typical answer is *No, I mean, yes. I mean, neither.*

"Um, Texas, actually. Born in the Alamo, raised in the capital," I said, smiling, adding a touch of Texas twang.

"Would you two like some O'Doul's?" Michael asked.

From the television I heard an announcer say, "Coming up next . . . *Will & Grace.*"

"Michael, turn that off," Elise said while slicing carrots very, very thinly. "I don't know who thinks gays are so funny."

"Well, some gay people are funny," I said. "And some aren't. Kind of like everyone el—" Before I could finish, I was interrupted by Michael banging something metal in his hand against the top of the glass coffee table.

"It's the laser-pointer batteries," he said. "I think they're corroded."

"Some things just aren't designed properly," Elise said while walking toward the window.

"They aren't speaking metaphorically, are they?" Sarah whispered. "You know, about gay people."

"Did you guys see the moon tonight?" Elise said. "Isn't it beautiful?" We followed her to the window. The sky was cloudless and sprinkled with stars. An almost full moon was rising between the trees.

"Too bad it needs to be dark in here," Elise said, lowering the first of many blinds, "if we're going to see the wedding pictures."

"Actually," Sarah said, "you showed them to me—"

"I know, but Alex hasn't seen them."

"Fixed it," Michael said. "All I had to do was replace the batteries. They'd just gone bad."

Elise nodded knowingly, then turned off the lights and directed us to the couch. Michael rolled the television to the side and flipped on a projector attached to a computer. A nearly life-sized photograph of a sunset appeared on the white wall. "This was the sun the day before our wedding," Michael said, spinning his red laser in tight circles around the glowing orb. He next pressed a button on another remote control. The first soft notes of Enya's "Sail Away" bubbled across the room.

"Hon, I think that was the sunset *two* days before the wedding."

"No. I'm pretty sure that was on the Friday."

Sarah dropped her head in defeat.

"This is a picture of the cake," Elise said. "And this one . . . oh . . . this is also the cake."

I bobbed my head to the song.

"And here is the reception area being set up. And that's Michael's grandmother," Elise said. "She flew in from St. Louis. Well, actually, she flew in from Baltimore, where she was visiting her sister. . . ."

"Unfortunately, guys," Michael announced, "dinner is ready! Come and get it!"

Michael and Elise seated themselves at the head and the foot of the table. Sarah and I sat across from each other. Their cat curled up under the table.

"So, I have to tell you guys what happened last Friday," Elise began as Michael set down a platter of poached whitefish, mashed potatoes, and boiled carrots—a culinary trifecta for those without teeth. "So, get this. I was watching television alone when Michael said, 'It's time for bed.' And I said, 'Right now? It's so early?' and he said, 'It's not that early.' And I said, 'It is early. It's only nine o'clock.' And he said, 'It's ten o'clock.' Get it? I had thought it was only nine o'clock. Ha! Ha! Ha!"

I looked at Sarah, who smiled and nodded, clearly thinking suicidal thoughts.

"Can you believe it?" Elise continued, clearly enjoying her second crazy-passage-of-time joke of the day. "It was ten o'clock, and I thought it was nine o'clock. Ha! Ha! Ha!"

Right then genius struck and the planets aligned as the solution came. I began to vigorously rub both of my ankles against the side of their cat, thankful for the first time in my life that I'm allergic to cats.

"I mean, who goes to bed at that time?"

I slipped off a flip-flop and gave the cat a final caress with the inside arch of my foot—the place where I figured blood vessels were closest to the skin. Within seconds, the backs of my knees started to itch.

"Hon, this is really good," Elise said to Michael in a way that suggested we were supposed to follow suit.

"Mmmm," Sarah and I both said loudly.

I saw Elise staring at my face. "Hey, Sarah, is Alex OK?" I wondered why she didn't just ask me.

"I'm fine," I said.

"I'm not sure," Elise said. "His eyes are really red."

"Oh, yeah. I'm fine. I'll be fine," I said, just before sneezing. I then sneezed again, punctuating it this time with a loud stomp on the ground. Sarah, Michael, and Elise recoiled, and the cat walked away. I hoped I'd given myself a big enough dose of cat. Turns out, I had.

"Michael," Elise demanded, "get the paper towels."

While Michael fetched an entire roll of paper towels, I began to frantically scratch the front of my neck with the kind of startled, jerking motion one might use to remove a large insect. Or jellyfish tentacles.

"I think there is something wrong with him," Elise said.

"Alex?" Sarah said.

"I'll be fine," I said. "Really." I sneezed again, causing my head to lunge forward and my chest to thunk the side of the table. The ice cubes in our water glasses clanked noisily as they sloshed back and forth.

"His ears are turning red," Elise said. Her insistence on talking about me as though I couldn't possibly hear suggested she thought I might already be in a mucus-induced coma.

"So, how long ago did you guys get married?" I said, bending over to scratch the backs of my knees again.

"Maybe Alex is allergic to the potatoes," Michael offered.

Elise put down her fork. "Who's allergic to potatoes?" she said.

"Not sure," he said.

"Well," I interrupted, "I am allergic to cats." For credibility, I added, "And penicillin."

"That's a definite negative on the penicillin," Michael said as though he occasionally added a half cup of general antibiotic to the marinade, "but we do have a cat."

"Oh," Elise said, "you're probably allergic to Tabatha, our tabby."

"You have a tabby cat named Tabatha?" Sarah said, incredulous.

"We do," Elise said with a grin. "She is so, so, *so* sweet. Just last night, for example—"

I sneezed again, this time glazing the top of my potatoes with a fresh film of, well, me.

"I think we should get going," Sarah said.

"I'm really sorry," I said. "It's just that . . ."

"Sarah's right. You really should go," Elise said. I started to apologize, but Elise stood and walked us briskly to the door.

Outside, Sarah turned to face me. Her expression was skeptical.

"What?" I said with a snuffle. "I'm allergic to cats."

After dinner, Sarah and I decided to take a short walk up the hill by her apartment. For the first time since either of us had been in Palau, the temperature felt cool. Not jeans-and-light-sweater cool, but at least not swelteringly, self-pity-inducing hot either. Optimistic and feeling a bit cheesy, I stopped by my motel and grabbed a blanket and a book on the way out. Reaching the top of the little knoll, we lay down and took turns reading aloud poems by William Blake, guided by the dim light of a radio or cell tower just behind and above us. One of our favorites was "The Laughing Song," the last lines of which read:

> *Come live, and be merry, and join with me,*
> *To sing the sweet chorus of "Ha, ha, he!"*

I set the book down. I have no idea what we talked about, but as we talked, the sides of our legs touched. I felt the smoothness of her skin touching mine. She didn't pull her leg away. Clearly, a good sign.

Normally when two people meet, they have some common point of orientation: a job, a friend, or a church. All we really had in common was geography: we were both *here*, which at least suggested a shared disposition—dreamy yet practical enough not only to consider moving to a place like Palau but to take all the steps to actually do it. But we knew next to nothing about each other. I knew she was a lawyer. She knew I'd once lived in New York. All we had in common was Palau, and with her contract ending, we might not even have that for much longer. But at least here our relationship could evolve at a more natural pace, unencumbered by a hectic schedule or friends nagging for developments. At least that's what I told myself after I turned my head to kiss her—and found that she'd fallen asleep.

CHAPTER 47

What You Can Expect to Learn in This Chapter:

➤ Which of the following should you not bring to a Palauan chief-swearing-in ceremony?
a) a life-sized chocolate cake in the shape of a manatee?
b) a very long and interesting book?
c) beer?

➤ Should you or should you not soak betel nut in vodka before consuming it for the first time?

As I stepped out the door on the way to meet Gibson for the chief-swearing-in ceremony, I realized I didn't have a gift. But what do you give to a man being sworn in as chief? A tie? A fruit basket? Thinking the event might be kind of festive, I decided on beer.

On the way to the store, I wondered why he'd invited me. Was it some sort of test to see how well I comported myself, the Pacific-island equivalent of a credit check? Perhaps he regretted not doing more due diligence on his other tenants before renting to them. I did know that if I was going to create a life here, in the possible paradise of Palau, I was going to need a place to stay beyond a motel room.

Apparently, beer was a bad choice.

When Gibson saw me walk down the crumbling concrete dock carrying a six-pack of Bud Light, he grimaced.

"Beer?" he said.

"Umm . . ."

Gibson yelled up to the balcony of Pirates Cove. "Anwar!" Anwar stuck his head out the sliding-glass door. "Alex thought he should bring beer. Get some ice!" Anwar popped back inside.

"Oh?" I said, stepping into the boat. "Should I have . . ." But before I could finish the sentence, my attention was snagged by a dead body, lying on a piece of plywood under a white sheet, in the middle of the boat. Oh, my God, I thought, there's a new chief because the last one died and here is his body. Either that or it was the last guy who had brought beer to a chief-swearing-in ceremony.

Before I could ask Gibson for details, he again yelled up at Anwar, "Anwar! Bring me my shoes!"

"Gibson," I said, "I know I asked before, but are you sure Anwar isn't your slave?"

He shook his head, and then called up again, "Anwar! And a quart of oil!"

"Really?" I said.

"He can go back to Bangladesh whenever he wants."

"Assuming he can afford his own plane ticket?"

"Yes," Gibson said, and looked up, likely wondering how much longer he'd have to wait for his ice, shoes, and oil.

A moment later, Gibson's wife, Mariana, came running down the stairs. Stout and dark-skinned, she looked like a miniature version of Gibson, though that could have been because she was wearing a plain white T-shirt that hung down below her knees and looked like it could have been his. She gave me a warm, friendly smile and waved, as if apologizing for the delay. Anwar followed close behind, carrying ice, shoes, and oil.

As Gibson started the engine and we pulled out of the harbor, I moved to a little bench at the front of the boat, away from the body and closer to Anwar. Confident neither Gibson nor Mariana could hear over the sound of the engine, I asked him where he was from.

"Bangladesh," he said.

"You like it here?"

"Yes," he said. "Better than Bangladesh."

"Where do you live?"

"At Gibson's. Gibson and his wife, they are good to me," he said.

"Really?"

"Better than Bangladesh," he said.

The engine quieted as we slowed down to thread our way through a channel. "Gibson," I said, "if you don't mind me asking, who is under the sheet?"

He smiled, stopped the boat, and, magician-like, ripped back the sheet with a flourish. It was a dugong, the Pacific relative of the manatee.

"We used to eat real ones," he said, "but the Germans made us stop. This one is made out of chocolate."

"Oh," I said, nodding in that knowing way that says, *I was going to bring the new chief a life-sized chocolate dugong, but they were sold out, so I brought a six-pack of Bud Light instead.*

Gibson started the engine again. For the next half hour, the thick green hills of Babeldaob rose and fell to our right as we continued north, well past where Gibson and I had first fished.

Finally, Gibson made a sharp turn toward the mangroves. I looked around for something to brace myself with for the coming collision, but there was nothing to hold on to. At the moment I expected the boat to crash into a thick clump of mangrove, a channel only a few inches wider than the boat appeared. We turned sharply to the left, and then right, but Gibson never slowed. I leaned into the curves and looked at Mariana.

"Gibson knows this well," she said loudly. "He used to hunt for crocodiles here at night. When he was a boy."

"Why at night?" I said.

"Easier to find. Their eyes glow red when you shine a flashlight. Gibson would shine the light, and then someone else would shoot them. Gibson's job was to jump in from the boat and grab 'em before they sunk."

Grab them? My natural history book said that saltwater crocodiles in Palau grow up to seventeen feet long.

"How many did he catch?"

"Around six hundred," she said matter-of-factly.

"Are there any left?"

"Plenty," she said, "plenty."

A moment later, we slowed to a set of concrete steps descending
into the water. "We're here," Mariana said.

Here was a small patch of cleared jungle surrounded by crickets
whining from the nearby bushes. After Anwar tied up the boat, each
of us picked up a corner of the plywood holding the dugong. Awkwardly, we carried it up the steps.

"Where are we?" I asked Mariana.

"Ngerdubech."

"Oh," I said.

A man appeared in a pickup and drove us and the dugong a few
minutes up a rutted dirt road to a *bai*, or community meeting
house—basically, some wobbly wooden benches under a metal roof.
In the old days, these buildings would have been built out of wood
and thatch, but thatch frays after a few years, and wood is prone to
termite problems.

The room was filled with people—113, by my later count—men
on one side, women on the other. A few sat on benches or leaned
against wooden posts with peeling green paint. Almost all wore
T-shirts and shorts. In the very center of the room towered a mountain of Mountain Dew cases—by my later count, 117.

Gibson mumbled something to Anwar, who promptly disappeared down a narrow path into the jungle.

"What should I do with this?" I asked Gibson, holding up the
beer. He gestured for me to follow him to the men's side. Mariana
joined a group of women sitting in a circle on the concrete floor.

"Should I introduce myself to the chiefs?" I asked, looking toward
a group of older men sitting near Dew Mountain.

"Not now," he said.

"Can you tell me what is going to happen—"

"Alex, relax," he said, sitting down on a bench. I sat next to him. No one in the room talked. No one, for that matter, moved. About half the room was asleep. Not a nodding-in-and-out sleep, but a deeply restful wake-up-and-not-know-where-you-are kind of sleep.

"When does the ceremony start?" I asked Gibson in a soft voice.

"It already has," he said.

I wondered if there was so much going on that I was missing all of it. Maybe I'd wandered into a poker game where every gesture and passing glance communicated information. If so, I had arrived with no chips and my cultural translator was snoring, loudly.

According to the nonzesty book *The Endangered Peoples of Oceania*, 60 percent of Palau's traditional customs remain. As the book points out, many islands are in worse cultural shape. For example, 90 percent of the people of Nauru have left their island, having sold (or had stolen) almost all of the rocky island's topsoil (mostly to the Japanese, who used the phosphate-rich soil for either fertilizer or bombs). The Marshall Islands, in the Southeast Pacific, literally have been nuked. So 60 percent isn't great, but it could be worse. And new traditions are being created or rejuvenated. A good portion of tourists to Palau, for example, return home with storyboards: arm-length pieces of wood carved with island myths. The storyboards themselves are actually kind of a myth too. The Japanese introduced them to Palau in 1935, apparently disappointed that Palauans weren't carving their myths into wood like other islanders. It stuck, sort of. These days Palauans still carve them, but the myths are mostly Yapese, the wood is imported from the Philippines, and most carvers are inmates in the prison in Koror—the only Palauans with enough time to fulfill the quaint expectations of cost-conscious tourists.

I broke ranks with the men and wandered over to the women's side. A few were weaving. Others stared at the jungle. Mariana sat on the floor staring, the best I could tell, at her toes. "Pardon me,

Mariana," I said, "but is there anything I can do? Maybe Anwar needs some help?"

"He's fine. He's getting firewood. You can sit with Gibson," she said.

I went back to sit with Gibson, who was now lying down where I'd been sitting. The bench, however, was too narrow for his body, so his arms just hung to the ground, his palms skyward and his knuckles resting on the floor. I sat on the ground and leaned against the bench.

No one spoke and no music played. In the U.S., there would have been music to fill these silences and to keep us entertained. Here in the heat, even the jungle crickets grew silent, leaving only the sound of the occasional dog's nails scraping across the concrete.

I'd later learn that the place was, in fact, buzzing with activity. Palau is a strict, hierarchical society based on clan and matrilineal descent. Every gesture—where people sit, whom they sit with, even which direction their knees point—carries meaning about their position in that hierarchy. But I understood none of that. Instead my notes filled up with fascinating observations:

12:45: Woman in the pink T-shirt just stood up.
12:52: Remember to tell Sarah that China's Three Gorges dam holds so much water that it is slowing the earth's rotation.
1:03: Dog just brushed past Gibson's leg. Without opening his eyes, Gibson kicked at it. Missed.
1:10: Woman in pink T-shirt just sat back down.

By three p.m., the room had never felt hotter. The tin roof had absorbed an entire afternoon's heat and was now radiating it downward, stilling even the dogs. I did, however, hear an occasional *pat-pat* sound. I looked around to find the source of all the racket and came up short, until, finally, I figured out that the *pat-pat* was the sound of spit hitting the dusty concrete floor. The dried red remnants of betel nut spit were, in fact, all over Palau. I'd noticed that the buttons of both of the country's ATMs were stained red with the stuff, as were the floors of most public buildings. That's why, I'd later learn, the floors and walls of the courthouse were painted red—some practices are easier to conceal than to change.

Finally, at no point in particular, Gibson slowly sat up and blinked his eyes a few times.

"Gibson, do you have any . . ." I gestured as though I was putting chewing tobacco in my mouth. He opened up a handwoven purse and gestured for me to take one of the green seeds, which were about the size of large acorns.

"Umm. Not sure how to do it," I said. He cracked one open. Then he opened a baby-food jar without a label and pulled out a pinch of tobacco that had been marinating in a clear liquid.

"What's it soaked in?" I asked.

"Vodka," he said.

I nodded, as though that was what I had assumed. He placed the tobacco and betel nut in the center of a green leaf and, twisting open a glue bottle, squirted some white powder on top.

"What's that?" It looked like cocaine. Or at least what cocaine looks like in the movies.

"Lime," he said. It looked nothing like a lime. "From burning coral." He carefully folded the leaf back over the top; the result looked like a small green samosa, only instead of chickpeas and dough, this one was a green nut, vodka, tobacco, and burned coral inside a thick leaf. I put the wad into my mouth and thought, Now that I've established some Palauan street cred, I should ask Gibson about renting that apartment of the Philippine ambassador.

Within seconds, though, I felt my face flush. Vast vats of saliva began to well in my mouth. The room spun. My cheeks swelled. My stomach retreated. In my haze, I thought back to the billboard I'd seen when I first arrived in Palau, "RUNNING AND CHEWING = DEATH."

Could anyone really run while on this stuff? As far as I was concerned, just CHEWING = DEATH.

In defeat, I spit the glob onto the floor. I was thinking ungenerous thoughts when I realized I had poisoned myself at just the wrong moment—as I started to recover, the room began to churn with activity. By *churn with activity,* I mean a couple of people stood up. A woman rubbed her eyes with clenched fists, babylike. Even Gibson lumbered into a standing position. When another woman slid on her flip-flops, I was so excited, I was on the verge of tears. It's happening, I thought. It's happening!

I looked over at Mariana. She raised both her eyebrows, so I walked over. "It's time to meet the chiefs," she said. As we walked over, she explained that her uncle was Ngardmau's new chief. I asked her how a new one was decided. "If a chief dies," she said, "the older women nominate a new one. Then the existing chiefs vote on their nomination. Either it's accepted or it isn't."

We approached six men seated in a semicircle of white plastic chairs. They weren't speaking but rather appeared to be gazing out over the assembled masses, appreciating the day. Mariana said something in Palauan and then said to me, "These are the chiefs. And this is my uncle." She directed me to an older man in slacks and a short-sleeved, button-down white shirt. He had thick wrinkles and shiny brown eyes. He stood awkwardly. I noticed crutches resting against a nearby chair.

"Go ahead," she whispered.

"Hello, my name is Alex," I said. "I'm here with Gibson and Mariana. Congratulations on becoming a chief."

He smiled. Because many older Palauans spoke Japanese instead of English as a second language, I had no idea whether he understood me. Awkwardly, I extended my gift of beer, but he only looked confused. Before I could explain how I felt like a dolt for bringing beer, someone reached out and spirited the cans away.

"OK. Time to go," said Mariana. Later, I saw my six-pack of Bud Light resting on the very summit of Mountain Dew, an alcoholic cherry on top, courtesy of the ceremony's only foreigner.

The *bai* emptied rapidly as all 113 of us walked uphill along a small dirt road. I lost Gibson in the crowd. A few minutes later, we came to a small green house with only one room. It was made of wood and had louvered glass windows on all sides. The chiefs were already inside—how Mariana's uncle beat us, I had no idea. Everyone was jostling for a view. I craned my neck and saw ten men sitting cross-legged against all four walls. In front of each was a basket wrapped in cloth. Suddenly, the chiefs began chanting melodically, deeply enough to make the wooden sideboards vibrate.

After about ninety seconds, some young men carried the chocolate dugong inside and placed it in the center of the room. The chief on the end made the first cut, along the largest cocoa vertebra, followed by Mariana's uncle and the other chiefs. When the last vertebra was sliced, the chiefs stood and walked out. There were no cheers, no ringing bells. No one opened a soda. And no one even ate the dugong. Still, Rekemesiik Ngiliti Idesmang was sworn in as Ngardmau's second-highest-ranking chief, although how or when that happened remained a mystery.

I would later meet an English-speaking Japanese anthropologist studying traditional Palauan ceremonies, and ask him if he'd been to a chief-swearing-in ceremony. He said he had. "Oh, good," I said. "Can you explain to me what goes on? Because—"

"To be honest," he interrupted, "I can't. I've been to a few of them and I don't understand a single thing that happened."

On the boat ride back, I asked Gibson if he had found a tenant for his place on the hill. He didn't respond. I recalled Jim, the public defender I'd met at the bar, telling me to just let things work out by themselves in Palau, yet now I'd forced the question. Ten minutes passed in awkward silence before Gibson stopped the boat. We rocked in the ocean. Well, I thought, this is the moment. Either he says I can rent his place, or he baits me on a hook.

"Awex," he said, *"err ca re ta place."*

"Gibson!" his wife yelled. "Your betel nut."

He spit it into the water and repeated himself, "Alex, you can rent the place."

"Great. But, umm, what is the rent?"

"Eight hundred dollars. No contract. Just month by month." That seemed a lot by Palauan standards, yet half as much as I'd been paying for my New York studio. "You'll have neighbors, though—"

"I've met some of them."

"All of them?" he asked with a smile before Mariana waved at him to shush.

"Alex, I want to show you something," she said, opening a little basket with two white envelopes resting on the bottom. "Our relatives paid us back for the food we brought." One of the envelopes had *$1216.76* written on it. The other was blank. Though we were floating in a small boat in a very big ocean, she looked around nervously. Slowly, she peeled open the unmarked envelope. Inside were two pebble-sized pieces of yellow coral. Through the center of each was a small hole.

"Palauan jewelry," she said, and looked me in the eye. "Very valuable."

"Are you going to wear it?" I said.

"Oh no, no, no. Of course not. I wouldn't want to show off," she said before sliding the top of the basket closed again.

CHAPTER 48

What You Can Expect to Learn in This Chapter:

➤ How do you flip an unflippable outrigger canoe?

➤ If you meet a brawny Palauan man named Marcus, why should you kick sand in his sandwich and run, very quickly, away?

I was on the back of an outrigger canoe—my feet dangling over each side, soles skimming the top of the eastern Philippine Sea—when something dreadful happened. The canoe had been designed for six, but we had an extra person—me—so I'd been assigned to the back. Instead of having a seat, I was perched up high on the little piece of fiberglass that held the back of the canoe together. For a while, at least, I felt I was more than pulling my weight. Every ten strokes someone yelled *huute!* and all six of us yelled back *ho!* before switching our paddles to the other side. For the first time, I understood how ancient Pacific Islanders could have crossed great stretches of ocean in one of these—a stabilizing pontoon jutted out on one side like a sidecar on a motorcycle, and as a result, these canoes were, basically, unflippable.

Earlier that morning, I'd met Sarah and a half-Palauan, half-expat group of a dozen others at the harbor to go camping. (She actually knew the woman who'd left me the errant voice mail and, kindly, had arranged for me to tag along.) The plan was pretty simple: paddle these two boats seven miles from Koror to the uninhabited island of

Ngermediu, spend the weekend camping, and paddle back. As we stood ankle-deep in the water, preparing to depart, a very fit, thirty-ish Palauan man named Marcus said something about wind direction and weight balance, handed Sarah an elaborately carved wooden paddle, and said she should go with him. "See you at the beach," she said chirpily, stepping into the Palauan's canoe. For my taste, a little too chirpily. Especially when I saw that Elise was among the people I'd be sharing a boat with.

"Hi, Elise," I said.

"Hi," she said.

"Is Michael coming?"

"No," she said, and walked away, concluding what would prove to be our most lighthearted conversation of the weekend.

Almost immediately, Sarah and her boat pulled far ahead, perhaps a mile or two, as we passed steep rock cliffs. The cliffs, topped by a narrow fringe of dark jungle, dropped down into an ocean so deep, it was dark blue, almost black. Black frigate birds with angled, double-jointed wings soared high above. A wispy layer of clouds protected us from the searing midday sun. A gentle breeze blew at our backs. The water was warm and calm. Riding high on that outrigger canoe, I was living the dream life I'd envisioned. I took a big sip of water out of my plastic water bottle, closing my eyes so I could better imagine it as a coconut.

A few minutes later, I must have leaned out too far or dipped my paddle too far into the water because my shorts, already damp, started to slide. At first just a bit. Then much faster.

As long as they notice me fall off, I thought, this won't be a big deal. The water will feel good and everyone will have a chuckle at the new guy. On the other hand, if I slid off the back unnoticed, the shorts that had caused the trouble would be all that remained of me. If they didn't disintegrate first, they'd wash up on some Indonesian beach and that would be that.

I let out a plea for help. Not a loud plea. Just a little call for my boating companions' attention. "Ahhhmmm?"

I don't know if anyone heard me, but I did get their attention. Because of some mysterious and complicated confluence of physics, geometry, and the will of an angry, angry God, as I slipped, the boat also flipped. Not a slow-motion roll, either. More a stomach-churning wallop.

The water felt refreshing. And I, for one, appreciated the break from paddling. Yet when I bobbed back up to the surface, I found otherwise-composed human beings in an angry flurry of activity. A few feet were already in the air, their owners diving for whatever might still be recoverable: wallets, sandwiches, cans of beer. I too dove down, but being reluctant to open my eyes in the salt water, I just made a few random waves through the water and, as expected, came up empty-handed. Fortunately, some gear had been placed in garbage bags in case of rain. These floated on the surface next to our capsized boat.

"So," I said to no one in particular while treading water, "any idea what happened?"

"I knew it was unsafe to have Alex in the boat," Elise snapped. "It's made for six people. Six people who know what they're doing."

"I'm really sorry. I think I leaned out too far."

"Well, you shouldn't have leaned out too far," she said, the contempt hissing through her teeth.

"Well, leaning out too far is, by definition, leaning out too far," I was about to say, before being interrupted by Monica, a sensible Peace Corps worker from Houston.

"Hey," Monica said, "has anyone seen my glasses? They're prescription."

"I can't find mine either," someone else said. Not only had I achieved the impossible—flipping a nearly unflippable canoe—I'd also blinded two people in the process.

Even though sight-impaired, Monica took charge, directing us all to one side of the overturned canoe to flip it back. "Watch your heads," she yelled as the pontoon whipped over our heads.

All I had to do now was get back in the boat. At first, I tried simply to pull myself up but found that five years' sitting at a computer had done a lot more for my typing speed than for my upper-body strength. I *really* didn't want to be the last guy back in the boat. Not only was there pride on the line, but I felt there was an outside chance—5 percent? 10 percent?—they might leave me behind. I flopped quickly, if awkwardly, back into the boat.

For the next two hours, no one said a thing as we paddled by a long and mostly featureless jungle-covered island. The hot afternoon sun soon baked our clothes dry, leaving behind a salty residue that, in turn, led to chafing. Not a funny amount of chafing as in *Ha! Do you have that sandpaper-rubbing-on-your-inner-thigh feeling too?* More along the lines of *Oh, my, this is really, really terrible.* Given my role in making everyone's clothes wet, I could only hope the others found their own chafing a welcome distraction from the monotony that is long-distance travel in an outrigger canoe.

Finally, we paddled over a submerged reef and onto a palm-fringed crescent of sand known as Margie's Beach. Behind the beach, a thickly forested hill rose steeply and seemed to be home to a very large population of crickets. A few crabs scuttled into holes in the brownish white sand. It seemed the other boat had arrived long before. Marcus was just finishing a story. Our group was met with a sigh, as though the others had been laughing for the last four hours and knew that the fun must end. I grabbed a Ziploc bag with a turkey sandwich. Water had leaked inside.

"Alex, how was your trip?" Sarah said as she approached us. "You need help unloading?"

I didn't like that she used my name. It felt so formal, as if she was trying to show she'd remembered it.

"Pretty peaceful," I said.

"Great! Ours too." Strange, I thought, for her to say *ours* instead of *mine.*

"You guys didn't bring much stuff," she said, looking into our boat, adding, "How was it paddling with Elise? Oh, my God. Marcus told this story. Hold on one sec. . . ."

She scanned the beach, making eye contact with Marcus, then slapped her butt and yelled, "Hey, Marcus, who's the Colombian now?" At least four people bent over in laughter at this apparently hilarious joke.

As Sarah and I carried the remains of our gear to a little grassy spot under a canopy of palm trees, Marcus passed us, shirtless. In one hand he carried a coconut. In the other, a chain saw. As he walked past on Sarah's side he did a funky chicken dance.

"Hey!" said Sarah before pretending to kick sand at him.

At this point, I considered throwing my sandwich at his temple, but I worried about the awkwardness that would follow if, instead of killing him, I just landed a soggy turkey and cheese on his neck. So instead I just waited for him to pull ahead of us and said to Sarah, "Who brings a chain saw camping?"

"Marcus does," she said. We then set down some stuff next to a small mountain of gear: three ice chests, a charcoal grill, a case of Pepsi, four cases of beer and half-a-dozen cardboard boxes of who knows what.

"Did you guys really bring all this stuff in your boat?" I said but before she could answer Marcus pulled the cord on the chain saw. It started immediately. On the way back for a second load, I told Sarah about the flipped canoe and the role I might have played.

"Really?" she said. "I thought those couldn't be flipped."

Though we'd been away from camp for just moments, when we returned Marcus was almost finished sawing his first chair out of driftwood. He set it in front of Sarah and said, "In Palau, the most beautiful always sits first." I rolled my eyes. Sarah, however, sat down with a smile. I refrained from pointing out that the chair looked not just unsafe, but so structurally unsound that in any other country there would be serious liability issues.

"You know, in the outer islands of Yap, they don't sit on chairs," I said, finding a place on the ground and trying to be conversational. My comment, however, went unnoticed. Marcus picked up a machete, sliced the top off a coconut with a clean whack, and handed it to Sarah.

"I am sorry, Sarah," he said, "but I forgot the straws."

"No problem," she said. "Thank you."

As I went to barf in the seaweed, I saw Marcus running down the coast, probably to find a quarry of granite with which to build his princess a castle.

"You want a sip?" Sarah said. "It's good."

"Coconuts aren't my thing," I said.

"It's delicious," she said, surprised.

"Too many worms," I said. "That's why the FDA won't allow them into the U.S."

"That's not true," she said, laughing. "Wait. . . . Are you jealous or something?"

"I'm not," I said. "I'm just not one of those guys who has to go around cutting stuff up with chain saws and hacking coconuts to impress girls."

Just then, Marcus yelled up from the beach. "Hey, guys! It's time for Ultimate Frisbee!"

"We're coming!" Sarah said.

"I'm going to take a pass," I said.

"Why's that?"

"Not sure. Maybe, I'm just tired from the paddling."

I wanted her to say that she would take a pass too, that we should just hang out together and have crazy sex in the jungle, but that wasn't exactly the gist I picked up from her response.

"OK," she said.

While Marcus dug lines in the sand with his heel, I sat on the beach and wondered if Sarah had invited me out of politeness. Or, worse, pity. I looked over at her. She didn't seem especially engaged in the game, though she did have a charming tendency to take about three steps more than allowed when holding the Frisbee.

When the game was finally over, Sarah came and sat next to me.

"Good game?" I said. "Or just so-so?"

"It was fun," she said, just as Marcus walked by, holding a fish—almost but not quite—as long as his arm.

"Dinner in ten minutes," he said.

"When did he have time to catch that?" I said after he passed.

"Do you need us to help?" Sarah yelled after him.

"No, thanks," Marcus said. "You just stay there and be beautiful."

"You got to be kidding me," I blurted out loud.

"He's just being nice."

Just then, Elise plopped down in the sand next to Sarah and said, "I hate mosquitoes." She had a can of insect repellent in one hand and a can of Pringles in the other. "Good thing Michael isn't here. He really hates them."

"That was a good game. You had some nice catches," Sarah said.

"Personally," Elise said, "I didn't really care who wins. For me, it's like politics. Democrats. Republicans. Republicans and Democrats. Whatever. You want a Pringle?" We both declined.

"That's interesting, though," I said. "Do you find you ever lean one way or the other?"

"I'm all for helping people—" Elise said, digging in for another snack chip. "I just think people should get a hand up"—*chomp, chomp, chomp*—"and not a handout."

"I agree," I said. "You know who that really applies to? Kids. The young ones, especially."

Sarah's head sank.

"Whatever," Elise said. "I'm going to get in line for dinner. I don't want to get the side of the fish with all the little bones."

Once Elise was out of hearing range, I said to Sarah, "*Hand up, not a handout?* What does that mean anyway? And how could you not know if you're a Democrat or a—"

"Alex," she said, "look around. . . . Do you see where we are?"

I looked around. Marcus was working on the fire. Elise was rummaging around in a backpack, probably for some ranch dip. Other people were setting up tents, taking photos, opening a beer.

"We're on a beach on an uninhabited island," Sarah said. "The sun is setting. The waves are crashing over the reef. Someone is making us fresh fish for dinner."

"Well—"

"But if you want to ignore all of that and pick a fight with Elise, at least be clever about it. You know, like, do something to her tent."

"Like what?"

"Not sure yet," she said, "but let's brainstorm after dinner."

We approached the fire and found Marcus breaking branches over his thigh. He was saying something about the weather. "Tomorrow, the reef may be more difficult to cross," he said. "It might take longer to get home." I hadn't noticed before, but the wind had changed, and the air had cooled a few degrees.

"So you're telling me we're going to be stuck here?" Elise said.

"No," he said, "but we should leave early." Marcus handed me a plate with fish on it. I took a bite. Then another. It was good. Marcus was a decent cook, I had to admit. And when talking about the weather, he'd sounded reasonable, responsible, even. I was about to forgive him for whatever it was he'd done or not done when he picked up a guitar. We stepped away from the light of the fire just as Marcus and another guy started singing, I swear, "More Than Words" by Extreme.

I turned to Sarah. "So, any ideas about Elise's tent?"

"I do, but let's go somewhere private," she said. The beach was narrow and the jungle hillside steep; the only option seemed to be the ocean.

"To the water?" I asked.

"Sure," she said.

We started to change into our bathing suits, but both were

wet and sandy. "There's no moon," she said. "Maybe we shouldn't bother."

"Good point."

She then slid off her shirt, shorts, and underwear, unclipped her bra, and ran naked into the ocean. It seemed the only reasonable option was to follow suit. Or unsuit. So I did.

CHAPTER 49

What You Can Expect to Learn in This Chapter:

- ➤ How do you effectively yet respectfully woo a woman with Pringles?

- ➤ Should you always respect the power of the sea? What if that sea is warm and a lovely shade of blue?

According to one of my books, Western scientists found the story of the archerfish, a local species of snapper, so outrageous they didn't try to verify it until the mid-1970s, nearly 140 years after first reported. Archerfish live in the estuaries and mangrove swamps and, apparently, have developed a special groove in the top of their mouths that enables them to squirt a narrow jet of water up to six feet away at insects or lizards. They even take into account gravity and the way light bends when it passes through water. To improve their chances, archerfish occasionally drape their mucus-covered tails over logs to lure prey closer. When the curious animals walk up, they get blasted into the water. And eaten.

Not that I feared Sarah was going to eat me, but as I approached the water, I worried that she might be just flirting with me, just as she had flirted with Marcus.

"Check this out," Sarah said, waving a hand slowly through the water. In the warm water, each wave of her hand, each spin of her feet while treading water, produced a swirl of bright blue-green bioluminescence. Whenever she paused, these would fall, briefly illuminating the sand below before growing dark like the spent embers of a sparkler.

"It's . . . incredible," I said.

"So," she said, looking up, "you're from Texas, but you don't have an accent or boots. You lived in New York for five years and then bought a bunch of books and a ticket to the Pacific. Now you're swimming here, wondering . . . well, wondering what?"

"I guess I was wondering what you were wondering," I said lamely.

"I just told you what I was wondering," she said.

"Well," I said, "to be honest, I was wondering if you have a boyfriend. You know, like some guy who's into chain-saw art or something?"

"You mean Marcus?" she said.

"Oh," I said, "I didn't think of him as an artist, but—"

"I'm not seeing Marcus," she said. "And you? What about you?"

"No one," I said. "I'm not seeing anyone." We treaded water for a few seconds, before I added, "But I just got out of a long relationship."

Oh, God, why did I say that?

"How long is long?" she said.

"Three years or so," I said. "Not that long."

"That's pretty long."

"It took us a year and a half just to speak each other's language. She was from Spain."

"What language did you break up in?"

"English," I said. We treaded water for another moment in silence. "It isn't sexy to talk about your exes, is it?"

"Not really," she said before asking, "So, what are we going to do to Elise?"

Whatever moment we had or could have had had passed. Ugh. How had I screwed this up again? This time we were even naked.

"Yeah, Elise," I said. "What were you thinking we should do?"

"Not sure. I know Elise isn't that comfortable camping . . . especially so near the water. So maybe a tidal wave. We wait till she's in her tent, then yell *tidal wave*—"

"—and throw a bucket of water against the side of her tent."

"Exactly."

We swam back to the beach, slid on our clothes, and together filled a cooler halfway with seawater. Per our plan, we crept up to her tent, flung the water, and yelled, "Tidal wave!"

"Hey? What are you guys doing?" we heard Elise say from over near the fire.

Sarah and I spent the night side by side on the beach, our ankles turning into novellas in Braille by the overnight work of sand flies. Rats rustling in the dried thatch of nearby palm trees had kept many of us awake, and on several occasions, the coconuts they dislodged landed nearby with startling thuds on the humidity-soaked sand. Just as I was finally deeply asleep, I awoke to a strange buzzing noise; wrenching my eyes open, I found Elise standing by my feet, an electric toothbrush whirling in her mouth. She stood in orange pajamas with her feet together. Her frazzled hair was in a ponytail tied at the top of her head. Seen from the ground, the effect was not dissimilar to looking up at a giant carrot with the roots sticking out the top. She walked to the water's edge and spit out her toothpaste.

"Is she gone?" Sarah said without opening her eyes.

"For the moment," I said. I was wrong. She came back.

"Hey, Sarah, you're up, right? When we get back, I was thinking we could do some macramé. I have a lot of new cords and patterns."

"Sure, Elise," she said. "Sure."

Thinking this would be the perfect time to impress Sarah with my camp cooking skills, I asked Elise if she had any Pringles left.

"For breakfast?" she said.

"For breakfast." She walked over to her backpack, found the can in the outside pocket, and returned. She started to shake a few out for me.

"Actually, I need the whole can."

"Bet it's going to be good," she said, handing me the canister.

I then found a skillet in the cooking area, a few sticks, and some relatively dry leaves and started a little fire. I poured some water into the skillet, then dropped in a few crumbled Pringles. Marcus can make chairs with chain saws, I thought, but can he make camping hash browns?

A few minutes later, I presented Sarah a smoking plate of mushy—and yet also somehow burned—Pringles. (For the full recipe, see Appendix A.)

"Umm, thanks," she said, picking up a tiny piece, just as a cold rain began to fall.

"Everyone!" Marcus yelled from the cooking area. "We need a meeting."

"I think we gotta go," Sarah said.

"Do you want a doggy bag?" I said.

"Sure," she said, handing the plate back to me. "That would be lovely."

We all gathered around Marcus. He said the tide was much lower than it had been when we arrived, and now the waves were breaking right on top of the barely submerged reef. There was no going around, he said. Either we left now, before the waves on the reef got any bigger, or we waited until late that afternoon for high tide. I looked out to sea. In my view, the waves looked manageable. And I wanted off the island. Besides, I thought, this is the South Pacific—the water is warm. Worst case, we get wet.

"If we wait till high tide," I said, "won't it be dark on the way back? That seems not great."

"We can paddle at night," Marcus explained. "The issue is more whether or not we want to cross the reef. Anyone else have a view?" No one did.

"OK, then," he said. "Let's give it a go. Let's pack the canoes and try to cross over."

We then grabbed our stuff and ran to the beach. Having no doubt heard of my paddling skills, Marcus had arranged for his and Sarah's boat to take the extra person, leaving mine with the proper six: myself, Elise, Monica the Peace Corps volunteer, and three Palauan men who seemed to know what they were doing. We paddled the few hundred yards out to the reef. Waves that had looked manageable from a distance looked quite unmanageable up close. They were at least six feet tall—a considerable height in any circumstance, but these were breaking over sharp coral. And the canoes rode low in the water, which meant out heads were not more than a foot or two above the surface, like little round bowling pins.

"Wait for a lull," Marcus shouted from the other boat. "Then we'll go—fast!"

We hung back a bit, waiting for a smaller set of waves. Sensing a lull, Marcus yelled, "Paddle! Now! Paddle hard!" Both boats sluggishly moved forward; then a little faster. But not fast enough. Just as we approached the reef, a huge wave's smooth convex curve began rising in front of us.

"Oh, shit," I said.

"Paddle! Paddle!" people yelled.

We were committed, but clearly we weren't going to make it. Monica, seated in front, took the full force of the wave. Jesse, a Palauan man sitting in front of me, ducked into the canoe. I ducked too. Mesmerized, I simply watched as all went bubbly and dark. I then felt a heavy weight press against me. The boat bobbed to the surface, perpendicular to the still incoming waves. Monica had been pushed against me, somehow. We untangled ourselves and looked around. Sarah's canoe hadn't made it across either. It had flipped. Paddles, water bottles, and flip-flops floated everywhere on the surface. Immediately, we readied for another attempt.

Another lull, another frantic paddle. And again, a monster wave formed just as we were about to cross into deep, safer water. This time, Monica ducked into the canoe. Jesse jumped overboard. I ducked into the boat again. The boat flipped. When I surfaced, Monica was screaming, "My back! My back!"

The front of the wave had forced her against the canoe's support beam behind her seat. "My back! My back!" she kept yelling. I looked around for Sarah. Her canoe had made it across somehow. We were still on the wrong side and another wave was approaching.

I asked Monica if she could move her legs.

"I'm not sure," she said just as a wave crashed over us. We bobbed up again.

"What do you mean, *Not sure*?" I said. "Try."

She tried moving her legs again.

"I think I can move them," she said hesitantly, "At least my feet." We then dog-paddled together to shallower water and away from the breaking waves.

I felt embarrassed for having been so ready to believe what I wanted to believe about the tranquil turquoise waters of the Southwest Pacific. Why would they be less treacherous than waters anywhere else? You can't rent a car at the Honolulu airport without at least one finger wagging about the power of the ocean. Even lifeguards at the local YMCA pool will warn you to beware of the riptide.

I looked at Monica's back. She had a small wound, which was bleeding a little. She calmed down. "I'll be OK," she said, holding her back.

As we prepared the boat for another attempt over the reef, I wondered what other obvious lessons had slipped through the wide-gauge net of my mind. Next week, would I plant some moss on a rolling stone? Perhaps dive back into the shrubbery, grasping for two more birds?

We startled paddling earlier than the previous two attempts, but again, a massive roller formed just as we approached. Rather than waiting to see what would happen, I dove overboard. The wave rumbled noisily overhead. I popped up and looked around. To my astonishment and dismay, the canoe and all of its passengers had paddled through the wave and beyond the reef. I was the only one who had jumped.

Between waves, I quickly swam across, grabbing a few bobbing water bottles on the way. The only thing worse than abandoning ship, I thought, is being the only one to abandon ship.

Later, I learned that after her boat had flipped on its first attempt, Sarah's foot had become stuck in a Japanese fishing net that had floated onto the reef. Underwater, she freed herself only by un-Velcroing one of her shoes. As it happened, eleven of us lost at least one flip-flop in the process of crossing the reef—not exactly *Perfect Storm* material, but enough to warrant my sixth Life Lesson. I later wrote it down on my ticket sleeve: "If you ever decide to cross a sharp reef with big waves breaking over it, wear shoes . . . with laces. And don't try to woo women with rehydrated Pringles."

CHAPTER 50

What You Can Expect to Learn in This Chapter:

➤ How many years, on average, can you expect to live on a small island before you start painting an endless series of naked self-portraits?

➤ Is Styx, in fact, the most kick-A band ever?

While waiting for Gibson to give me the keys to my new place, I stopped by the local chapter of the Nature Conservancy to ask about work. The bureaucracy didn't permit me to be paid—not until a formal job announcement was posted—but there was plenty to be done, so they gave me a chair and a computer. By the end of the week, I still didn't have an apartment, but I felt good about going in to the office every day. I appreciated the work they were doing, mostly supporting like-minded Palauans trying to protect the more fragile bits of the country. Not surprisingly, no one really wanted me meeting with members of parliament or arranging loans to finance boats to enforce protected marine areas, so I just wrote and edited reports to send back to headquarters. I'd rather have gone scuba diving every day, but my budget didn't allow it, and I did like feeling productive. Or at least as productive as I could feel writing and editing reports no one would ever read.

While I was driving back to my motel at the end of my first week, it started to rain again. It had been raining most of the week, but that didn't feel like a big deal. I wasn't on vacation; I lived here! It would probably be sunny next week. If not, then the week after that. In the light Friday afternoon traffic that passes for rush hour in Palau, I slowly passed Koror's weird—yet increasingly familiar—strip of little bodegas. One sold purses and shoes out of giant wire crates. Another bolts of fabric and mannequins. Another just restaurant take-out supplies made of Styrofoam. As I drove, I thought about how I'd always assumed my life would be located in the middle of a triangle loosely formed by family, work, and where I had gone to college. Yet now, slowly and piece by piece, I was constructing a life in a place far outside that triangle. It was good for my confidence to know I wasn't as entrapped by New York as I'd once thought.

Finally, the next morning, a Saturday, Gibson opened the oversized doors to my new place. It seemed the Philippine ambassador, in his rush to flee the country, had left some items behind, among them a ripped couch, an old table, and, most curiously, a Wiffle ball and bat.

Gibson immediately noticed the bat and, without a word, tossed me the ball and pulled the bat behind his right shoulder. He nodded that he was ready for the pitch. I threw one, gentle and underhand. He connected. The ball whizzed through the nearly empty living room, bouncing off concrete columns and windows before rolling across the mahogany floors and stopping in the corner.

"Base hit," Gibson said. He tossed me the ball, and I pitched again, this time harder. Strike. Another pitch. A solid drive that bounced off a few walls and windows before landing somewhere in the kitchen.

"Double," he said. I wondered what he would consider a home run. A hole in the wall?

I then threw a fast pitch. Gibson swung hard—or as hard as a three-hundred-pound man can swing a small plastic bat. He connected. I ducked. The ball whizzed past my head, ricocheting wildly off every wall and window. I was pretty sure he must have broken the bat.

"Holy crap!" I said as the ball rolled toward the entranceway before coming to a stop at the feet of an angry mustached man standing in the doorway.

"Hi," I said, startled. It was Randall, the man I'd met on the USS *Frederick* who longed for the clean floors of the Dole Pineapple Factory in Hawaii.

"It's a good thing Gibson doesn't know what's going on up here," he said, stepping inside.

I was about to say something about it having been Gibson's idea when, in one of those superb sitcom moments that occasionally intrude upon real life, Gibson rounded the corner, the bat dangling from his huge hand as a child's swing might from an oak tree.

"Oh," Randall said, "he is here." They simply looked at each other for a moment before he added, "Gibson, you know I can hear everything downstairs."

Gibson shook his head and handed me a set of keys, then waved at us both as he walked out the door.

"So," Randall said, "you're Gibson's new tenant."

"Seems that way," I said, and smiled. "I believe we met on the boat—"

"I live downstairs," he said, apparently not recalling that we'd already met and he'd already said that he lived downstairs. "I'm Randall Cook, prosecutor. That's Cook with two O's, no E." Without offering to shake hands, he stepped inside and walked in a tight circle around the middle of the living room.

"Looks like your movers haven't arrived yet," he said. "That's no surprise. Movers here are terrible."

"Well, I just have this one bag and a few boxes, so it's not—"

"These Palauans. They're so goddamn lazy. Took them two days just to move my wicker furniture from my old apartment."

"Sorry to hear that," I said. I was being truthful: I was sorry to hear that. I tried to change the subject. "Can you believe Gibson built this place himself? How amazing is that?"

"Could have done a better job. Palauans are lazy because we gave them so much money. They don't need to work. U.S. money runs this place, and it's ruining this place." Then it was his turn to change the subject. "Hey, you don't make a lot of noise, do you?" he said, looking behind me suspiciously as though I might be hiding a copy of *Stilt Walking and Jackhammering for Dummies*.

"Nope, just me," I said.

"Good. You like sticks, don't you? I just got a new stereo." I understood each individual word he was saying, but not in that particular order.

"Sticks?" I said.

"You know, 'Domo Arigato, Mr. Roboto.'" He hummed while tilting his head robotlike from side to side.

"Oh. The group Styx. I remember that song— "

"Come by tonight and I'll play some for you. I just got the new Sony Subwoofer 4000." Apparently, he assumed I too had just read the latest issue of *Pacific High Fidelity* magazine and couldn't wait to get in a good listen. Without waiting for a response, he walked out to our shared driveway and around the corner. He didn't bother to close the door behind him.

Alone for the first time in my place, I was eager to have a look around. There were two bedrooms but both had small windows, so I dragged a bed into the living room. Out of my car, I grabbed everything I currently owned: a suitcase of torn T-shirts and shorts, an answering machine, a toaster, and my box of books. I opened a window to let in some fresh air, but feeling the heat of Palau's midmorning pour in, I closed it quickly.

For the first time in four months, I fully unpacked, laying everything out on the wooden dining room table—my own dining room table. I was only renting the place month to month, but the moment felt momentous. Or semimomentous. Like buying a used car.

That evening, as I walked down the outside steps to Randall's apartment, I heard dogs' nails running across a tile floor. Before I could knock, Randall opened the door. Two small white dogs leapt out the door and ran into the bushes, as if making a break for it. "That one is Aloha and the other one is Hula. Aren't they cute?" Randall said before adding, with a theatrical sweep of his arm, "Welcome to my humble abode."

His abode was very similar to my abode except in one respect: every wall was covered in richly hued floor-to-ceiling oil paintings of the same naked redheaded woman. Naked redheaded woman on bench. Naked redheaded woman on swing. Naked redheaded woman watering a cactus. Just then, a woman walked around the corner. She was tall, in her midforties, and had red hair.

"You haven't met Rebecca," he said. He was technically correct but I felt like I had.

"I like to paint," she said. "Mostly people."

"More like person," Randall said, guffawing with his hands on his hips. "More like person." As he repeated his own joke, I noticed that Randall's bushy mustache wasn't symmetrical: it tapered on one end, like a squirrel's tail.

Randall directed me to the kitchen, where Rebecca handed me a prepoured glass of wine.

"You guys been here long?" I said.

"Five years," Randall said, adding, "But it only feels like five minutes . . . underwater."

Rebecca nodded in agreement: Five years in Palau did feel like five minutes underwater. She then asked me where I was from.

"Well, I grew up in Texas, but—"

"Interesting," Randall said. "Let me show you my new Sony."

As I walked out, I glanced over at four framed diplomas hanging on the kitchen wall. They weren't arranged symmetrically. Instead, three were clumped together, with the fourth all by itself. I looked closer. They were diplomas for a wine-appreciation course. Three had been awarded to Randall, one to Rebecca.

Their living room, located directly below mine, had large windows and, unlike mine, seating for at least sixty. All of it was made of wicker. Wicker chairs and wicker couches and wicker lounges were spread around wicker coffee tables—enough wicker, in other words, to keep a few movers busy for a month.

"Take a look at this stereo," Randall said. "You can't buy anything like this here. These Palauans, they have no appreciation of quality."

Rebecca handed me a plate of yellow cheese cubes.

"Listen to this reverb," he said, cranking up some classical music. Rebecca looked at him admiringly. I assumed, she was thinking, Yes, let's listen to his reverb.

"Sounds nice," I said.

"Nice? Nice? This is Beethoven's Ninth Symphony performed by the Berlin Philharmonic played on a Sony 4000 Double Blast Sub-woofer. Listen!" He then turned up the volume, almost to the point of pain.

During a softer moment in the symphony, I asked if either, by chance, had read the book *Let Us Now Praise Famous Men*.

"*What?*" Randall said, annoyed.

"A book called—"

"What?" Randall said again.

I wanted to go upstairs and grab the book, as I was sure they'd appreciate the incredible preface in which Walker Evans explains how to fully experience music. "Get a radio or a phonograph capable of the most extreme loudness possible," he suggests . . .

> and sit down and listen to a performance of Beethoven's Seventh Symphony or of Schubert's C-Major Symphony. But I don't just mean sit down and listen. I mean this: Turn it up loud as you can get it. Then get down on the floor and jam your ear as close into the loudspeaker as you can get it and stay there, breathing as lightly as possible, and not moving, and neither eating nor smoking nor drinking. . . . You won't hear it nicely. If it hurts you, be glad of it. As near as you will ever get, you are inside the

music; not only inside it, you are it; your body is no longer
your shape and substance, it is the shape and substance of
the music.

But it was too late. Randall was gone, vigorously air-conducting
with his eyes closed. Rebecca's eyes were closed too.

While Beethoven transported them to some far-off place, I just
looked around the room. Every cushion—and there were a lot of
them—was decorated in the same orange floral pattern. The same
pattern, it just so happened, as was printed on Randall's shirt.
Between Rebecca's paintings of herself on the walls and Randall
blending into the chairs, I wondered if they ever had difficulty finding each other.

When the music finally ended, both kept their eyes closed for a
very long time. A minute. Maybe more. I shuffled a bit in my seat,
knowing that the wicker would creak. Finally, Randall's eyelids fluttered, then opened slowly. With a deep exhale, he said, "OK." But he
drew out the word so it was more like *Ohhhkaaaaaaaaaayyyy*.

Consciousness fully regained, Randall popped out of the chair.
"You know what time it is now?" he said.

"Seven twenty?" I said.

"No. IT'S STYX TIME!"

"More cheese cubes?" Rebecca asked, handing me a platter.

"You know, of course," Randall said while fiddling with his new
stereo, "that Styx is the most kick-A band ever." I wanted to suggest
some alternatives as the most kick-A band ever, but he was already
standing with his eyes closed. As Randall tapped out the first tender,
tender notes of "Lady" on his air piano, I began to worry about the
island's long-term effect on foreigners . . . and vice versa.

CHAPTER 51

What You Can Expect to Learn in This Chapter:

► If you ever find yourself in charge of building a road through the jungle, is it necessary to take rain into account?

► What is the best long-term business opportunity in Palau?

andall's comment about U.S. money *running and ruining this place* reminded me I still didn't understand America's intentions here and, getting my mind around that increasingly felt central to understanding Palau itself. Unsure of whom else to ask, I decided to go straight to the top. In the slim Palauan phone book, I looked up the office of the president.

"Hello. I'm a reporter visiting Palau," I said to the woman who answered, though I didn't feel much like a reporter or a visitor. "And I was hoping to arrange a meeting with President Remengesau." Not that I pronounced it *Remengesau*—more *Romans Must Go*.

"OK," the woman said. "What time is good for you?"

That wasn't the answer I was expecting. "Oh, anytime really." That sounded a little wimpy, so I added, "But mornings are best."

"Well, he's out of the country at the moment, but he jogs in the morning. Would you like to join him when he gets back?"

"Sure," I said.

She told me she'd call back that afternoon after she checked with scheduling but it could be a few weeks before I could meet them. I called Sarah. "My first interview as a journalist will be with a head of state," I said. "We're going to go jogging together. I haven't been jogging since I was on the cross-country team in junior high."

"Hmm," she said, "what are you going to talk about?"

I told her my plan to ask about the Compact Agreement, the $150 million road, and the rest of the money.

"Well, that will take about a minute," she said. "Then what?"

I wasn't sure.

"I read that he walked the whole length of that road during his campaign," Sarah said. "You could ask him about that. He said he was the first Palauan to walk across the entire island of Babeldaob in one trip."

"Maybe we should be the first Americans?" I said, suddenly excited by the idea of walking across an entire country. It would give me something else to talk about during the interview, and what better way to get your mind around a place than walking all the way across it? Most important, I'd have a lot of quality time with Sarah.

"Well, I've been wanting to see the new capitol. The U.S. is building it," she said. "I heard it's crazy big and very odd. Apparently, no one wants to work there."

"It'd be a tour of America's pork projects in the Pacific!" I said. Sarah said she had a long weekend coming up; we could do it then.

That we'd just hatched a plan to do a sixty-mile jungle hike hadn't really occurred to either of us. Nor, until I met an official with the U.S. Army Corps of Engineers at the Pirates Cove, did we know we'd be walking mostly through mud. "A complete disaster," he said. "The road was supposed to be eighteen feet wide, like secondary roads in the U.S., but the Palauans made it twenty-four feet for no particular reason. It doubled the cost, but the budget was already fixed. The whole thing is sliding into the jungle."

About ten days later, Gibson took Sarah and me by boat to a

simple concrete dock at the northern tip of Babeldaob. The engine still on idle, I asked him what Palauans thought of this road.

"Everyone jokes that when it's done, the best investment won't be in land, but in tow trucks to drag all the drunk drivers out of the ditch."

"Good to know. Any advice?" I said as we stepped out of the boat.

"Watch out for snakes," he said, putting the engine into gear. With a smile and a wave, he turned toward the reef.

"Was he joking?" I said.

"I don't think there are poisonous snakes on Palau," Sarah replied.

"You sure?"

"No." There wasn't much else to do except strap on our packs and start walking.

"Kinda warm," Sarah said about ten steps later.

"Not over where I am," I said. "I must have found a little microclimate."

It wasn't, in fact, easy going. Though the road was fairly level, we felt like we were walking uphill. It had recently rained (it had always recently rained in Palau), making the road—more of a wide path—slick. With each step our heels slid to the side and sank into the dark-red mud, then lifted with a little *pop*.

"Can we just cover some basics?" I said.

"Like the birds and the bees?"

"Kind of. I was thinking more where you're from and stuff like that. I know you're a lawyer. Shouldn't you be working at a law firm or the ACLU or something?"

"I've done both. I interned at the ACLU and liked it but they don't hire many people right out of law school."

"And the law firm?"

"I was just a summer associate at a place called Brobeck, Phleger, and—"

"Ha! They used to do the legal work for my little company! Maybe you did some of it?"

"I doubt it. After about two weeks, they realized reading contracts wasn't my strong suit, so they gave me various research projects. My real specialty was the coffee breaks."

"It's good to know what you're good at," I offered.

"They didn't invite me back. It was mutual."

"The dress code didn't suit you?"

"Yeah. Or the steak nights and golf."

"Got it," I said. "You have any siblings?"

"A younger sister," Sarah said. "She's always been perfect." She didn't seem as much jealous as admiring.

"And you haven't been?"

"My parents were once so worried that my sister was too focused on making good grades that they said they'd buy her a new pair of shoes if she made an A minus without getting upset."

"Did she get the shoes?" I said.

"No. To her, it wasn't worth it. Hey. It's pretty hot," she said. "Can we stop talking for a while?" It did feel about a thousand degrees, so we walked in sweaty silence, pausing only to pass a water bottle back and forth. The road was far short of twenty-four feet across, more like six—and it rarely touched the coast. Instead, it mostly ran through the middle of the island; as a result, we saw only jungle. Thick, steaming, prickly jungle. There wasn't a piece of machinery in sight. Nor a tire track or footprint.

After nearly two hours, I suggested we look at a map. Pulling out the detailed printout I'd been given upon first arriving in Palau, I could see we'd traveled about an inch. The entire island was thirty-five feet long.

Just as we started walking again, it began to rain. Not a cooling rain, but a warm, fungus-inducing downpour. But stopping wasn't an option. We pulled garbage bags over our packs and kept walking. Silent and wet, we trudged forward, only now wrapped in garbage bags.

I later read that the engineers who had planned the road had not taken Palau's literally twelve feet of annual rain into account. Nor had anyone tested the soil, which is apparently something you need to do before building a road. Not helping matters, the Army Corps of Engineers, which oversaw the project, gave the actual construction work to the lowest bidder: Daewoo, a Korean conglomerate that would later declare bankruptcy, its chairman jailed for fraud.

"How are you doing?" I asked Sarah on one downhill stretch.

"OK," she said. "I'm OK. You?"

"I'm going to pull through, I think."

This would be our last conversation for two hours.

Had Daewoo actually done the work on the road, things might have worked out better—after all, they built complicated things like helicopters, skyscrapers, and nuclear power plants. Instead, Daewoo subcontracted most aspects to cheaper, smaller, shadier companies. The subcontractors, in turn, relied on imported contract labor, mostly from Bangladesh, Vietnam, Nepal, and China. Workers complained they were not being paid and that living conditions were terrible. Meanwhile, with every afternoon rain a little more of the road's red clay washed into the jungle. By the standards of the U.S. Army Corps of Engineers, an agency famous for draining the Everglades and building the protective dikes around New Orleans, it was a total success.

Just before sunset, the road took a much-appreciated turn toward the ocean. Soaked yet dehydrated, and nearly delirious, we limped into a four-house fishing village. An elderly man sitting on his concrete stoop pointed us to a pier where we could sleep. Fortunately, the pier had a little gazebo at the end to shield us from the rain. We organized our gear, then sat and watched waves crash over a distant reef. Gray clouds turned the water a dark steely blue. If we hadn't been so exhausted, it would have been pretty.

"Eight miles," I said, looking at the map. "Fifty-two to go. Beef jerky?"

"Who is that?" Sarah said. A Palauan man in his late forties approached. His shirt was tucked awkwardly into his pants, and he walked with a slight limp. He was carrying something. A tray?

"Ungil kebesengei," Sarah said as he got closer.

"Good evening," he replied in English, and smiled as he set down the tray. He'd brought us two glasses of water in which the remnants of ice cubes clinked gently, two hamburgers, and a large plate of French fries. Clean knives and forks were wound tightly in white paper napkins. I realized that the closest house, and therefore the closest kitchen, was at least half a mile away. We thanked him repeatedly and invited him to join us.

"Welcome," he said before turning back to his house.

"Total prick," I said once he was out of earshot.

"What an asshole," Sarah said.

We then pushed our burgers together in a thankful and mushy toast. "To the good people of Palau," Sarah said.

"And their crap-ass jungle," I said.

Ten minutes later we saw the same man returning.

"He heard what you said about him," I said. "And he's angry."

"Ungil kebesengei," Sarah said when he was close enough to hear. Without a word, he set a bottle of ketchup on the tray and returned the same way he'd come.

Within moments of swallowing our last bites of our hamburgers, we fell soundly asleep. If our legs touched that night, neither of us noticed.

CHAPTER 52

What You Can Expect to Learn in This Chapter:

➤ What is the best way to carry a large fresh fish while hiking through the jungle?

➤ What children's game must presidential candidates in Palau excel at?

The following morning, we rinsed our dishes in the ocean, dropped the tray at one of the houses, and resumed walking before sunrise. The mud had dried somewhat overnight, speeding our pace. Crickets, birds, and frogs chirped and croaked from both sides of the road. As the village disappeared behind us, fruit bats swooped low and just over our heads before fluttering back into the trees. Here, the road was wider. Or at least the jungle had been cut farther back, leaving a wide swath for the shadeless straight road. The sun rose fast and very, very hot.

About midmorning, a truck, the first we'd seen, approached us. A full-figured middle-aged woman with a soaring Afro tumbled out of the driver's seat. She said that she was a relative of Gibson's and that she'd been looking for us since yesterday. "I have something for you," she said before walking to her truck and returning a moment later with a fish wrapped in a newspaper. Its head and tail stuck out each end; it was three feet long.

"Oh, thank you," I said, "but we couldn't." I was being honest. We really couldn't.

"I've been looking for you," she said, looking deflated.

"*Sulang, sulang,*" Sarah said, taking the fish. "Thank you. Thank you." The woman got back in her truck, turned it around, and headed back in the direction she'd come.

"That was so nice," Sarah said.

"We're not going to carry that fish."

"It's a gift," she said. "What are you gonna do, chuck it into the jungle?"

"That's exactly what we're going to do." But Sarah wasn't listening. I could feel the straps loosening on my backpack. "No, no, no. You are not going to put that in my pack."

"You'll be fine," she said. "Let's go."

I heard the snap of a clip as she closed the top of the backpack over the fish. The head and tail stuck out on each side, like one of those wacky arrow headbands.

"Bitch," I mumbled.

"Dickweed," she said.

We continued our march up and down hills along the compacted red clay road. The heat of the sun, the weight of our packs, and extreme dehydration made further conversation, once again, impossible.

About fifteen miles into the day, we came upon a crew of road workers. At a seemingly random spot, five men were heaving shovels of mud and dirt into the jungle. As we approached, they set their shovels down. We slid our backpacks off. All of us were caked in mud. Unable to speak one another's languages, however, there wasn't much to do except stand and look around. Yet the absurdity was lost on no one: seven foreigners, one carrying a giant fish, were standing on a desolate, half-built Palauan road that the Palauans themselves didn't seem to want.

Finally, one of the men noticed our nearly empty water bottles and offered to refill them from his large jug. We accepted gratefully.

"Hot," I said, wiping my brow to add clarity.

"Hot," they said, nodding.

"Well, good luck," I said.

Everyone smiled and waved.

Sarah and I must have looked in pretty bad shape, because one of the men ran to catch up with us. He offered us his sandwich: two pieces of fresh bread with mustard and some kind of meat in between.

"Thank you," I said, accepting.

Sarah took it from my hand and gave it back to him. "Thank you, but we're OK," she said, pointing at the fish sticking out of my backpack. He offered again, and she refused again.

"What were you doing?" she said as we continued walking.

"It looked good," I said.

"You can't take food from a Bangladeshi road worker."

"But you can from a Palauan woman?"

"That was different. She was looking for us. You were going to take that guy's lunch."

"He offered."

"We have plenty of food! We packed a ton of spaghetti."

"I know," I said, spinning quickly in an attempt to thunk her with the head of the fish.

"Let's just keep going," she said.

"Is this our second fight?"

"It's not. But if it were, I would have already won."

"Oh my God," I said. "Was that—I dunno—a conditional, pluperfect declaration of victory? You really are a lawyer." Apparently, that was the wrong thing to say. She stopped and glared at me. "OK, OK," I said. "You're right. But you have to admit that sandwich looked good."

For the next few hours we passed not a single house or person. Just red clay and jungle. Up and down hills. More fucking red clay. More fucking jungle. Finally, from the top of a hill, we saw a dome sticking out of the canopy far in the distance.

"Is that the capitol?" I said. "No one would build a capitol here."

"Well, I doubt it's a Wendy's," said Sarah. "A Taco Bell, maybe. But not a Wendy's."

Part Graceland, part Parthenon, the new Palauan capitol complex rising out of the jungle of Babeldaob was nothing if not ambitious. Its location, on a hill above the small village of Melekeok, allowed for views along the central spine of Babeldaob and white-water views up and down the eastern coast. When Sarah and I arrived, exhausted after twenty-five miles of walking, the site was deserted.

"Hello?" Sarah said, announcing ourselves as we approached the door to a columned building with the word *Parliament* etched in the triangular pediment of its facade. The building's shape was almost identical to that of the U.S. Capitol, its scale that of a medium-sized state capitol building. Bigger than Kansas', say, but smaller than Texas'. Yet it represented the seat of government of a country with just twenty-five thousand people.

Sarah knocked on the steel-and-glass door. "We could have designed something cooler," she said as we waited.

"You mean more original?"

"You know, just something that would fit in more with the surroundings." She knocked again.

"Like something made out of thatch?" I said. "Or shaped like a giant coconut? That would be kind of cool."

"No. I think a building should honor its environment more. Not feel like something dropped in by helicopter from someplace else."

"OK, Frank Lloyd—" I said, reaching for the handle. The door opened. Inside, we found giant rolls of thick carpet lying under a gilded rotunda lit by a giant chandelier. A spiral staircase with a curved brass banister circled up and around to the second and third floors. Plaster statuary sat on the concrete floor, each piece waiting for a perch on one of the empty pedestals nearby. Though it appeared no one had been here in weeks, the air conditioner was on full blast.

"Hello?" Sarah called again as we wandered upstairs, our hands following the dusty banister. We passed more rolls of carpet, more empty pedestals, and various wood-paneled committee rooms, then the parliament floor itself. There was a bunch of little desks with wires sticking out of them, presumably awaiting voting buttons.

Outside again, the late-afternoon sun reflected hard off the white buildings and the exposed dirt of the construction site. I looked up at the birds and fish embedded in the columns. Just as the ancient Greeks built bulges into the middle of their columns to make them appear straight from a distance, these too bulged in the middle. But they bulged *way* too much, giving them a cartoonishly bloated look, like a snake that's just eaten a gopher. I tapped one. It was hollow.

We skipped the building labeled *Judiciary* and made our way to the *Executive Branch*.

"I like how they all have such clear names," I said as we walked. "It's like someone designed a government complex after reading a social studies textbook." The Executive Branch wasn't as fancy as the Parliament building, consisting of a few plain offices, most with views of the jungle instead of the ocean.

I was coming to learn that Palau's small size allows for such simplicity. In the United States, a building marked *Executive Branch* would have to include the entire U.S. military as well as the IRS and a few dozen other massive bureaucracies. But Palau doesn't have a military or much in the way of taxes. And unlike in the United States, Palau's small size allows almost everyone to have a role. Each of the thirteen states has its own council of chiefs and elderly matriarchs who select those chiefs, a state assembly, elected members of Parliament, and a governor. It's not much of an exaggeration to say that everyone has a voice in how the place is run.

The flip side to all this democracy, of course, is that Palauan politics is extremely personal. Traditional political parties don't exist, their roles filled instead by extended families and networks of business contacts. Running for president is a bit like running for student

government, only with more beer. (Election season is the only time
that the entire island runs out of Budweiser and Bud Light.) Most
campaign events are casual all-day affairs that culminate in games of
musical chairs. For real. If a current president is running for reelection, he's always allowed to make it into the final rounds, a perk of
incumbency. But when the music stops, he lunges for the last chair
just like the other guy.

Sarah and I walked down the hill to Melekeok and arranged to sleep
in the simple concrete community center. Perhaps it was the mud and
exhaustion or perhaps the wastefulness of American aid, but I was
grumpy. Just as we slipped inside, it started to rain.

"I read there is a shortage of textbooks in the schools here," I said.
"Why don't the Americans pay for that instead?"

"That would be better," Sarah agreed, spreading a mat across the
linoleum floor.

"You know a third of Palauans live abroad because of the lack of
jobs?" I said.

"What about the Parthenon? When it was being built, don't you
think people wagged their fingers at its garishness, its wastefulness?
Everyone wants to feel proud of something."

"Of course. But the newspaper has stories every day about Palau's
drug problem. Shouldn't we—"

"I'm going to try to figure out what to do with this fish," she said,
walking to the door.

She returned almost as quickly as she'd left. "I gave someone the
fish," she said. "We have another twenty miles tomorrow. I'm going
to sleep."

We turned off the lights and climbed into our sleeping bags, the
rain pinging the tin roof above us—the same steady rain that in two
hundred years will have long since melted away America's gifts of
papier-mâché capitols and roads to nowhere.

CHAPTER 53

What You Can Expect to Learn in This Chapter:

▶ While jogging with the president of Palau, is it appreciated to bring up a movie about a fictional small country that invades the United States only to find its invasion ignored?

▶ What might the president have hidden in his exercise towel?

The day we finished our hike (still friends but not exactly boyfriend-girlfriend), I found another message on my answering machine—usually a cause for celebration in itself, but this message was from the president's office! Apparently, President Remengesau was available. If I still wanted to meet, I should go to the jogging track on Wednesday at five thirty a.m. That gave me just two days to recover and prepare.

Shortly after finishing a sixty-mile jungle trudge, however, you don't much feel like jogging or cramming, especially a book titled *Overreaching in Paradise: United States Policy in Palau Since 1945*. But I hoped it could provide some context for why the U.S. threw so much money at Palau.

Turns out, *O.I.P.U.S.P.P.S.N.* wasn't so much an overview of U.S. policy in the Pacific as a collection of the world's most boring quotes. The sad thing is the quotes weren't even good quotes; in fact, each one managed to make everything else in life, including watching socks wick the sweat off your ankles, sparkle with urgency. Then there was this text from the back cover—traditionally, the part of a book used to grab the interest of the reader:

> In the process of insisting on the "ratification" of what by 1986 had become a non-negotiable Compact, the United States has overreached its rights as administering authority under the Trusteeship Agreement for the Trust Territory of the Pacific Islands which it entered into with the United Nations Security Council in 1947.

Text that good needs to be printed more than once—that same sentence also appears in the preface. Perhaps I read it too quickly to fully appreciate *O.I.P.U.S.P.P.S.N.*'s subtleties but reading it reminded me of a line from that old Peter Sellers movie, *The Mouse That Roared:*

GENERAL SNIPPET: I warn you, madam—I know the entire Geneva Convention by heart!
GRAND DUCHESS GLORIANA: Oh, how nice! You must recite it for me some evening. I play the harpsichord.

Most disappointing, however, was that *O.I.P.U.S.P.P.S.N.* didn't answer my $447 million question about the intent behind America's largesse. All it said was that the U.S. gave all that money to Palau for *significant economic, political, and foreign policy reasons.*

I called Sarah the evening before my jog/interview. She asked if I was ready.

"Not really," I said. "But I took a shower and stretched."

"Do you have a notepad?"

"Good point," I said. I rummaged around and found a sticky one at the bottom of my backpack. I even found a pen.

At five twenty-eight a.m., I pulled up to Palau's only running track. It was still a half hour from sunrise, and the parking lot was empty except for a Chevy Suburban with tinted windows. Leaning against it were two large men, both awake but not especially anxious about security.

"I'm here to meet with the president," I said.

They pointed me to the track. On the far side a man jogged alone, the only one on the track. Shit, I thought, he's early. As he approached, I could tell he was about five foot ten, sturdy but not overweight, his gait swift for a man in his early fifties.

I double-knotted my shoelaces and scribbled with my pen on the pad to make sure it was working. I'd never done an interview before, much less one with a head of state while jogging at five thirty in the morning. Actually, I was pretty sure I'd never done anything at five thirty in the morning.

"Hi, Alex," he said in a rich baritone without slowing his jog. "Join me." He wore white tennis shoes, white socks, gray sweats, and a white shirt and carried a white towel in his right hand. Even though the sun wasn't up, he wore sunglasses of the same oversized mirrored style favored by Nigerian generals who promised free elections once calm was restored.

I had only one question I really wanted to ask, but I thought I should work up to it. "So, what's it like being president of a small country?" I said, though even as the words came out, I realized what a stupid question it was. Compared to what? Compared to being the president of a big country? How the hell would he know?

"I asked for it, and it's a privilege to have gotten in," he said, sponging his brow with his white towel, "but there's sacrifice to family, to friends. You know, I'm a fisherman. I'm grateful we only have smaller problems. Nobody is starving here." I was writing as fast as possible while trying not to bump into him, especially on the curves.

Just as I asked how Palau had changed since he was younger, a blister on my left foot burst. "Of course, there have been many changes," he said, "but the thing that has changed the least is our culture. Governments have changed and the way we run businesses has changed, but holding on to our culture is still the most important thing." I wasn't sure what this really meant, but before I could follow up, he asked how long I had been in Palau. I told him only a few months, but that I'd developed an appreciation for the country after walking across Babeldaob with a friend. To my relief, he immediately stopped jogging.

"The whole thing?" he said to me as I reached down to shift my left sock around.

"The whole thing," I said. "North to south. With all due respect to your country, it was terrible."

He smiled. "I thought I was the only person who'd ever done it," he said. "Congratulations." He shook my hand and started jogging again.

Even this early in the morning, my notepad was wet from the perspiration cascading off my face. You can't walk from a car into a store in Palau without bursting into a full-body sweat and looking for a place to take a nap, yet now I was jogging, writing, and talking at the same time. I felt like one of those reporters summoned to George W.'s ranch to do an interview while clearing brush. But given the heat and humidity, this was more like water aerobics.

Without prompting, he returned to his earlier subject. "I wouldn't want a McDonald's here. Our traditions are still strong and extended family is still our core obligation. But to hold on to all of that, we need our environment. Some take it for granted. But some portions must be left undeveloped. We need peace and quiet, nature, trees, and greenery also."

A half dozen other people were now walking around the track, all with little towels around their necks. No one paid any attention to their president. I asked what he thought about the proposal then floating around to build a casino in Palau.

"We can survive without a casino," he said. "If the people want one, that is one thing, but the social factor is the liability. People also say we need a golf course. But we don't have the space. We might have room for a driving range." Perhaps that was the essence of political compromise. Some folks wanted a golf course. Some didn't. So you gave 'em a driving range. I didn't know how much more time the president (or my body) would give me, so I started to ease into my main question.

"Once the Compact Agreement with the United States runs out, where will jobs come from?"

"Growth needs to come more from the private sector than the public. There may come a time to freeze hiring. Rightsizing, I think, is the term. I'm doing things not for popularity but in the interest of Palau. I don't want to be the president who bankrupts Palau."

"Is there anything that you would want Americans to know about Palau?" I said, panting.

"It would help if Americans would understand that small Pacific islands believe in democracy and the ideals the U.S. espouses. It would help a lot if Americans could know about our special relationship. This is my last turn, by the way. Then I'm stopping." Time, in other words, for one more question.

"So," I said, "any idea why the U.S. gave Palau all that money?" As far as question phrasing goes, I knew it was artless, but I was dizzy. And at least it got to the point.

"America gave us that money," he said slowly, in the same tone your grandfather might use to tell you always to take care of your mother, "because Palau is America's best friend."

Drenched in sweat and delirious, I didn't really get what he was saying, but later I had a chance to think about it. Like a lot of foreign aid, the money the U.S. gave Palau had nothing to do with the needs of the recipient and everything to do with the needs of the donor. The only remaining superpower, the U.S. likes to know it has a friend, not so much a "brokenheart necklace" *best* friend but at least a loyal sidekick of a friend. The kind of friend who will willingly join any coalition we propose and vote for us if we run for class treasurer, even if we ignore him in the cafeteria.

As we pulled off the track, I caught my breath and said, "Have you, by chance, read a book or seen a movie called *The Mouse That Roared*?"

A crazy question, granted, but it seemed relevant, and the 1959 Peter Sellers movie had been on my mind recently. It's about a tiny country in Europe called the Duchy of Grand Fenwick, which, falling on hard economic times, declares war on the United States; their thinking is that the U.S. has a habit of destroying countries and then rebuilding them better than before.

"Is that about the country that invades the United States?" he said, stopping. "I've seen it."

"Maybe if tourism doesn't work out . . . ," I said.

"Yes. We'll need to give it some consideration," he said, chuckling.

I then thanked him for his time and extended my hand for a handshake. As I did so, he switched the towel he'd been carrying from his right to his left hand, revealing a tape recorder that had been hidden in the towel's folds. He pressed the stop button and, with a confident smile, shook my hand and said, "Good to meet you, Alex."

Even on a small island, it seemed, the motto was *trust, but verify*. Even while jogging.

CHAPTER 54

I was asleep when my mother called. "I finally got ahold of your brother," she said without introduction. "He's all right. He was late to work, thank God."

"Good to hear," I said. I had no idea what she was talking about. "And you, how are you doing?"

"I'm fine," she said quickly. "Nothing's happened in Texas."

"Good. Not much in Palau either . . . Hey, can I call you back in the morning?"

"I think we should talk often. Maybe every two hours."

That did seem often. I looked out the window. A half-moon shone. Light reflected off the big banana leaves drooping outside my window. The wind was completely still.

"Mom, it's midnight here."

"I know. We just don't know what else could happen."

"Well, sleep. That's one that comes to mind," I said.

"Turn on the television, for fuck sake," she said. "Two planes hit the World Trade Center this morning. They both fell down. Your brother was getting a haircut."

I called Sarah and turned on the television. Halle Berry was being interviewed on *Good Morning America*. For reasons having to do with copyright and broadcast licenses, (nonsatellite) Palauan television is delayed one week. More or less the same channels are on offer as in the U.S.; they're just a week late, plus an extra twelve hours to account for time zones. Thus, on Monday evening in Palau, you can see the previous week's *Monday Night Football,* last Monday's *ABC World News Tonight.*

As a result, Sarah and I watched September 11 on September 18. A week's worth of news supplemented by the Internet hadn't shed much light on what happened that day. I could, however, make out a certain emotional arc to the coverage: what started as confusion evolved into shock, passed through fear, then anger, before concluding with confusion of a deeper, more fundamental sort than the day had started with.

The coverage also shifted from the cinematic to the personal. Instead of just the towers falling, we saw the face of a taxi driver in tears. The banker who lost hundreds of colleagues, including his own brother. The family of that fireman who went up one last time.

Palauan angles on September 11 were not in high demand, so not surprisingly, the American media didn't report this item: on September 11, a Palauan delegation was in Manhattan to visit the United Nations. They were staying at the Hilton Millenium Hotel, a slender building located directly across from the World Trade Center. It was the first time many of the delegates had ever left Palau. After the first plane hit, they ran from the hotel. Many carried their luggage; a few carried pillows. None of them knew a single person in the city. So they walked north, in a daze, up to the middle of Broadway. No doubt some were thinking of their island, 8,700 miles away and without a single streetlight. Eventually they found themselves, as one does on occasion, camped out on the apartment floor of the Italian ambassador to the UN.

On September 19, the same day the Palauan legislature voted to send $50,000 to the American Red Cross, I checked out *A History of Islam* from the local library. I felt naive and earnest doing so, but I didn't know what else to do. Not that the book helped much anyway. After I read most of it, the same questions still swirled in my mind as had on September 11 and September 18, and that would still years later: how do you respond without creating more enemies? How do you wage war against an idea? After Islamic fanaticism, what next? Selfishness? Then envy? Perhaps someday, I thought, my children will explain it all to me.

One thing I knew was that I'd never live in New York again. After watching those interviews on television—many of which took place in my former West Village neighborhood—the crush of guilt was too great, the shame of not being there too intense. "Where were you that day?" people would ask, as previous generations had asked of December 7, 1941, and November 22, 1963.

"I was on a remote Pacific island," I would have to say, "reading books and watching Halle Berry talk about *Monster's Ball*."

CHAPTER 55

What You Can Expect to Learn in This Chapter:

► Is the presence of dolphins a sign that you're approaching paradise? What about seasick, barfing boat captains?

► Is a positive experience assembling a desk from IKEA worth making life plans around?

efore September 11, Sarah and I had made plans to visit Angaur, the only one of Palau's three hundred islands located outside a protective barrier reef. Reachable only by an occasional ferry, Angaur was where expats went to get away from getting away from it all. It was said to be beautiful, covered in fruit trees and cooler in temperature than the rest of Palau. As far as islands go, the grass doesn't get much greener than on Angaur. Yet we debated not going. It was late September but only a week since we'd first seen the towers go down on television in Palau.

"It's kind of bad form, right?" I said a few evenings later while we sat on my couch with the television on mute.

"It is and it isn't," Sarah said. That was one of the things I loved about her—she could see at least two sides of just about every issue. "Say you had died in the World Trade Center and could, somehow, watch what people chose to do afterward. Would you want your loved ones to watch endless replays on television or continue on? Not just live their lives but celebrate life itself?"

"You are a lawyer," I said.

"I'm serious," she said. "Why empower those assholes by giving them anything more than they've already taken?"

"In other words, *We'll show them by spending the weekend on an island*?"

"Yes," she said.

And so it was decided.

In retrospect, it was a good decision, though we almost didn't make it to the island at all. As we drove up to the harbor, deckhands were untying the little ferry from the dock—Angaur's ferry is, apparently, the only public transportation in the world that sometimes leaves early. The shiny steel boat was quite small, the size of a one-bedroom house and, as was my experience so far in the Pacific, seating was limited. There was only one short bench, already filled with elderly people. Most of the twenty or so other passengers sat on the floor, where they leaned against pallets of rice and soda or sprawled across multicolored plastic mats. We found a place to one side, next to a small stack of lumber.

For the next three hours, we puffed our way south through the Rock Islands. Though it was lovely to watch these green-and-gray isles slide by, Sarah and I quickly fell asleep, unable to overcome the drone of the engine, the humid heat, and the ferry's lumbering sway. That sway became a shudder, however, as we passed through a break in the protective reef and hit the first swells of open ocean. The ferry's bow smacked into the water of each rising swell, sending a spray of salt water over everything and everyone on the boat. Deckhands who previously had been sleeping or fishing scurried about, securing the front-loading ramp with extra lengths of thick rope.

The ocean in this six-mile channel separating the last Rock Island and Angaur was different from what I'd seen in Palau or, for that matter, anywhere else. Big dark blue swells that had been gaining momentum for thousands of miles rose and fell, their tops scattered by a strong wind blowing in the opposite direction. Meanwhile, currents so strong you could actually see them swirled in the water, spinning the boat in sudden, unexpected directions. We'd heard the crossing took over an hour, despite the short distance, and now understood why. In effect, we were being pushed by four different forces: wind, current, swell, and, hopefully strongest of all, the engine. We were, therefore, relieved (and soaked) by the time the first hazy hint of Angaur's green northern shore finally come into view.

"Not the easiest place to get to," Sarah said.

I nodded in agreement, noting the steady flow of passengers, alone or in pairs, running to the railings to throw up. I closed my eyes and tried to sleep, but Sarah kept making comments . . . helpful comments like . . .

A deckhand just tied himself to the boat.

I hope this doesn't disrupt the after-dinner show.

Wow. A triple barfer. Very rare. I think one of them is the captain.

Finally, we made it past the island's tip and into calmer waters. Angaur's shoreline seemed to alternate between jungle and palm, volcanic rock and white-sand beaches. A pod of maybe twenty dolphins swam to the side of the ferry. Each one leapt grandly out of the water before turning sharply out to sea. Halfway down Angaur's coast, the captain turned us toward shore, waited for a lull in the waves and, between breaks, accelerated quickly before sliding into a harbor that couldn't have been twice the size of the ferry itself.

Even before the engine stopped, children jumped off the boat and into light green water, maybe ten feet below. They were joined by children onshore jumping off the concrete walls of the harbor. Half a dozen adults leaned against a rusting white pickup. They wore shorts and T-shirts and looked pleased, if not ecstatic, that the ferry had once again arrived.

Sarah and I joined a spontaneous bucket brigade of people tossing cases of beer, faded Tupperware containers, and hand-labeled boxes from the boat into the back of the truck. Within five minutes the ferry was locked up and empty; the pickup, along with all the adults, gone. Only a few children remained, taking turns doing flips into the water.

We asked the oldest, a boy of about ten, for directions to the island's guesthouse, and he said he'd just take us. He walked, barefoot, ten yards in front us, kicking leaves onto the side of the dirt road as he went. Angaur felt about ten degrees cooler than Koror. I wondered if that had to do with the lack of a barrier reef. Perhaps the beautiful, shallow lagoons that surrounded most Palauan islands also absorbed and trapped the sun's heat. Far ahead of us, I thought I saw a monkey run into the bushes.

"Are there monkeys here?" I called ahead.

"Yeah . . . they're pests."

"Cute pests, though, right?"

"They eat my grandmother's fruit," he said. "She doesn't like them."

We passed a small open-air building. It had a concrete floor and tile roof. "Community center," the boy said.

Just beyond, we passed a handful of cinder-block houses painted bright hues of blue and red and yellow. A few elderly women smiled or nodded from chairs placed in the middle of wide, weedy yards. "Is this downtown?" I called out to the boy, now maybe twenty yards ahead. He waved his arm as if in agreement.

A few minutes later, we arrived at the guesthouse, a one-story wooden bungalow with a wraparound porch. Once white but now well faded, the house felt like the kind of place you might have found on Oahu's North Shore in, say, 1949. Its louvered windows were coated with a film of sea spray; its plywood floorboards sank slightly underfoot. There was running water and a small fridge but no phone or television.

I glanced at the guestbook. The few entries were long and rich in adjectives; many were drawings. A short path through the trees led to a small beach.

"It's twenty dollars a night," the boy said. "You can pay Leon when you leave."

"Are you sure it's available?" I said, unsure if such a young concierge could be trusted.

"Yes," he said matter-of-factly. "It's always available."

Estimating from a map left on the kitchen counter, Angaur was about eight miles around. A road appeared to circle the island. There was a lake in the middle. Perhaps some hills. Sarah and I set down our bags and set out walking. We figured we could walk around the southern tip and cut through a path across the middle and be back before dark—happy to have a much smaller island to traverse this time.

The road on the map proved to be more of a path. How long it would remain even a path seemed uncertain. Every thirty feet or so, we passed a fallen coconut, its roots just starting to take hold in the short green grass. We were both struck by Angaur's beauty. Neither of us spoke as we passed alongside white-sand beaches barely visible through the trees that arched over the path, a shaded tunnel formed by huge Pacific banyans, short flame trees bursting with red flowers, and slender ironwoods, pinelike trees with dark red trunks that seemed to belong more to the Cascades than to a remote Pacific island. The banyan trees were the most impressive. Though their trunks were ten feet around, most of the epiphytic plants' canopy was supported by aerial roots growing down from the branches, like buttresses on a Gothic cathedral—if Gothic cathedrals were ever green and covered with pink flowers. Amazingly, banana, papaya, and mango trees also lined the path. They produced so much fruit that most appeared to have fallen on the ground where they were left to reseed and grow anew, just as fruit is supposed to do.

We were also struck by Angaur's sounds: not just the din of birds and whine of crickets but the constant crash of waves on empty beaches, or later along our walk, against the island's limestone cliffs. Occasionally, we'd even turn a corner and surprise a troop of monkeys— descendants, we'd learn, of a group of long-tailed macaques introduced a hundred years earlier by the Germans. The monkeys would leap around, sometimes even throw branches at us, before disappearing into the thick forest in a noisy shudder of broken twigs and angry screeches.

A few miles from the guesthouse, we came across what looked like an abandoned *bai*. It was tucked among the ironwood and banyan and set just back from a long, thin crescent of sand. We sat down on the wooden platform, our legs warmed by the late-afternoon sun, and watched birds swoop bugs off the surface of the calm blue water.

"This is the most beautiful place I've ever been," I said.

"Me too," Sarah said.

"The old-timers who built this," I said, "chose this spot. Picked this design."

"They did a good job," she said. We watched a fruit bat lazily flap its way across the little bay.

"So," I said, "any ideas about what you're going to do after Palau? You know, after your contract is up?"

"Not sure," she said, circling the sand with the tip of her flip-flop. "The court already bought me a ticket, but I think it's changeable."

"Well, if you could do anything, what would it be?" I'd been coming to learn that this was an essential question. Given that compromises were inevitable, if you don't start with the ideal, you certainly won't get there. Put another way, people rarely exceed their own expectations so might as well start big and work backward from there. And at that moment—anything seemed possible. It was as if by going to Palau and then on to Angaur, we'd reached escape velocity and were now beyond the gravitational pull of our old lives, our old expectations.

"Remember, I'm a fox," she said. "I find everything interesting. What about you?"

"Well, I rarely describe myself as a fox, but I've been thinking about my house in Koror."

"Feeling house proud, are you?"

"Yes and no, actually. It's an incredible house, but it was Gibson who saw that steep hillside and thought to build something there. It was Gibson who dragged the trees out of the jungle. I just rented the place."

"Oh, God."

"I think that's part of what I was missing in New York."

"Deforestation?"

"So much of my life was online. And all of our lives are only getting more that way. Life here isn't exactly digital, but we'll go back on Sunday and the first thing we'll do is check our email."

"To communicate with *people*."

"Maybe it comes from having built and, basically, lost that online company, but building a house feels fundamental and practical."

"Practical?" she said.

"I know that getting a master's degree in accounting or something would be more practical, but at least building a house would be *real*. Not pixels on the screen, but dirt under your nails, a roof over your head."

"And a hole in your wallet."

"We could do it cheaply," I said. "I'm thinking something really simple. Look at this place. It's just a floor and a roof. You don't even need walls here. And labor is the biggest cost of building. We could get friends to help us. I bet we could do the whole thing for a few thousand dollars in materials."

"Do you have any friends?"

"Well, I could make some. But I do think anything you do yourself has more meaning. Whether it's making dinner or making babies, it's better to do things yourself than just buying—"

"What's the going rate on a baby these days?" she said. "And do you know anything about construction? Just because you've lived in a house doesn't make you qualified to build one."

"I assembled a desk from IKEA once. And in college I built a shelf."

"Me too," she said.

"For some reason, the brackets didn't hold."

"Sounds like a metaphor for your life," she said, hopping down off the platform. "It'll be dark soon. Let's go."

While we walked back, I was actually encouraged by Sarah's response. She'd asked questions—good questions—but she hadn't said no.

That evening, while Sarah took a shower, I sat at a table with a piece of paper and a pen.

"What are you doing?" Sarah said, coming out in a towel.

"Sketching out the house."

"What?"

"Only as a thought exercise. I'm just imagining what it would look like."

She glanced over my shoulder. "You want to live in a chicken coop? I gotta get dressed. Then let's make dinner."

After a simple meal of spaghetti and red sauce, we sat together on a wooden swinging bench out on the porch, our feet perched on the railing. As the ocean churned in the distance, we watched a pair of geckos that clung to the plywood ceiling overhead. Occasionally, one would lunge toward a bug attracted to the porch's single yellow light. Most were misses.

"It's so simple," I said. "Just two people on a swing on a porch, the ocean in the distance. Life should be this simple."

"I think it's deceptive," she said. "Palau just *looks* easy. They speak English and use U.S. dollars. And in a way it *is* accessible, but in most ways it isn't. Long-term expats, the ones who have been here twenty, thirty years, all say that they underestimated the difficulty of navigating the culture." We watched a gecko grab one of the bugs and swallow it.

"It's so clichéd," I said, "this screen saver idea of paradise, but this is pretty close, right?"

"It is pretty close," she said. "And clichéd but so what? No one really thinks paradise exists, do they? Didn't Gauguin paint a lot of his paintings of the Pacific before he even left Paris? He found, just like everyone finds out here, that places, people—they're always more complicated and more interesting than we expect."

We then sat for a long moment while a small gecko on the ceiling leapt at a gnat, only to fall and catch himself on the nearby wall. Sarah rested her head on my shoulder. I found her hand and held it. She didn't pull away. I leaned down and kissed the side of her forehead. She didn't pull away. But she didn't turn either. I leaned farther down, at an awkward angle, and kissed her cheek and the edge of her lips. Then she turned. Slightly. A millimeter at most. But enough.

We kissed, and then we kissed a little more. And then we fell asleep, enfolded in each other's arms—two people on a little swing on a little island, never more untethered from the rest of the world yet never more safe.

CHAPTER 56

What You Can Expect to Learn in This Chapter:

- ➤ What, if any, is the relationship between having a lot of choices and happiness?

- ➤ If you put two goats in a corral, will they eventually fall in love?

The afternoon after returning from Angaur, I went snorkeling just off the shore of a city park and found myself swimming parallel to a four-foot-long cornet fish. I was focused on it, and I am pretty sure it was focused on me too, because as I swam, it kept looking at me, until, bonk, it ran into a rock. This was very exciting. After meeting Sarah and hanging out with those elderly topless women folding laundry in Yap, this was the third most exciting thing that had happened to me since arriving in the Pacific. I was, therefore, thrilled to tell Sarah about it that night when we planned to meet for dinner.

I also was anxious to find out what she felt our kiss had meant.

For dinner, we chose a place called K-Café. Expectations were high. It was a new restaurant in a place that doesn't get many new restaurants. And it had *café* in the name. Sarah ordered the fish with sauce. I ordered the pasta.

At first, neither of us mentioned the kiss. We talked about the weather. Given that Palau has the most consistent weather of any place in the world—from day to night and month to month, the temperature is almost constant; in the dry season it rains once a day and in the wet, twice a day—it wasn't a sizzling topic. We then talked about the restaurant and how its handmade mosaic map on the wall placed Palau in the very center.

"I'm glad we kissed," I said abruptly.

"Me too," she said. "Me too."

"Me too," I said.

"I know," she said, "because you already said so." We just looked at each other for an awkward moment.

"Your contract's up in four weeks, right?" I said.

"Yep," she said.

"And then?"

"Not sure." This seemed like an opening. "I don't want to stay in Koror, though. I've already been here a year."

I again brought up moving to Angaur, maybe building a small bungalow. She raised an eyebrow as I repeated my pitch about anything you do yourself having more meaning than just buying it. And what could be more fundamental than housing?

Seeing that I was serious, she rattled off the dozen or so reasons why it wasn't a good idea. I sensed that underlying all of them, however, was the questionable sanity of building a house with someone you've kissed once. Fortunately, before she could definitively say no, our food arrived. Sarah's fish was soaked in a gravy of cold mushroom soup.

"Huh," she said, chewing. "This tastes like halibut. Halibut comes from Alaska." Considering the amount of fresh fish available in Palau, this was akin to eating frozen bagels from Texas in New York City. The waitress returned with my plate.

"Looks like you got the alphabet soup," Sarah said. "Tasty." It was, indeed, standard-issue Chef Boyardee alphabet soup. Even though the preparation of my $18 entree required nothing beyond a can opener and a microwave, at least it came with a side. In this case, Triscuits.

"I'm not sure this is a great value," Sarah said, chewing slowly on her fish. "But you can't be too particular on a small island."

"What do you mean?" I said. Was she speaking indirectly about our relationship? About me?

"Well, in a big city, you fret a lot about where to eat, because you could conceivably end up at one of the best restaurants in the world. But in Palau, you just go with what you got."

Oh, shit, I thought. She *was* talking about me. I'm the canned alphabet soup, the defrosted halibut of eligible men in Palau.

"Do you think this is a *Z* or an *N*?" I said in a near daze.

"It's definitely a *Z*," she said. "But I'm serious. Here you maximize appreciation for what you have. And spend less time worrying about what you don't have."

"But it doesn't mean you don't have high standards, right?" I said.

"Well, it does kind of mean that," she said, reaching over to grab one of my Triscuits. "If I lived in Paris, the K-Café would be a huge disappointment. But in Palau, it's . . . I dunno. It's something else. It's the OK Café, just without the *O*." She laughed a little at her own joke, but I was beginning to feel sick. "What I mean is that having lots of choices isn't always a good thing," she continued as she stood to go to the restroom. "A lot of choices just makes you choosy."

In any other context, that observation might be profound—I even wrote it down as my seventh Life Lesson, but that was later. Now it just made me feel deflated. Apparently, she kissed me because she had so few choices: As my grandmother used to say, "Put two goats in a corral, and eventually they'll fall in love."

When Sarah returned from the restroom, I got defensive—and incoherent. "For a small country, I think Palau has a lot of good restaurants, a lot of great choices. Don't you think? I mean, it's not that small. Some islands only have one grocery store. Have you been to Yap? They have fish the chefs wouldn't piss on."

The expression on her face was a mixture of astonishment and addled fear, like the one you'd see on a moose that has just fallen through a swimming pool cover.

"Are you OK?" I said.

"The bathroom."

"Was it gross?"

"You need to see it," she said. Happy to be talking about something other than lowering standards on a small island, I excused myself to go check it out. The men's room, at least, appeared normal enough: two urinals and a stall, all pretty clean. I returned to the table, reporting that all seemed normal.

"You need to see the women's," she said.

"Really?"

"Really."

I went back into the hall but, after walking back and forth a few times, couldn't find it. I asked a Filipina waitress, who pointed me back to the bathroom marked *Men*. Maybe she hadn't understood? It was, after all, strange for a man to be asking for directions to the women's bathroom. But I went back into the men's room anyway. A large man with dense neck hair was standing at one of the urinals. I scanned the room again. Plenty of paper towels. The linoleum and sink counters looked fine too. The man at the urinal looked at me from the corner of his eye.

"Just looking," I said. He responded with the kind of glare one might expect and left without flushing.

I then poked my head around the other side of the stall, and there, at the back of the men's bathroom, just past the urinals and the last toilet, was a narrow door marked *Women*.

"At least they capitalized the sign," I said, sitting back down at our table.

"Yeah," she said, reaching over to grab my last Triscuit, "but maybe a few more choices wouldn't be a bad thing."

CHAPTER 57

What You Can Expect to Learn in This Chapter:

- ► Is being called the Rosa Parks of the driveway slur a compliment?

- ► Is there ever a good way to tell someone, "Your spouse is an asshole"?

In one of the books I brought with me, *Discipline and Punish: The Birth of the Prison*, Michel Foucault says that the way a society handles its prisoners reveals a great deal about that society. Palau may be no exception. Though not mentioned in the book, the Republic of Palau opens its prison doors during the day—at six a.m.; guards simply let the inmates out and gently remind them to be back in time for dinner. Thus from six to six, everyone from drunk drivers, rapists, and murderers to assassins of Palauan presidents is free to hold normal jobs, to meet their friends for lunch, or just to hang out by the docks. In that sense, the inmates aren't really inmates. Nor are they outmates. More just mates. (The only exception applies to those convicted of drug crimes. These scoundrels, the U.S. government insists, require incarceration 24-7.)

Palau takes the six-to-six approach for all other crimes because locking criminals together to seethe their days away seems like a crappy way to rehabilitate them. But it's also a function of geography. There is simply nowhere for them to run. (And the customs officials at the airport know pretty much everyone by name.) But Palau's prison policy did underscore what I was coming to realize about islands: from prisoner to President, all are trapped by collective recognition as much as the sea.

My problem: I wasn't just trapped on a small island.... I was trapped on a small island with Palau's special prosecutor. One evening, our relations grew especially tense after I made the mistake of walking from my bedroom to my kitchen. As I opened my refrigerator, I heard three loud bangs on the floor. They were coming from downstairs. Seconds later, my front door opened without a knock. It was Randall.

"What the F, Alex?" he said, the veins bulging from his temples. "You gotta stop walking funny. Your heels always hit the ground."

"What?" I said, confused. Didn't most people's heels hit the ground when they walk?

"Yeah, you walk funny," he said. "You gotta be more quiet when you're walking around up here." He stepped inside, uninvited, and began walking around on his heels, imitating me as a kid might a duck.

"Oh, is it loud—"

"Loud?" he was yelling now. "It sounds like . . . it sounds like . . . jackboots up there."

"Jackboots?"

"Yeah, like Nazi jackbooted thugs." I blinked several times. "Whenever you walk, it sounds like a . . . like a herd of . . ." He licked his lips as he searched. I wondered what he was going to go with? Elephants would be the obvious choice. Or perhaps giraffes. Do giraffes travel in herds? He'd probably go with elephants. Finally, he found it . . . again. "Nazi jackbooted thugs."

"My walking sounds like a herd of Nazi jackbooted thugs?"

"Yes." He nodded. "It does. That's what it sounds like."

"Well, I've never heard such a thing myself, but I have lived in a lot of apartments—"

"Look, pal," he said, tapping his index finger on the top of my chest. I wondered if he was going to do that thing where you pretend to point out a stain on someone's shirt but instead slide your fingers up and flick the person's nose. If only I had been so lucky. Instead, he said, "If you want war, you can have war!" He spun officiously—you might even say Nazi-like—on his heel, or at least as Nazi-like as one can spin on the heel of a flip-flop.

The next afternoon, Gibson came by the house with a high-pressure water pump and sprayer. He wanted to wash off the layer of slick green moss that Palau's humidity periodically grew over the driveway. The pump was noisy, so instead of talking, I just watched as he sprayed. Each pass removed about a three-inch swath of dark green algae that contrasted nicely with the light gray concrete below. About ten minutes into this process, inspiration struck. I stood and grabbed the handle of the sprayer from Gibson. Thinking that Randall wouldn't be home till that afternoon, in blocky letters, I wrote, *Randall Sux*. And I wrote it big, about the width of two parked cars.

I know it was wrong. Wrong. Wrong. Wrong. And terribly immature. But it also felt so good! Randall had slandered Palauans, had jabbed his finger in my chest, had compared me to a Nazi. And I was still smarting from my dinner with Sarah the previous night, so now I was lashing out.

Gibson must have had his own grievances because he took the hose, added the word *Asshole*, and handed the hose back to me. We had a good junior high chuckle at that one. It was a nice moment for us.

Our previous attempt at cross-cultural communication—trading computer lessons for Palauan language lessons—had failed. Gibson liked the idea of spreadsheets for his restaurant's budget, but liked the idea of his wife doing it even more. And she had no interest in computers. Palauan, meanwhile, proved impossible for me to learn. Mostly because, as far as I could tell, Palauan has only three letters: N, M, and P. For another, almost everyone who speaks Palauan also speaks English. I gave up after only a dozen or so polite phrases. But in our mutual contempt for Randall, there was complete, shared understanding.

I, however, was the one holding the hose when we heard a car coming up the driveway. The car turned out to have only one person inside: Randall's wife, Rebecca. By the time she stepped out, I'd only had time to remove one letter, so that our eight-foot-wide note to self now read: *Randall Sux Asshol.*

"What's THAT?" she said, looking over my shoulder as I shifted from side to side to block her view. "'Randall Sux . . .'" She craned over my shoulder to read the rest. "'Randall Sux . . . Asshole.' Who wrote this?" Though I found it hard to believe she disagreed, the angry tone of her voice suggested she wasn't going to it that way.

"Not sure," I said. But that didn't seem right. Not only was I busted—I was holding the (still dripping) hose, after all—but I'd also just read a book by Joan Didion in which she'd said, "Character is the willingness to accept responsibility for one's own actions."

"It was my idea," I said.

"Alex wrote the first part," Gibson added, "and I wrote the second."

"We were just about to add a question mark," I said—Didion says nothing about spin.

"This . . . this . . . this . . . is . . . incredible," Rebecca said. Gibson and I looked at each other. She was right. It was incredible. She then leaned over and whispered something to Gibson before marching down to her apartment.

I felt like a jerk. Her husband was, of course, an asshole, but perhaps I didn't need to tell his wife that . . . on their driveway (which, in my defense, we shared). As I washed away the letters, I wondered if I lacked the discretion necessary to navigate island life.

I asked Gibson what she'd said.

"She said, 'You're going to regret this.'"

"And? Do you?" I said.

He thought for a moment. "Not yet," he said, smiling, "but I probably will."

When I told Sarah the story, she wasn't impressed.

"I have to work with him," she said. "At least for a little longer.
And it's mean. What did you think was going to happen?"

"I figured we'd erase it before he saw it," I said.

"Of course, because no one actually parks in their own driveway."

"Well, for the record, we were right. He didn't see it. And I had
the landlord's permission. Not just his permission, his assistance. He
aided. He probably even abetted—"

"How *old* are you guys? Eleven?"

"We were speaking truth to power," I said, trying to cast my little
civil disobedience in grand terms.

"Really? Who are you, the Rosa Parks of the driveway slur?"

"I'll take that as a compliment," I said, "but I think more Paul
Revere."

"Well," she said, slowly cooling down, "it's a good thing he doesn't
know we're seeing each other. I think we should keep it that way."

I stopped talking. I couldn't believe what she'd just said—we were
dating! Or at least *seeing each other*. Sure, she'd said it angrily, and she
wanted it kept secret, but she'd said it!

That night, I sat on my bed and wrote my eighth Life Lesson on my
ticket sleeve: "On a small island, don't insult your neighbor in the
moss of your shared driveway." (A pledge, so far at least, I've managed
to keep.) As I thought more about the day, I realized that one positive
aspect of small-town life was being forced to associate with people
you wouldn't normally associate with. That is, after all, the essence of
community. Yet small-town life was feeling increasingly small. Perhaps that's because on an island the stakes are bigger, the cost of mis-
behavior higher. Slowly and embarrassingly, I was learning that island
life is really small-town life writ large. Or writ small. However it is
writ, it benefits those who are careful in their dealings. Evidently,

some folks already understood this—like the fellow Germino who wrote this letter to the editor in the local newspaper, *The Palau Horizon*. "To whom it may concern," he wrote . . .

> *I would like to convey this apology to the driver of a black Jeep whom I treated rudely on February 27 at about 8:00 in the morning. I admit I was out of line and had no justification for my behavior. I hope you will find it in your heart to forgive me.*
> *Germino*

The takeaway? Screw up in a place like Palau and pretty soon you're apologizing, publicly, because as someone pointed out about small-town life, the woman you just cut off in the grocery store parking lot might be your son's music teacher, and now she is going to assign him the trombone.

CHAPTER 58

What You Can Expect to Learn in This Chapter:

➤ In an emergency, how far can you throw a partially formed chicken fetus?

➤ Are people who are attracted to work-for-food schemes in exotic places typically what one might call *skilled*?

A few weeks before Sarah's contract was set to expire, I woke up early one morning to make her a great breakfast. The previous night had been the first night I'd spent in her apartment.[1] An important milestone but one that also felt natural, given the amount of time we'd been spending together. Most mornings, she'd stop by my house to chat before work. During the day, we'd email or call each other. After work, we'd go swimming or for a hike, then out to dinner. More and more, we'd finish each other's sentences, anticipate each other's jokes. Sarah didn't seem to fit into any of my tidy categories or any categories at all. I simply knew she was someone I wanted to be with, to grow with, to fight with, to be the full person of myself with. In short, I was crazy about her.

That morning's breakfast started normally enough. I began by heating olive oil in the skillet. Then I tossed in some thinly sliced onions and garlic. While they sautéed, I found a tray, folded a napkin, and plucked some flowers from outside her apartment. Without

---

[1] !

incident, I cracked the first two eggs into the pan. The third egg, however, was not like the others. It felt heavier. Strange, I remember thinking, that one egg would have frozen in the refrigerator but not the others. Perhaps this one had been closer to the back? No big deal—I'd eaten more than my share of defrosted eggs. I cracked the shell and dropped the egg into the skillet. But it was no longer an egg. It was a chicken fetus, and the smell was intense—an aromatic sizzle of rotten cheese and sulfur, with a hint of asphalt.

"Oh, God," I yelled while crouching to avoid seeing it.

"What? Are you OK?" Sarah said from her bedroom.

"Oh, God!" I said again.

I stood, slowly, and just enough to look over the rim of the skillet. Everything inside was vibrating in the heated oil—and purple. Purple head. Purple beak. Wet purple wings. Little purple chicken feet.

"What's going on?" Sarah said, again from her bedroom.

I then made the first of two decisions that seemed, somehow, right at the time. "Sarah," I said, "you have to come see this!"

She opened her bedroom door and walked into the kitchen, the hem of her pajamas tucked under her heels. "What's that smell?" she said just as she glanced at the skillet.

"Aaaaaagh!" Sarah screamed. "Get it out! Get it out!"

"I made you this special breakfast—"

"Get it out! Now! Now! I'm gonna throw up!" Bent double, she lunged toward the bathroom.

Clearly, this was an emergency calling for quick thinking and even quicker action. Throwing my sizzling chicken fetus into the trash didn't seem a good option—the smell would still be a problem. And I couldn't slide it past the little metal parts of the kitchen drain—little parts that exist, as far as I could tell, to keep people from doing just that. I could have flushed it, but Sarah had already run into the bathroom. That left one option: outside. I ran the skillet to the balcony and hurled the simmering mix into the bushes behind her apartment. I'm not sure what the world record is for the chicken-fetus toss, but I doubt mine made it seven feet. The smell lingered for a week. The memory for much longer.

Later, after the smell had settled, we lay in bed as I stumbled through the same question I'd been bringing up a lot.

"So," I said, a bit nervously, "have you thought more about what you might do after your contract's up? When your contract is over? Are contracts up or over?" I wanted her to say it didn't matter, just as long as we were together.

"I think either is fine," she said. "Up or over. I guess I could go back to the Bay Area and look for a job, but"—and here she paused for a long time—"we can come up with something better, right?"

"Of course! How would you feel about just staying here?" I said. Though my feelings toward Palau had cooled recently, I thought that might be a function of a more mature understanding, or just what happens when a traveler finally unpacks his bags for a while.

"I dunno," she said. "I could try to extend my contract, but the chief justice has concerns about my work ethic."

"That's bullshit," I said.

"I agree."

"But aren't there other legal jobs here?" I said.

"I could probably find something," she said, "but there are so many other places too. What about you? There must have been other places you were thinking about?"

"Kinda. But I'm not sure geography is as important as I once thought it was."

We both sat in silence for a moment. "Let's step back," I said, repeating my words from Angaur. "If you could do anything, what would it be?"

"Well, I've been thinking about building that house, that bungalow as you call it. It sounds like an adventure."

"Really?"

"I have some savings from this year. Not much to spend on here.

But this house, it wouldn't be anything complicated, right? Wood posts. Thatched roof."

"Like that *bai* we saw," I said. "We're doing this on Angaur, right?"

"It's far but—"

"Cheaper than Hawaii. Can foreigners own land on Angaur?"

"No," she said confidently, as though she really might have been a lawyer who'd spent the last year practicing law in Palau. "But they can lease."

"Perfect," I said.

"But whose land can we lease?"

"No idea, but it's eight miles around. Surely someone would, right?"

"Yeah, probably. But with all due respect to that IKEA desk you built," she said, "I do think we would need some help."

"We must know someone who knows something. . . ."

"My friend Butch once built a cabin in Alaska. Maybe he'd help."

"You know a guy named Butch who built a cabin in Alaska?"

"Yeah, but he's originally from Louisiana. A small town called Morganza."

"It's probably hot there," I said. "Sounds like our lead contractor."

Sarah then came up with a reasonable plan. "Before we start nailing wood together," she suggested, "let's just see if anyone would want to help. You know, send a few emails and see what happens."

That evening we drafted an email to those we thought might be interested in joining us.

Subject: Swiss Family Robinson Meets the Jackson Five

Dear Friends,

We have an idea: move to a Pacific island and build an elevated house/bungalow. Almost certainly there have been worse ideas: hip air bags for the elderly and invading Russia in the winter both come to mind.

But we need your help. We have an island in mind—Angaur—
a beautiful outer island of Palau. All we need to do is lease
the land, design the house, and build it.

It won't be all heavy lifting. Other activities include: kayaking,
caber tossing, scuba diving, potato-sack races, playing doctor
and light cannibalism. Plan on about six months.

We can't pay much—well, anything—but we can provide a
lot of canned food. Let us know if you're interested, and we'll
send follow-up details as they become available.

Sincerely,
Sarah & Alex

We looked over the email again before sending it but then I
paused. "Are we sure about this?" I said.

"Pretty sure," she said, "but that's why we're sending it, right?
To see—"

"I mean *this*," I said, pointing back and forth between us. "Us."

"Well, pretty sure," she said, smiling. "But you're not going to just
keep looking for the next thing, right? The next island?"

"This is what I want," I said. "If you're there too." It was hokey but
also true.

"Great," she said. "Send it."

A few days later we met at Sarah's apartment to review the responses.
Surprisingly, about twenty people responded favorably, including Sarah's friend Butch. Unsurprisingly, people who are attracted to work-
for-food schemes in exotic places are rarely endowed with what one
might call *skills*. Other than Butch's, almost every email of interest
started with some variation of "I'm not sure I'd be much help but..."

"If we are really going to do this," Sarah said, turning from the screen to me, "I'll need to go to San Diego first. At least for a little while. I haven't seen my family for a long time. You should come too."

I wasn't eager to leave Koror. There was so much more to see, so much more culture to try to get my mind around, and I liked my friendship with Gibson and liked the place I was living in. But paradise, I was coming more and more to think, was being around people you care about while also feeling productive—all, ideally, in a pretty place. And what better way to do all of that than by building a house on a South Pacific island with friends?

"I'd love to," I said. "We can take some building classes or something while we're there."

Then, at the same time, we both said, "How hard can it be?"

That afternoon we went online and bought round-trip tickets to San Diego. There, we'd learn construction, earn some money somehow, and figure out exactly what we were going to build. At the least, it did seem a good rule of thumb that before moving to a remote island to build a house with your girlfriend, you should at least introduce yourself to her folks. I then ordered one last book—this one to be sent to the house of Sarah's parents. I knew *Post-and-Beam Construction for Beginners* wasn't one of the Great Books, but Thucydides didn't have much to say about attaching headers to joists.

STEP 7

REGROUP

CHAPTER 59

What You Can Expect to Learn in This Chapter:

► Is a free one-hour class from Home Depot on *flower box construction* sufficient training to build a house?

► What if that class is taught by a man who lost his thumb in a Skilsaw accident?

When we arrived at the San Diego airport, Sarah's father shook my hand firmly, his arm stiff, as though not sure exactly what to do with his daughter's souvenir. He was completely bald and wore long, baggy shorts that almost, but not quite, reached his tennis shoes. Sarah's mother and sister, however, gave me a much warmer greeting: they both smiled and gave me a hug. Their heads came up to my chest, making me feel, at least among the four of them, like a giant.

We packed ourselves and our luggage into a new Toyota Camry with Sarah's mom in the driver's seat. As we left the airport, we made small talk about our flight and Palau. "It's good to be home," Sarah said, looking out the window, "but not sure how long we'll be back for."

"What?" her mother and sister said at the same time.

"I think we're going back to the Pacific," Sarah said.

Sarah's mother glared at me in her rearview mirror as though I was to blame. Sarah explained we were going to build a house. Her dad, silent in the front seat, looked out the window, watching the two-story houses and their tidy suburban yards slide by.

"And are you going to live in it?" her mother asked.

"For a while. It may end up being a second home."

"Do you have a first?" her sister asked.

"No," said Sarah.

"And you, Alex," her mother said, "do you know anything about building a house?"

"No, ma'am, not really." Sarah nudged my leg. "I mean, a little." She nudged harder. "We're getting some friends to help. Maybe you guys would like to—"

"Mom," Sarah said, "what would you like Alex to call you?"

"I don't know. My name is Sue."

In Texas, you don't call your girlfriend's mother by her first name. "How about Mrs. Kalish?" I said.

"No way," Sarah said. I thought for a second.

"How about Mama Kalish?" I said. Sarah's sister smirked.

"Sue! Stop!" Sarah's dad yelled. "I saw something. Stop here. Right here."

"Lyle, you're not . . . not now."

"It will just take a second," he said. She pulled over. "Just back up a bit . . . great. Pop the trunk."

"Please, Lyle," she pleaded.

"Alex, follow me," he said. I looked at Sarah. She shrugged. She had no idea what he was doing, either.

I got out and stood next to him as he reached into the trunk and grabbed a small trowel and a brown bag. "Follow me," he said. "We have to be quick." Bent double and glancing quickly left and right, we cut across a lawn. Not too far from the living room window of a Tudor-style house, he dropped to his knees. With the trowel he dug out a softball-sized white mushroom from the grass. "Hold the bag open," he said, carefully lowering the fungus inside. "OK. Let's go! Go! Go!"

There was no irony in his voice—he really didn't want to get caught.

The car doors barely closed, Mama Kalish hit the accelerator. Clearly, this had gone down many times before.

"It's a *Coprinus comatus*," he said, smiling.

That evening, in the living room, Sarah's father gave me an old copy of a book called *The Territorial Imperative.* "It's not too technical," he said, which, coming from an economics professor, was a relief.

The central premise of its author, Robert Ardrey, is that humans, especially male humans, are just as territorial as any other species. Humans may cloak our territoriality in business ventures and flower gardens, but like dogs and worms, the real priority is access to food and mates. I wondered what message he was sending. Did he approve or disapprove of our plan? And was there a subtext about his daughter? Was he saying I should view her as a resource—no doubt precious—but still, a resource? In any case, I took it as tacit approval of our plan.

Sarah showed me the room we'd be sharing. I'd been worried about the sleeping arrangements and was thus relieved to see two twin beds, each tucked into a corner of the room. That seemed like a good compromise, I thought. Yes, Sarah was an adult, but this was her family's house.

Like the childhood bedrooms of many adults, Sarah's was a time capsule of her youth. Soccer trophies lined the top of a bookcase. High school notebooks still crammed the shelves. A Depeche Mode poster hung on the wall. Though I wasn't expecting many red flags (e.g., a skull collection or a self-taxidermied raccoon), seeing such a normal room in such a nice and normal house felt grounding and important in a way that probably wouldn't have had we met someplace other than Palau.

We brushed our teeth and climbed into our respective beds.

"I like your family," I said.

"My parents can be really annoying," she said, reverting to the teenage tone adults seem to find when back in their childhood home.

"Mine too," I said. "But they mean well."

"I know they do. Anyway, good night, Alex," she said before switching off the lamp.

"Do not start the saw while resting it on your thigh," the Home Depot clerk explained at our free evening class: Power Tools 101. We were the only students at Terry's lesson. I opened my notepad, and Terry switched on the saw, careful not to let the straps of his trademark orange apron catch in the whirling blade. He said he always liked to begin with Skilsaw safety. As he stepped away to get a piece of wood for a demonstration, I asked Sarah, "Do you think we should be worried about, you know, his missing thumb?"

She thought for a moment before responding with a riddle, "Would you rather sail under a captain who has lost a ship or one who hasn't?"

I was thinking about which I'd prefer when Terry rounded the corner, carrying a long piece of knotty pine. As he cut it into five pieces, I jotted down Terry's tips. They seemed more inspired by the Home Depot's sales goals than by our educational needs:

—don't be afraid to ask for help.

—make sure you have the right tools.

—always buy extra material.

Terry then connected the pieces with a half dozen screws. "Now you should have no problem," he said, concluding our first and only lesson, "building yourself a very nice flower box."

Beyond construction skills, we figured we'd need $20,000—about $3,000 for travel, $8,000 to lease the land, $3,000 for materials (wood, canvas, and screws), $1,000 for tools, $3,000 for food, and $2,000 for miscellaneous expenses. Accordingly, over the next few months, we lived with Sarah's parents and saved up money. Leaning on my Internet and political experience, I did some consulting work for a political campaign while Sarah found legal work on a contract basis for the State of Alaska (where she still had good contacts). Living rent-free with Sarah's parents and, with income from subletting my old apartment and office in New York, we managed to save most of that $20,000 in about six months.

Away from Palau, however, we began to second-guess our Angaur decision. Perhaps we could find a place that was closer, more practical, or, at least, less hot? One afternoon, as Sarah's father watched television in the den, we rolled out a map on Sarah's kitchen table.

After spending so much time in the Pacific, the Caribbean seemed kind of wimpy. Hawaii, New Zealand, and Australia were out because of cost. Tahiti, where Sarah had spent a year abroad during college, was out for the same reason. American retirees had made waterfront property in Mexico too expensive. Same with Costa Rica. Panama's laws regarding foreign ownership of beachfront land were murky. And river runoff made Nicaragua's Pacific coast brown and silty. We'd heard New Guinea was pretty rough and American Samoa filled with fast-food restaurants. And radioactivity was still a lingering problem in the Marshall Islands. That left us with basically two choices: Fiji and the Cook Islands, two English-speaking island groups to the left (west?) of Tahiti and far enough from the equator to be temperate but not cold.

We chose Fiji because tickets were less expensive—an important consideration for us and the half dozen friends who still wanted to help us build a house. Surely, we figured, somewhere among Fiji's three hundred or so islands we could find a place to build.

Within days of arriving on Fiji's northernmost island, Vanua Levu, we found a little house by the water to rent for $300 a month and began asking around about buying or leasing property. We quickly learned, however, that disputes over land dominated Fijian life and politics. It was as if we'd waded into the lives of a couple in the middle of a divorce and asked to sublet the guest room.

Turns out that of the million people who live in Fiji, half are native Fijians and half are descendants of Indian laborers imported by the British in colonial times—and they hate one another. With neither side able to gain a solid majority, political power switched constantly, and along with it, the laws governing land ownership.

Just when we were deciding what to do next, a man came into our bedroom while we slept in our little rental house. I was woken up by the sound of our bedroom door opening and saw a man in the doorway holding a flashlight. "GET THE FUCK OUT!" I yelled. Having played my only card—yelling an obscenity—I was, of course, relieved when he turned and ran away.

The next morning, we found that Sarah's tennis shoes were missing. Our landlord said we should go to the police. "They'll use some jungle justice," he said. We didn't know what he meant until we arrived at the police station, parked out back, and saw a wall covered with bloodstains. We decided not to make a report.

Perhaps word had spread that we had gone by the police station: that night while we were eating dinner, a guy of maybe seventeen knocked on our door. He said that he had taken our shoes, that he was sorry, and that his coming into our house must have been scary. Looking forlorn, he handed Sarah her shoes back.

We sent our friends an update that we were continuing our search in the Cook Islands and bought tickets to Rarotonga, a beautiful island with steep, jungle-clad mountains plunging into the sea. Short on cash, we found jobs teaching at two local high schools (an experience that compelled us to send every teacher we've ever had a letter apologizing for not appreciating their efforts). Meanwhile, we rented a house and found a small piece of available property in the mountains with a distant view of the ocean. We even managed to negotiate a mutually acceptable deal with the owner. The government, however, saw things differently.

On paper, foreigners could own land in the Cook Islands, but when we actually sat down with a local lawyer, we found out leasing was out of the question; foreigners could only own land if they also started a business that *benefited the island*.

"Umm, what kind of business?" I said.

"Well, at the moment, only dry cleaning is on the list. So if you want to start a dry cleaning business you can own land."

"Is there a minimum investment?" Sarah asked. She was plucky that way.

"Five hundred thousand dollars."

Sarah and I sat in bed one evening and discussed our next move. "It's far and hot," I said, "but Angaur's looking better."

"It is," Sarah said, "but as you said back in Palau, we shouldn't let the perfect be the enemy of the good. Or the friend of the so-so. Or whatever that phrase is."

"At least we know our way around, culturally. And you have contacts at the court."

"And Butch," she said, "is champing at the bit to go. All our friends are." Over the previous few months, we'd learned that people who are keen to build a house on a tropical island with friends don't care that much which island.

"OK, then," I said, "to Angaur."

"To Angaur," Sarah said.

We opened up a computer and drafted a final email to our friends. We told them we'd settled on Palau, specifically an outer island called Angaur, and to give us a month to secure the land. They should buy their tickets to arrive in early September and the house should be done by mid-December. In other words, we'd have the troops home by Christmas.

CHAPTER 60

What You Can Expect to Learn in This Chapter:

► What shall we actually do with the drunken sailor?

► Why should you always bring a pair of scissors while traveling by ferry to Angaur?

Of the 6,973 miles that separate San Diego from Angaur (via Honolulu, Guam, and Koror), the last six were the most difficult. Twice as perilous as our last attempt, this particular crossing was complicated by a storm, a broken steering system, and a (very) drunk captain.

It had started normally enough. Arriving early, we'd found a bench on the tiny second-floor area outside the captain's bridge. The ferry threaded easily between the densely forested Rock Islands while frigate birds soared overhead in an overcast sky, the gray of which made the normally turquoise waters seem cold and milky. But when we passed the end of Peleliu and entered the channel, the boat started to rock violently, and passengers who'd been asleep on mats or slumped against pallets of soda just moments before leaned over the railing, hurling a chunky shower of betel nut and off-brand cola.

Angaur, just a long, faint shadow on the horizon, disappeared behind a curtain of rain. Not a warm, tropical cloudburst, but blowing sheets of cold rain. A canvas awning snapped; ropes whipped about; paper and trash flew off the boat, vanishing into the waves.

"If it was an easy place to get to," I yelled to Sarah, "we couldn't afford to build there."

"I think we're turning in circles," she responded.

I looked around. We did seem to be turning. I glanced into the bridge. The captain, a skinny, bearded man in his thirties, was alone at the helm, staring toward the horizon, his eyes severe yet also blank. A half dozen empty beer cans slid back and forth across the equivalent of a dashboard. His arms were crossed, not touching the wheel, yet we were definitely turning.

"Do you know the second line of that song 'What Shall We Do with a Drunken Sailor'?" I said to Sarah. She shook her head. "It's 'Soak him in oil till he sprouts a flipper!' That's weird, isn't it?"

Before Sarah could respond, a Palauan woman in her fifties with a responsible way about her turned to us and said, "The steering was supposed to be fixed weeks ago. Now it's broken again." She pulled a cell phone from her purse but, unable to get reception, slid it back in.

The captain tapped on the window and gestured for a young boy to come inside. As they spoke, the island of Peleliu suddenly spun back into view. Some combination of wind and currents was pushing us toward its rocky shore.

The boy ran out of the bridge and yelled, "The captain wants to know if anyone has a pair of scissors!" I calculated that this was in at least the bottom third of the list of questions you want to hear from your ship captain. Sarah's face started to turn a little pale.

"Have you ever heard of the Dutch Admiral Problem?" I said, "It's a true story about two farm boys in Holland. They both dreamed of a life on the sea, but neither knew how to sail."

"Not really in the mood for a parable," she said.

"Who ever is? But these two boys, they got accepted into the Dutch navy by telling anyone who would listen how experienced and wise the other one was."

As I spoke, I heard something metal being tapped against the captain's window. A woman held up a pair of scissors for the captain.

"So, these two guys aren't good at much, but they are good at talking about how talented the other one is."

Inside, the captain unscrewed the top of a little metal box with the tip of the scissors. He slid off the lid, then blinked several times at a tangle of wires. We were now close enough to Peleliu and its reef to make out individual coconut trees on the rocky shore. Running aground, as now seemed likely, probably wouldn't kill us, but scrambling over jagged metal and sharp rocks wasn't something to look forward to.

"These boys quickly began to rise through the ranks," I said as we watched the captain repeatedly poke the scissors inside the box of wires, recoiling each time in a sparky shower. We how could see crabs scrambling over rocks for safety.

"Eventually, they became admirals, despite knowing next to nothing of the sea!" I smiled. "Amazing, isn't it?"

"Alex," Sarah said, "never speak to me again."

About a hundred yards from the reef, the boat's course straightened, and through the salt-sprayed window, the captain flashed a two-tooth smile and a thumbs-up. Each time we started to turn, he'd grin, then maniacally jam the scissors into the box again.

Slowly, Angaur started to take shape. Waves slammed against its north coast, occasionally pushing dramatic sprays of water through holes in the limestone. Down the west coast, a steep, empty beach. Then more rocky shore. Then palm trees and huge banyans growing to the water's edge. For a while, a child raced us on a bike, his knees coming up to his chest at the top of each pedal. Just as he disappeared into the forest, a pair of dolphins sidled up to the side of the boat, then worked their way forward to ride the ferry's bow wave. Finally, five hours after leaving Koror, we turned sharply into Angaur's little harbor.

As we drifted to a stop, the sun appeared through big gray clouds.

Light reflected off the still dripping leaves of the tall trees that lined the harbor. The little shelter was empty. Except for a monkey that screeched from a distant tree, no one on the island seemed to notice we'd arrived.

After just a few minutes, people from the island started to pull up to the harbor: kids on bikes, then a person on a scooter, then the same rusting white pickup we'd seen on our first visit. We walked the half mile to the guesthouse where we'd stayed before and where our group would live during construction. Some of the dirt roads had been paved, but little else appeared to have changed. Same with the guesthouse, whose wooden floors sagged only a little more than I remembered. In the distance, through some squat bushes and across a yard that was half dirt, half stubby grass, we could see the ocean.

Sarah and I set down our bags and stepped onto the porch. After a week of traveling, months of preparation, and years of dreaming, we were finally back. The island, with its thick forests and hidden beaches, felt just as remote and wild and full of possibility as I'd remembered. Yet doubts persisted. What if we couldn't get permission or couldn't find land? Or what if, an hour into building, we realized we were in way over our heads? That didn't just feel likely; it felt inevitable. Most concerning: even if we managed not to destroy our relationship with each other and our friends, would it be what we wanted? Not just the house itself, but the experience itself.

Not that there was time to really consider these questions. Our first friends were arriving in three weeks. Per Gibson's suggestion back in Koror, we left the guesthouse in search of the island's matriarch.

After walking a few minutes down the little road, we saw the truck from the harbor, now full of boxes, rumbling slowly toward us. I waved and the driver, a shirtless man with a very high Afro, pulled to a stop.

"Hi," I said. He just stared at me, so I kept talking. "Pretty hot . . ."

His expression said, "It's always hot, you fucking idiot."

I glanced up and down the street. "Umm. Do you know where the chieftess lives? Oh, by the way, I'm Alex and this is Sarah."

He pointed at a nearby house. I thanked him, but he didn't respond. As he drove away, he spit red betel nut juice onto the dusty road.

"Good energy here," Sarah said.

"Yeah, I'm feeling the love."

A few houses down we saw a middle-aged woman gardening. Sarah asked for the chieftess. Without saying anything, she pointed to the house next door.

We found the high chieftess sitting alone in a plastic chair in her backyard. She was in her seventies and was wearing an orange dress with a white floral pattern. A fire in a fuel drum smoked nearby.

"*Ungil tutau,*" Sarah said.

"*Ungil tutau,*" the chieftess said.

"My name is Sarah and this is Alex." The woman nodded. "We just came in on the ferry. We used to live in Koror but fell in love with Angaur."

"Welcome," she said.

"We think Angaur is the most beautiful island in the Pacific," Sarah said.

The chieftess smiled and said, "Thank you. We are very lucky."

"We brought you this," Sarah said, and gave her a handwoven betel nut holder we had bought at the senior center in Koror.

"It's beautiful," the chieftess said, gesturing for us to sit.

While I just smiled, the chieftess and Sarah spoke for some time about Angaur, about how it had changed and not changed since the chieftess was young, and how extremely difficult it had become to keep people on the island, given the lack of jobs.

"Now, how can I help you?" the chieftess finally said.

"Well," I said, "we know land is very precious in Palau and because of that foreigners aren't allowed to own land. That said, if it suited you and the community, we would be interested in renting a little spot. But again, only with your blessing."

"What for?" the chieftess said, frowning.

"We would like to build a house, a small house we could visit on occasion with our families," I said.

The chieftess looked at us for a while, then said, "The last foreigner to build here was a U.S. soldier after the war." I assumed that on Angaur, the scene of much fighting, *the war* still meant World War II. "And we haven't seen him in many years."

"I'm sorry to hear that," Sarah said. "For us, it is very important to be an active part of the community."

"I see." The chieftess stared into the jungle for a minute, and then said, "We are repainting the school tomorrow. We can talk then."

Sarah and I were among the first to arrive at the school the following morning. A middle-aged man was unloading cans of paint from a pickup.

We told him we had come to help.

"Good," he said, and handed us a can and two paintbrushes. Within an hour, maybe thirty folks—about a third of the population of the island—appeared to paint the front of the school bright blue. The chieftess and several other older women sat in folding lawn chairs under a nearby banyan tree. They appeared to be weaving, but we both felt carefully observed.

About midmorning, the school principal announced, "No more paint. Thank you all for your help." We'd finished only the front; the sides and back were as before.

We approached the sitting women afterward to introduce ourselves.

"Thank you for coming," the chieftess said before we could speak. "Some people wanted to know if you two are married." None of the others made eye contact, choosing instead to focus on their baskets.

"Yes," I said. "I mean, we will be getting married." Sarah looked startled, blinking several times.

"And you do not wish to make a development here?" the chieftess said.

"No. Definitely not," Sarah said, looking at me.

"We would like to build a simple house," I said, "for us and, perhaps someday, our family to visit."

"We know, by law, foreigners can't own land in Palau," Sarah added. "We just would like to lease."

"Well, the Council of Chiefs is meeting tomorrow," she said. "They will discuss your proposal."

We started walking to the guesthouse.

"What was that about?" Sarah said.

"I think they just want to know if we intend to start a business here."

"No, about us getting married?"

"Oh, you know," I said. "I just thought it would sound better."

"Right," Sarah said.

The following evening we found the chieftess making bread over coconut husks burning in an empty drum. She motioned for us to sit. When the last clump of dough was done baking, she sat down next to us.

"The chiefs met," she said. "Look around, find a spot that you like, and we'll find the family that owns it. We will be happy to have you on our island, as long as you don't commercialize it."

Early the following morning, machete in hand, we started slicing our way around the eight-mile circumference of the island. It was a classic boyhood dream made real: marching around a forested isle in search of the best place to build a tree house. Except for the guesthouse and the crumbling harbor, nothing was built on Angaur's coastline. Occasionally, however, we'd come across someone gathering crabs or fishing. After we explained what we were doing, they always encouraged us to build on their property. And why not? We weren't buying land—just leasing it—and who wouldn't want some starry-eyed foreigners to build them a house?

Picking a specific location, however, wasn't easy. Every peninsula, rocky cove, and white-sand beach seemed to offer an equally captivating combination of sea spray, shade trees, and wondrous seclusion. Yet each offered its own unique characteristics as well. We could cut a trail to the beach here or build a bridge to that little rocky island just offshore there. Perhaps a sleeping platform in that tree or stairs down to the sea over there.

Paradise, as usual, felt just around the corner.

CHAPTER 61

What You Can Expect to Learn in This Chapter:

▶ Is it a good idea to build a house on someone else's land? What if one of the twenty-three members of the clan who owns the land puts his hand on your shoulder and says, "Go ahead and start. It will be fine"?

▶ When friends, who have turned their lives upside down to help you build a house, arrive after traveling twelve thousand miles, should you greet them with:
a) a hug?
b) a lei?
c) a note handed by a stranger, explaining that your plans have changed and that you hope to catch up with them Stateside?

Over four dirty but fun days of searching for land, our questions had become increasingly practical. Did we want to face sunrise or sunset? (Sunset.) Electricity or no electricity? (Power would be nice but not a deal breaker.) Coconut trees or Australian pines? (Pine needles don't hurt as much as coconuts when they hit your head.) Beach or no beach? (To avoid the sand flies, best to avoid sand.) We settled on six possible sites, but it ended up being an easy choice: Sarah checked with some contacts at the land court in Koror and found that five of the six sites were tied up in land disputes—a common problem in Palau after the Japanese destroyed all the property records.

The undisputed site also happened to be our favorite. To get there from the harbor of Angaur's little village, you could either walk four miles around the southern half of the island or a mile and a half or so directly across the middle. Either route was along a narrow path made of crushed coral lined with dense vegetation. The entrance to the property was along a tiny footpath that began between the stately buttresses of two giant Pacific banyan trees and wound a few hundred yards along the forest floor before finally arriving at the sea. Except at the water's edge, the site was thick with banyans, ironwood pine trees, and pandanus. The most intriguing part of the property was along the coast where a little peninsula jutted into the sea, forming the far-eastern point of the island. Because of that unusual geography, the site had long views north and south along the coast, and enough elevation (on cliffs about twenty feet above the ocean) to protect us from flies and global warming. Other features: a little cove once used by Angaur's chiefs for bathing offered easy access to the ocean, and the coral reef out in front was said to be among the island's richest. The closest electrical outlet or telephone was two miles away, granted, but so was the closest neighbor.

When we asked the chieftess about the property, she said it was owned by one of the island's four clans. Fortunately, its most senior member, Blumel, lived on the island. We got directions to her house and found Blumel sitting in a chair on her porch, wearing a purple muumuu. She was around eighty years old, but you could tell that not too long ago she'd been a strong and active woman. When we introduced ourselves and presented gifts, she smiled politely, but she couldn't understand a word we said. (She spoke only Palauan and, having grown up before World War II, a little Japanese.) Her granddaughter, a teacher in her early thirties visiting from Guam, happened to be there and could translate. We explained our intentions again. After waiting for the translation, Blumel nodded, as though she knew these kinds of offers would be coming eventually.

Sarah and I had discussed the uncomfortable neocolonial aspects of white folks buying land on the cheap from the natives. We decided, perhaps conveniently, that Palau was different from other places. For one thing, people here were doing pretty well financially. No one was hungry; most everyone had cable television and a car. For another, we weren't buying land, just leasing it. (If anything, it was the Palauans who had been fleecing the Americans: $40 million for a bridge, $150 million for a road, $447 million for an agreement on foreign policy— pretty soon that starts to add up for a country with only twenty thousand people.) And while we would be taking up some space, it wasn't highly sought-after space: no one in the past fifty years had built a house beyond the main village. Even so, it felt important to be accepted by all involved. And on that point, the clan's matriarch agreed.

"I am only one member of the clan," Blumel's granddaughter translated. "You must get everyone else to agree and to sign the papers. But it sounds like a good idea."

I asked how many other clan members there were.

"Twenty-three," she said. Oh, shit.

"Do most of them live on Angaur?" I said.

"Only a few live on Angaur," Blumel's granddaughter said. "Some are in Koror. A few of us are in Guam. One in Saipan. A couple in Hawaii. One in California."

"Do you have their phone numbers?" Sarah said, undaunted. "Or is it better for you to contact them?"

"Don't worry about it," Blumel's translated reply came back. "Sabino, my nephew in Koror, will help you with it all. Do you two already belong to a church in Palau?"

"Not yet," said Sarah without pause. "Do you have one you like?"

I thought it was an amazing question, coming, as it was, from the only Jew on the island.

Back in Koror, we went to church with Sabino, a soft-spoken man in his fifties who worked for the local utility company. More than anything else, he seemed driven to get to know us and our intentions. After the evangelical service, we went out for coffee. The following day, lunch. Then drinks. Then another church service. But whenever I brought up the property, he said he needed more time to check with other family members.

While Sabino didn't share our sense of urgency, Sarah and I were starting to panic. Our friends were about to arrive, all from a long way away. (The shortest trip took twenty-six hours; the longest, forty-two.) And they weren't coming all this way to get updates on our meetings with Sabino.

The following evening, Butch from Alaska landed at the airport in Koror. Wanting to set the right tone, we decided to meet every new arrival with a different practical joke. For Butch, we arranged for a stranger to hold up a sign with his name on it and hand him an envelope. Inside, a car key and this letter:

Butch,

Glad you made it. We had to go to Angaur, but we dropped off our car for you here. The key is enclosed. Catch the next ferry that you can.

Look forward to seeing you,

Alex & Sarah

The airport parking lot had maybe three hundred cars. We hid behind a low wall and watched him step out into the bright afternoon light and consider which car might be ours. Without even taking off his backpack, he began jogging, key in hand, from car to car.

Among the many reasons we were thrilled Butch was coming—beyond his easygoing manner and his building experience—was that he was in fantastic shape. He regularly did ultramarathons and organized two-hundred-mile wilderness races so grueling and so remote that every year one-third to one half of the participants were evacuated by helicopter.

Within three minutes of arriving, he'd found our car. Apparently, he recognized the shape of the key and knew to try only the Nissans. We watched as he tossed his pack in the passenger seat and leapt in. We jumped in behind him and yelled, "Welcome to Palau!"

It wasn't until much later that day that he said, "By the way, I think you forgot to mention which car was yours."

"I have good news and bad news," Sabino said when we met for what we thought was a final meeting over breakfast. "All have agreed to a lease . . . except one. A cousin in California doesn't think you're paying enough."

"We haven't even discussed how much we'd pay," I said.

"I know, but he doesn't think it's enough. He asked if you could wait until he comes to visit next year."

We told Sabino that we couldn't wait a year and that, unfortunately, we might need to find other property.

"Let me check with my cousin one more time," he said. "We'll meet again tomorrow."

That evening, Cabot, the younger brother of a friend of mine, arrived. Having never met him, Sarah and I were a wee bit nervous. Our initial email asking people to come help had gone, if not viral, at least slightly contagious as friends forwarded it to other friends and, in Cabot's case, family. Eventually, we had to invoke a rule of sorts: friends and friends of friends were welcome, but anyone beyond that felt too removed to be stuck with on a remote island. Cabot, of course, was pushing that limit. And at twenty-three, he'd be the youngest among us, but his sister swore he was handy, fit, and independent, so we welcomed him . . . with, of course, some gentle hazing.

Just as his flight landed, Sarah and I handed another stranger a note for Cabot, along with a little sign and a picture so he would know whom he was looking for. This note read:

> *Cabot,*
>   *Glad you made it. Unfortunately, our plans have changed. At the last minute Sarah and I had to go to the Philippines. Not sure this house-building thing is going to work out. Look forward to meeting up with you Stateside, if not sooner.*
>   *Our sincerest apologies,*
>   *Alex & Sarah*

Butch, Sarah, and I watched as Cabot emerged from customs. Thin and tall, he had short blond hair and carried only a small backpack. He took the note and read and reread it—probably three times—before sitting down on an airport chair and sinking his face into his palms. Feeling terrible, we ran from around the corner and yelled, "Surprise!"

"I'm glad it was just a joke," he said matter-of-factly as we shook hands and hugged as warmly as you can hug a stranger whose life you just pretended to ruin. But instead of punching us jokingly on the shoulder, he said something entirely unexpected. "I just spent the entire flight teaching myself to shuffle cards with one hand. Do you want to see?" He then pulled out a deck of cards and, sure enough, shuffled them with one hand.

When we walked out to the airport parking lot, we found our car on cinder blocks. All four tires were missing.

"What the hell?" Sarah said.

"Holy shit!" I said. "This is really weird. Do people just steal tires like that?"

Just then, a tall man with messy blond hair approached us, smiling. It was Darren, another friend who was going to help us build. He was supposed to arrive the following day but had tricked us and shown up early. While we waited for Cabot, Darren had snuck out and removed all of our tires. His joke made us feel confident: if Darren could remove four car tires in twenty minutes, he surely could build a house in four months.

Over breakfast the next morning, we asked Sabino if he'd been able to talk to his cousin in California.

"Don't worry about it," Sabino said. "He will eventually go along."

This time it was our turn to ask for a delay. After breakfast Sarah left a message for a local lawyer she knew for advice. While waiting for a call back, we met Steve, the last of the long-termers, at the airport. Steve was—and probably still is—a slender and affable Brit with short dark brown hair. To free up the time to come here, he'd quit his job at a comic book store in Nottingham. He'd flown to Palau on the cheap via Amsterdam, Dubai, Singapore, and Manila, and probably Cleveland. Once again, we recruited a stranger to hold a sign, a note, and, this time, a thick manila envelope.

> *Dear Steve,*
>   *Welcome! Glad you're here. We ran into a spot of trouble, as you guys would say. This is going to sound weird, but*

can you take a cab to the abandoned textile warehouse just
past the airport exit on the right? It should cost around $5.
Ten minutes after you get there, a man named Hans will
come by. Just hand him this package. That's it. We'll be by
not too long afterward and will explain it all later.
  Sincerely,
  Alex & Sarah

The envelope contained, of course, a small Ziploc bag of flour. Without hesitation, Steve climbed into a cab. We followed some distance behind. Sure enough, he got out at the abandoned factory, paid the taxi, and stood on the side of the road. Through binoculars, I watched him take a bottle of water out of his pack, then lean up against a concrete wall, just below a broken window. Though he had to be hot and exhausted, he pulled out a birding book and binoculars and scanned the treetops. After a few minutes, he put the book back into what he called his rucksack and slowly began opening the package we'd given him. He closed it immediately and looked around. Just then Darren, aka Hans, walked up, wearing sunglasses and carrying a backpack. Other than the former factory, there was only jungle around—not really the place you'd expect a man to be going for a midday stroll. As later reported, the conversation went like this:

HANS (in Austrian-Norwegian accent): Hello. You must be
    Stephán.
STEVE (in British accent): Steve actually. Are you Hans?
HANS: Yes. Do you have it?
STEVE: I think so.

Steve handed him the package.

HANS: This is it? There were supposed to be two!
STEVE: Just that one. That's all I was given.

HANS: Don't fucking fuck with me, you little fuck. Where's the
    other one?
STEVE: Umm. This is it. So, how do you know Alex and Sarah?

At this point Sarah and I ran out of the bushes. Steve, apparently, never believed our little prank, though he did say he found Hans quite unpleasant.

When we got back, Sarah had a voice mail on our cell phone (a new thing for Palau) from the attorney. He suggested we chance it without that one signature: If we could get twenty-two out of twenty-three, that would be pretty good by Palauan standards, especially if one of the signers was the matriarch, who carried a lot of weight legally and culturally.

Finally, we agreed on the terms: we'd pay a hundred dollars a month for twenty years—this was beyond our initial budget, but we had twenty years to make it work—and promise not to commercially develop the property.

"What about the signatures on the lease?" I asked Sabino. "Won't they take a long time to get?"

"Could be months," he said, "but go ahead and start building. It will be fine."

And with those calm words of reassurance, we began building a house on someone else's property.

STEP 8

BUILD A HOUSE

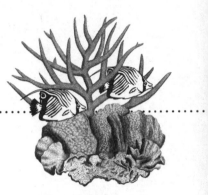

CHAPTER 62

What You Can Expect to Learn in This Chapter:

> ➤ What do the Empire State Building and the Pyramids have in common with a house on Angaur?

> ➤ Why should you look at the production schedule of *Survivor* before picking an island?

We were three whacks into construction when Steve, the affable Brit, hit something hard with his shovel. "Huh," he said, "that's interesting."

"Rock?" I said.

"Someone mentioned that to me," Darren said. "Probably compacted limestone."

"How compacted?" I said.

"Pretty compacted. It's the reason the island hasn't washed away," Darren said.

"It's bloody hard," Steve said.

"How deep do we need to go? Do you get typhoons here?" Butch said, looking out at the placid turquoise sea not thirty feet away.

"I don't think so," I said.

Darren thrust his shovel into the ground. Immediately, sweat started to cascade off his forearms. "The book says three feet," he said. "Maybe two and a half would be OK?"

"Welcome to paradise, Steve," Steve mumbled as he slammed his shovel into rock. "Welcome to paradise."

Under normal circumstances, we'd find some better tools back in Koror. But these weren't normal circumstances. The same week we started building, the television show *Survivor* came to Palau. Filming a dozen people eating raw crabs apparently isn't so easy—it took a crew of five hundred people to do everything from accounting to building cell-phone-repeater towers. As a result, Koror's two hardware stores, thinly stocked to begin with, were almost barren: Survivors, it turned out, had gobbled up the country's entire supply of ladders, wheelbarrows, and nails. When we were halfway through construction, a friend back in the United States went to Home Depot and mailed us 12,500 screws.

It was hard not to feel a bit resentful. For one thing, the Survivors had helicopters (two, in fact, shipped in by container and reassembled). More frustrating, their paradise was a stage set, an illusion; were the camera to spin just so, viewers would see that the *castaways* were equidistant from the frozen chi-chis of Palau's only four-star resort and the outflow pipes of Palau's Department of Waste Management. Our paradise was an illusion of sorts too, but at least it was an illusion we planned to inhabit and, over time, make real. Or so we hoped.

By about eight thirty a.m.—an hour into building—we'd dug an inch of our first hole. Cabot set out to see if he could borrow a crowbar from someone on the island and, amazingly, returned with one about an hour later. It weighed twenty pounds, and it vibrated painfully as it ricocheted into rock, so we developed a rotation system. For one minute each, we'd take turns pounding the crowbar while the others either rested or dropped to hands and knees to scoop out the hard-earned shards. We needed a new plan.

One option, of course, would have been to build a smaller house, but at nine hundred square feet, this one didn't seem especially large. Nor was simply digging fewer holes an option—we'd already planned them eight feet apart, which our book said was as far apart as they could be. In fact, our plan already seemed remarkably simple. We sketched it in half an hour:

We chose to build a square house—there are few shapes simpler than a square—with one-quarter set back as a deck. The remaining L-shape structure would orient toward the ocean. Since our bathroom would use a composting toilet, a technology none of us was optimistic about, we decided it should be built apart from the central house in a small box of a room in a grove of trees. The shower, meanwhile, would be built next to the ocean on a wooden platform. A narrow wooden boardwalk would connect all three parts.

We also figured Palau's warm weather would make building more straightforward. We were able to skip whole chapters in *Low-Cost Pole Building Construction* about walls because ours would be made from canvas. We'd simply buy the canvas online and roll the canvas down when it rained. And with no frost heaves to worry about, the holes for the posts could be only half as deep as the standard four to six feet. On a difficulty scale, it all seemed somewhere between store-bought cookies and homemade bread. In other words, an Easy-Bake bungalow.

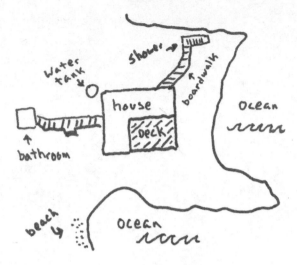

After two more hours of digging and only two more inches of hole, we took a break to make sure we were building in the right spot. One option was farther inland, closer to the narrow road/wide path that circled the island. There, the trees were huge—maybe a hundred feet high—but the ground was pockmarked with fist-sized crab holes. And we couldn't see the ocean. Closer to the water, along the northern, left side of the peninsula where two-story-high cliffs rose above the sea, there were no crab holes, nor was there any dirt. Just volcanic rock, sharp and windswept. Walking along the cliff top, we could see into nearly clear water, making out not just coral heads but individual fish between waves. Occasionally, a big wave would hit the rocks below, misting us in sea spray.

"Seems a little close," Sarah said. "Not even plants grow this close to the sea."

The cliffs on the right or south side of the peninsula were lower—maybe ten feet—and, at least at this time of year, the ocean was calmer on this side. But the ground was all rock: building this close to the sea wouldn't solve our hole problem and might expose us to others when the wind changed direction. So we went back to our original place, in the middle of the peninsula maybe forty feet back from the ocean on either side. Granted, the ground was hard, but we could build under the canopy of protective trees. And most important, the view of clear blue waves breaking up and down the rocky coast, often in the shadow of outstretched palm and banyan trees, was lovely.

As the others walked around looking for the best place to access the ocean, Darren and I did some math. At thirty inches deep apiece, forty-four holes worked out to 1,320 inches of hole. At one inch per hour that was 1,320 hours of work for a team of three. We could reliably muster two full-time teams, meaning 660 hours of work. Assuming ten-hour days of nonstop digging, the holes would take all of us . . . sixty-six days.

"That's a long time," I said.

"Not good," he said.

"We found a little beach," Butch reported. "There's an old plane half buried in the sand. Looks like it's from World War II."

"Any bodies?" I said.

"Nope!" Steve said brightly. "No bodies!"

That evening, back at the guesthouse, we tried to go online to look up how to best dig through compacted limestone but, as was often the case, our dial-up connection was down. I called a contractor friend of Butch's named Jim in Alaska. He looked it up while we talked.

"Hmm," he said. "Says here the Pyramids are built out of compacted limestone. They used slaves, right? Good thing you got some of those, heh, heh."

"What else does it say?" I said.

"The Roman Colosseum too. And the Empire State Building— compacted limestone."

"That's helpful but—"

"Did you know marble is actually limestone? OK, here it is. Says, 'The most common methods for extracting compacted limestone rely on hot acid and explosives.' Do you have either of those handy?"

Sarah and I took the next ferry back to Koror in search of better tools.

We returned a few days later with a quarry's worth of equipment: shovels, pickaxes, even a rented jackhammer powered by a rented generator, all mustered from back-alley shops the Survivors hadn't plundered yet. None of it helped. The shovel handles broke. The pickaxes could only go a few inches deep because of their shape. And though the jackhammer did dislodge fragments in small pieces, it required as much work as the others and a lot more gasoline. Nothing, it seemed, worked better than the crowbar.

So we found a second crowbar and returned to the old system: whack crowbar into rock; drop to knees; scoop up fragments; and remove salt and limestone dust from eyes while mumbling, "Welcome to paradise, Steve. Welcome to paradise."

Repeat for thirty-two days.

CHAPTER 63

What You Can Expect to Learn in This Chapter:

➤ On an island where no one uses cash or credit cards, how do you pay for a haircut?

➤ When the ferry is broken and you find yourself essentially marooned and out of food, what do you eat?

After a month or so of building—and with three months remaining—the ties that held our little boat together began to fray. Cabot had a habit of clinking his cereal bowl to get the very last bits. Every couple of nights, Darren would accidentally unplug the extension cord that led to Steve's fan. To most everyone's dismay, I was always second-guessing the placement of the holes—fifteen degrees this way, say, would have the sun come up over the end of the bed. Sensing this was heading south, Sarah started to create some systems, including a rotation for meal preparation and dish washing. All seemed to think it was a swell idea, but enforcing compliance proved difficult. How, for example, do you gently remind someone it's his turn to do the dishes after he's burned three thousand calories that day building you a house?

Though short on skills, our crew at least wasn't high maintenance when it came to sleeping arrangements. Cabot slept on the couch, even though it was a foot too short. Butch slept on a camping pad in the living room, Steve in a tent in the yard. Sarah and I took a bedroom, as did Darren. We all shared a bathroom—a bathroom with holes in the floor and one shower's worth of hot water. Food too was in chronically short supply.

As a group, we required an enormous amount of calories. An entire box of cereal for breakfast, for example. There was a tiny store on Angaur, but they sold mostly ice cream and beer, both of which we bought plenty of. The actual food they sold was patchy. Pasta, for example, but no pasta sauce. So every two weeks Sarah and I would go to Koror for building supplies and pasta sauce. If the weather was bad or the ferry was chartered for a funeral in Babeldaob (which seemed to happen frequently), we'd just have to wait. We once went a month between trips, the seven of us eating mostly rice and whatever canned food seemed the least botulized. Around this time, I asked one of the men who hung out by the store what they ate when the ferry stopped for a long time.

"We eat bananas," he said. "Just bananas."

What food we did have was under constant assault by rats and ants. On special days, you could see an entire food chain on our kitchen's warped Formica counter: a wandering ant might find a smudge of peanut butter left over by the sink. More ants would follow. Then larger bugs that came to eat the ants. Then spiders that came to eat the bugs. But it didn't end there. The spiders would attract wasps that, unable to consume such a bonanza, would store the spider bodies in clay nests, which they built nightly on our ceiling or, occasionally, on our clothes. About once a week, we'd knock the nests off the ceiling or shake out our underwear, sending desiccated mud and spider bits crashing to the floor or the kitchen counter. We tried our best to sweep it up, but some pieces might fall behind, say, the toaster and attract another battalion of ants.

With five men and only one woman, the vibe also grew increasingly mammalian. Every morning, for example, Steve refused to apply sunscreen to Butch's back. The conversation usually went like this:

STEVE: My mother told me never to lube another man's back unless I wanted to. Especially if that back is hairy and belongs to a man named Butch.

BUTCH: That's surprising because your mother told me she thought my back was sexy.

SARAH: Can't we talk about something else? You know, like, relationships? Fart jokes are funny but not, you know, forever funny.

Invariably, this would prompt five index fingers pointed toward her with a chorus of "Hey, Sarah, pull my finger."

No doubt, therefore, Sarah was thrilled when a Peace Corps volunteer named Maria returned to Angaur after a training stint away. Maria was in her early twenties, had long, curly black hair, deep brown eyes, a Southern accent, and, courtesy of a year in Palau, a rich tan. Though an alluring woman anywhere, as the only available female on the island between the ages of fifteen and forty, Maria's appeal to Cabot, Steve, and Butch was, well, singular.

One afternoon, after Sarah and I showed up empty-handed to an Independence Day celebration, Maria stopped by the guesthouse. "You should always bring gifts to community events," she admonished us.

"What kind of gifts?" Sarah asked.

"For a wedding, a case of beer. For a funeral, a case of Pepsi or a case of Mountain Dew."

As she spoke, Cabot, Steve, and Butch suddenly grew elaborate plumage and oversized antlers. A few started gathering sticks for a nest.

"Would you like to stay for dinner?" Butch asked. Maria smiled and said her host family was already making something. "I really should get going," she said sweetly in her Southern accent

"You sure?" Butch said. "It's penne . . . with sauce!" Even that, apparently, was not enough.

Within moments of her departure, Cabot started a wood carving for her. Steve started planning a surprise meal for Maria and her host family. And Butch, ignoring his penne with sauce, began a poem. Astonishingly, three months later one would end up proposing to her. And even more astonishingly, she'd accept.

In the meantime, there was a lot of house to build.

"Now we get to fill the holes back up," Butch said when we finished the last one. After a month spent digging down, it was satisfying to see the house start to go up, albeit slowly. The work was hard, but for the first long stretch since first coming to the Pacific, I didn't find myself thinking about a different island or wondering if I was doing the right thing with my life. There was simply too much to do.

The holes, for example, required concrete. Heavy concrete that had to be mixed with a shovel in a wheelbarrow. Four wheelbarrow loads for each of the forty-four holes. Concrete requires four ingredients—cement (whatever that is), gravel, water, and sand—none of which we had. Though we had a tarp at the building site for capturing rainwater, it didn't collect in the quantities we needed. Nor, beyond carrying bottles of water on our bikes, did we have any way to transport water from the guesthouse to the site. And though Angaur had lots of limestone, gravel was basically nonexistent on the island. Sand was abundant, but it had to be washed—plus, we figured it wouldn't be popular for the *haolis* to convert local beaches into housing material. Most problematic was the cement, since the Survivors had nicked all of it in Koror.

As we usually did when in a bind, Sarah and I asked Maria for advice on where we could find all of this stuff. Turned out, procuring concrete on Angaur required an understanding of the island's Byzantine barter system. She suggested we start by talking to a man named Xavier.

We found Xavier sitting on his mother's front steps. He was in his midforties and had deep furrows in his forehead. He said he had some bags of cement behind his house for a project he'd decided not to do. "Go ahead and take them," he said.

"Oh," I said. "If you're not using them, do you think we could buy them from you?"

"No," he said curtly. "Just take them."

"Really?" I said. "It must have been hard to get them—"

"Take them," he said, twirling a stick on the ground

"Well, that's really nice. Maybe we'll be back tomorrow then to pick them up?"

He half nodded and twirled his stick a few times before standing up and walking inside.

When Maria stopped by again that evening, sweating after a jog, I asked her how we should repay him. "People will be insulted if you offer them money," she said. "They do favors for one another out of neighborliness. Just give him a gift."

"What's the exchange rate for a bag of cement?"

"Whatever you like," she said. "I'm sure it will be appreciated."

Cabot was sitting on a couch, working on his carving. She sat down next to him. "What's that?" she said.

"Oh, just a thing," he said. It was, in fact, amazing. He'd taken a solid block of wood and carved it into a sphere. He was half finished inlaying wooden dolphins.

"It's lovely," she said.

"You can have it," he said casually, handing it over to her.

"Really?" she cooed.

Steve rolled his eyes.

"Maria, do you like cards?" Butch interrupted. "Gin rummy? Spades?"

Cabot suddenly got on the ground and started doing push-ups. Steve stepped onto Cabot's back, crossed his arms, and said, "Maria, would you like to go snorkeling sometime?" Cabot groaned slightly but, to prove a point, did another ten push-ups with Steve standing on top.

Perhaps worried that the expanding mist of testosterone might cause a rash, Maria again excused herself. As soon as she'd left, Sarah called a meeting. "You guys can't go on like this," she said. "Feelings are going to get hurt. We need another system."

"Like what?" someone said.

"How about each one of you guys gets a shift?" she said. "Say, forty-eight hours of exclusive flirting." Her mind was practical that way. "I know it's sexist, but we gotta do something."

"Done," Butch said.

"Best of luck, chaps," Steve said.

Cabot, however, was already refocused on his carving. "Maybe," he mumbled to himself as much as anyone else, "I should add a papaya tree?"

The following morning, Sarah and I found Xavier once again sitting on his mother's stairs. "I brought this for your family," I said, holding up a six-pack of soda and a loaf of bread.

"Thank you," he said, setting them down on the stairs next to him.

"You lived in Angaur a long time?"

"Yes," he said, looking at the ground but adding nothing more.

"We just got to Angaur," I said. "We're that group that's—"

"I know."

In silence, we watched a chicken appear from around the corner, then cluck away. A moment later, a dog with a belly full of nipples loped by. As if in passing, I said maybe we'd be by later to get the cement.

"OK," he said.

"OK," I said. "See you around."

Xavier just nodded and stared into the dirt, before sliding his foot out of his flip-flop and scratching the side of his leg with his big toe.

This was pretty typical of our exchanges with the locals. If anything, Xavier was more talkative than most. Up to then, Sarah and I had felt like high school foreign-exchange students who show up in the middle of the school year—no one knew where we fit in, so they simply watched us. Or ignored us. But rarely did they speak to us.

Fortunately, Maria was there to help with some of the cultural translation. When we ran into her on the way back to the site, I told her about our meeting with Xavier.

"You gave him gifts this morning, and you're picking up the cement this afternoon?" Maria said, wide-eyed.

"Was that not a good idea?" I said.

"It looks like you're paying him for it. It can't look like you're paying. You have to wait longer."

"So no one pays cash for anything here?" I said.

"Land and beer," she said. "They only pay cash for land and beer. Everything else is bartered."

"That's fine," Sarah said, "if that's how it's done." She then asked Maria how we might get a truck to help us move the cement in a few days.

"Ask the governor to borrow the island's garbage truck," she said.

"What should we give him for that?" I said.

"Not sure," she said, thinking. "But I know he likes Chivas Regal."

A few months navigating Angaur's barter economy started to make Yap's giant stone money system seem progressive and convenient. The possibilities for ambiguity and hurt feelings seemed almost endless here. I started to wish I could just roll a two-ton rock over to someone's house rather than have to guess what Margarite would feel was a fair exchange for borrowing her cousin's wheelbarrow for a month.

Slowly, however, we learned what each person in the village wanted for their goods. For example, a load of concrete in Angaur costs a frozen chicken for a bag of Xavier's cement, some newsmagazines for Trevor's washed sand, six cans of tuna for Jeronimo or Emeliano's gravel, a polite request for three coolers of rainwater from Linda's catchment system, and, of course, a bottle of Chivas to the governor for use of the island's garbage truck to transport it all.

CHAPTER 64

What You Can Expect to Learn in This Chapter:

► Imagine you're a Peace Corps volunteer on a remote Pacific island. How popular would you guess your aerobics class would be?

► How do you blend fruity drinks without a blender?

ithin two days of finishing the holes, we'd screwed forty-four wooden posts into place. The progress felt tremendous. For the first time in six weeks, we were working with wood instead of crowbars and concrete—working up rather than down. For six weeks, we'd come to the site and found it looking almost exactly the same as the first day Sarah and I saw the property. Yet now, as we turned the corner, we saw forty-four sprigs of wood sticking up every eight feet. They didn't look exactly straight—had the Sistine Chapel been made with the same precision, it would now be an Arby's—nor could they have looked less natural . . . or, to our eyes, more beautiful.

Our plan—build a house on a beautiful island with friends—was working! All we had to do from here on was connect cross-supports to the posts, technically called joists. Or joints. Whatever they're called, they'd hold up the floor. From there, we'd add the roof trusses, then the metal panels of the roof itself and some insulation to prevent the whole place from turning into a giant toaster. After the main house was complete, we'd just have to build the little room for a composting toilet and the path down to the outdoor-shower platform.

We knew the shower was a bit ambitious. We planned to catch water from the roof of the house and use gutters to run it through a screen before dropping it into a large metal catchment tank. From there, a solar panel and inverter would power a twelve-dollar on-demand water pump, similar to those found in recreational vehicles. That pump, in turn, would push the water through a propane-powered hot-water heater and down a pipe under the walkway to the shower, and, ultimately, down the rocks to the sea.

Yet, as with almost all of our supplies, the biggest problem was simply getting the wood to the site. Construction, I was learning, mostly involves moving heavy things. No lumber was available on Angaur, for barter or otherwise, so every piece of wood—and there were a lot of pieces—had to be carried from a rack at the hardware store in Koror (assuming it was available) to the checkout counter, then loaded onto the store's delivery truck, then lifted out of the truck and stacked on the ground at the harbor, then hoisted on and off the ferry, then loaded onto the island's (borrowed) garbage truck, then carried by hand the last few hundred yards from the road to the building site, then stacked before finally being held aloft as someone screwed it into place.

That's assuming, of course, everything else went right: that we'd remembered to recharge all the batteries, that the bolts were the proper size, that the brackets didn't rust before even putting them in place, and that the drill didn't start smoking and suddenly stop out of anger and pure exhaustion.

Pretty early on, Darren noticed a bigger problem: we had no idea how to ensure the joists were screwed into the posts at the same height. If we were off by even a quarter of an inch, the floor would slope. Measuring from the ground wouldn't work since the ground itself sloped. And a handheld level wouldn't work either; the longest ones left after the Survivors cleared out the hardware stores were only four feet long, and our spans were eight feet. To the enduring credit of either his research or his ingenuity, Darren came up with the solution: a long clear tube of water and just one air bubble. It worked perfectly. Everyone, except perhaps Darren, agreed that Darren should be our new lead contractor.

As I ran around the posts marking where we should hang the joists, I thought, forget thumbs—what most separates us from other species is an interest in straight lines. I wondered if that's why dome houses and yurts aren't more popular: they remind us too much of our cave-dwelling past. Straight lines were a mark of progress, and because of people like Darren and his water level, we could have them. Within a day, we'd marked lines indicating wherever every joist should be screwed in. In another two days, we had a floor—a straight and level floor. In two months—halfway in—we'd managed effectively to build . . . a deck. But a deck meant chairs. It meant barbecue. It meant fruity drinks and beer. In short: civilization.

Progress was now proceeding so rapidly that we allowed ourselves twice-daily breaks to jump off the cliff and swim. The ocean cooled us off a bit; the water temperature was about 85 degrees, only a few degrees cooler than the air. The snorkeling, though, was stunning. Lacking a protective reef, the open ocean directly in front of the building site allowed us to see almost anything passing by. In the clear bright blue water, you could count on reef sharks, schools of multicolored parrot fish, pairs of angelfish, and small packs of fast-swimming predators with blue racing fins called trevallies. On occasion you might even see dolphins, a sea turtle, or a manta ray. Twice, we saw oceanic whitetips—lovely, if scary, ten-foot-long sharks normally found far out to sea.

Each day, as the sun was starting to set, we'd ride our bikes back to the guesthouse, where most of us would collapse into chairs and moan softly while someone would start the sundowners. The drinks we sipped on the porch at, well, sundown were the highlight of each day. Displaying a kind of dedication not evident elsewhere in the project, each night we tried to improve on the previous night's recipe. Warm vodka and warm water, even when mixed with sugar, isn't nearly as good as it sounds. But everything changed one night, courtesy of an important innovation from Cabot. Lacking a blender, he realized he could bend a fork in half and insert the middle into a power drill. It worked perfectly. Newly empowered with a blending device, we tried at least sixty variations until finally happening upon *the* perfect sundowner. (See Appendix B for the recipe.)

Morale improved the most, however, whenever Maria wandered by the site. Though she might swim with us or help stain a little wood, she never seemed keen on any actual lifting. Which made sense. Few volunteers sign up for the Peace Corps because they want to build beach homes for Americans, even if those Americans are incredibly fun and charming. Besides, she had her own project, which was possibly even more daunting than building a house without access to electricity: teaching health education to the people of Angaur.

Of Angaur's approximately eighty residents, most were either very young or very old. But such was Angaur's importance to the U.S. government that it had sent a Peace Corps volunteer to the little island of Angaur. Her mission: teach aerobics to the locals.

The community building, however, was not the hippest aerobics studio. For one thing, it lacked windows; instead, it had big open holes in the walls, which enabled grasshoppers to jump in but rarely out. Once they died, ants would eat the softer bits, leaving behind desiccated carcasses that crunched underfoot unless swept daily to a corner morgue. Meanwhile, its open-air design had allowed the salt air to saturate the paint, which fell to the sun-faded linoleum floor like cornflakes from a slowly overturned box.

Despite her lackluster digs, Maria managed to get a program going. The first week, eight people showed up—a good turnout, percentagewise. The second week that number dropped to four and the third week to one. The fourth week, no one came at all. After no one turned up the fifth week as well, Maria called her supervisor in Koror and reported that the class was a flop.

Instead of suggesting a new approach, however, the supervisor reminded Maria that obesity was a growing problem throughout the Pacific and that she should continue, if nothing else, to set an example. So Maria did. Every week for the next two years, she walked to the open-air community center, plugged in a portable stereo, and grapevined, t-stepped, and punched the air . . . for the people of Angaur, for her country, and, most of all, for herself.

CHAPTER 65

What You Can Expect to Learn in This Chapter

► When a guy yells that he wants to fuck your girlfriend,
  do you
  a) grab a friend for backup and start a fight?
  b) offer him a beer?
  c) invite him over for a grilled-cheese sandwich?
  d) all of the above?

► What does the Transcendental Movement of the late
  1830s have to do with your project? (Trick question: I
  don't know either.)

A force of nature, Zephyr arrived for the last month of construction and brought a certain intensity to everything she did. Within twenty-four hours of arriving, for example, she'd conducted a handstand contest (so she'd have a reason to learn how to do handstands) and eaten an entire fruit bat (does not taste like chicken, especially when undercooked). I'd met Zephyr in college after she'd fallen in love with a friend of mine and introduced herself, one by one, to all of his friends. After helping us build that house, she'd write a book about corruption and democracy and run for governor of New York (and almost win).

Her professional life, however, didn't start off so glamorously. "I counted the other day," she said to Darren in an interview for a never-aired radio project. "I've had thirty-two different jobs. I define a job as anything you get paid for and do for more than three weeks."

"What was the most unusual?" asked Darren.

"I once had a friend drop me off in Memphis. I had fifty dollars. I took the first job I could get—cleaning rooms in a three-hour motel."

"A three-hour motel?"

"They rented rooms in three-hour blocks. Mostly to prostitutes and drug dealers. That wasn't my worst job, though. That was working for a New York socialite."

"What made it so bad?"

"She fancied herself a writer and had all of these little scraps of paper with thoughts lying around. My job was to type the thoughts into a computer, into a kind of database, a database of thoughts."

"That was worse than the three-hour motel?"

"You should have heard the thoughts!" she said, laughing.

Darren asked her why she'd come.

"Well," she said, "Alex and Sarah have this idea that you get more joy out of things you yourself help create. And I think it's true. Like growing your own food, there's something very natural about building your own house. And giving friends an opportunity to be a part of it is great. I've learned from campaigns that people don't just want to be a part of a community—they want to be a part of a purpose-based community. Our generation is really confused about purpose, but then Alex and Sarah came along and gave us a purpose, plopped it down in our lap. It's wonderful to feel you are working toward something. What's more weird to me is that more people aren't doing this. After all, being here is cheaper than paying rent someplace."

Their conversation then turned more philosophical. "To me," Zephyr said, "it's like the Transcendental Movement of the late 1830s. Do you sit in one place and really focus on it or move around a lot? Alex and I have talked about this a lot. . . ."

Actually, I never viewed what we were doing as part of a resurgent

Transcendental Movement. I didn't even know what the Transcendental Movement was.

At best, Sarah and I felt like imposing guests on Angaur. At worst, like imperialists in shorts. In our defense, nothing was happening with this land—or for that matter any land on Angaur—before we got there. And a lot of different folks approached us to build on their land. They thought it would be great to have some foreigners build them a house, and why not? At the least, we wanted to keep our promise to be a net contributor to the community. We volunteered (and presented traditional gifts) at every island event we heard about—everything from funerals to birth ceremonies to the Angaur Day celebration. If the community center or the school was being painted, we all showed up with paintbrushes. Regardless of the event, however, few people ever, technically speaking, talked to us.

Locals did come by on occasion: to pick fruit from the trees, to jump and fish off the rocks, and to cut down dead trees for firewood. But finally, after many weeks, those passing through would stop to chat. Most of these initial visitors were men in their thirties and forties. After asking where the walls were and listening to our answer, they'd nod and hop back on their bikes. "Drop by anytime," we'd say as they swerved to avoid a tree root. Sometimes they'd even wave back to us.

When word spread that we were about to install two trusses—large, heavy spans that would support the roof—three local men showed up and volunteered to help. In one dramatic morning, we muscled them into place. It was the closest we'd have to a classic barn raising and was one of our best interactions with the people of Angaur.

A few days later, however, we'd have our worst.

We were just starting to screw sheets of metal to the roof when we heard someone yelling, "Alex!" It was coming from the ocean. Two guys in their twenties were fishing in a canoe a few hundred yards offshore and seemed to be drinking. They kept yelling toward shore, but we couldn't make out what they were saying. It sounded something like "Alex, we wa u uk ur fred!"

"Hi!" I yelled back. "You guys need anything?" They must not have heard because they didn't respond. A minute later they yelled again, but the wind made it difficult to hear, so we simply waved.

"Maybe they've caught a big fish and they're excited," Cabot guessed. "Let's swim out to congratulate them with a six-pack of beer."

"Great idea," I said.

We put six loose cans in a plastic bag, jumped off the cliff into the water, and started toward them.

"They will really appreciate this," I thought as I swam, but progress was slow. The currents were stronger than we expected. After about ten minutes of hard swimming, Cabot noticed they were paddling away.

We waved at them to stop, but they kept paddling. "Maybe they don't see us," I said. We swam harder but finally turned back, exhausted.

"That's too bad," I said, when we were back onshore.

That evening Xavier came by the guesthouse. It was unusual for anyone to come by the guesthouse, especially at night. "I want to apologize for what happened today," he said, looking down. "The whole island is embarrassed."

"No problem," I said. "We're just sad we didn't get the beer out to them."

He gave me a puzzled look, then wished us a good evening.

The following night a muscular Palauan man with acne scars stopped by the guesthouse. He said his name was Jamie, that he'd been one of the guys in the canoe, and that he wanted to apologize.

"No problem," I said, confused. "Would you like to join us for dinner? We're just about to have spaghetti."

He looked very surprised.

"Really, come on in."

"Umm . . . OK," he said. All eight of us sat down together. Cabot brought him a beer. Reluctantly, Jamie took it.

"So you like to fish," Steve said, spinning a fork in his spaghetti. Jamie nodded.

"Where is a good place to fish?" Butch asked. "Over where you guys were in the canoe?"

"It's OK there," Jamie said without looking up. Sarah gestured to me that he wasn't eating.

"Do you not like spaghetti?" I said. "We can make you something else, but we don't have much."

"We have cheese and bread," Sarah offered. "Would you like a grilled-cheese sandwich?"

In disbelief, Jamie just blinked several times. "No," he said quietly. "No, thank you."

We made other attempts at conversation, but Jamie just sat uncomfortably, not saying a word. Unsure of what else to do, we started talking about the house and the plan for the next day. He skipped the chocolate pudding and said he needed to get going. After he left, we noticed he'd taken only a sip of his beer.

A week later, just as we were finishing the roof, Maria told us she'd heard about the fight.

"The fight?" I said.

"The fight with Jamie."

"The fight?" I repeated.

"Yeah, when Jamie yelled 'Alex, I want to f- your girlfriend' and you and Cabot jumped in the water and started chasing them, even though those guys were in a canoe and had wooden paddles."

"*What?* Oh, my God!"

"The whole island thought it was chivalrous and brave."

It was. Or, rather, would have been.

CHAPTER 66

What You Can Expect to Learn in This Chapter:

➤ Is a store that sells pasta sauce, but not pasta, also likely to carry monkey diapers?

➤ How do you carry a baby monkey while riding a bike?

It was raining the day the monkey arrived. A hard rain. The hardest, in fact, Sarah or I had ever experienced in Angaur. When the rain started, Darren happened to be on the roof screwing in the very last sheet of metal. He climbed down and we all shared a sweaty hug, happy to have a roof over our heads. Then we heard a voice on the path to the house.

"Alex? Sarah? Are you there?" It was Melvin, a Filipino man in his late thirties who worked at the island's store. "I have a present for you."

He then opened a white plastic bag, tilting it slightly for us to see. Inside, a baby monkey was curled up, snoring lightly in the corner.

"Melvin, where did you get this?"

"The jungle," he said, smiling. "It's a boy."

He reached in and lifted the monkey out of the bag. He was small—excluding the foot-long tail, he fit snugly in Melvin's hand. He had a tiny flat nose, oversized ears, short brown fur that grew thinly over pink skin, and, centered on the top of his head, a little mohawk. The umbilical cord was still attached. I brushed my fingers gently down his side. He (the monkey, not Melvin) squeaked softly and opened huge dark brown eyes. It is not an exaggeration to say he was the cutest thing I'd ever seen.

"Oh, my God," Sarah said. "He needs to be with his mother."

"Sorry. It's too late."

"Why?"

"I shot her."

"Melvin, really?" I said. "Why?"

"I need to send money to my family. We get ten dollars for every monkey tail we bring in."

"I thought they stopped the bounty program," I said.

Fed up with the monkeys eating their betel nut, the government of Angaur had introduced an eradication program, but it had been suspended after the governor decided the long-tailed macaques might someday have value to tourists. (Never mind that in three months, we'd yet to see a tourist.)

"They did stop it," he said, "but who knows? Maybe they'll start it again. So I'll keep them until then, but I just thought you might like this one." He then picked the monkey up by the end of his tail, causing it to scream while reaching out his hands and feet in an attempt to get away or hold on to something.

"Give him to me!" Sarah said.

As Sarah comforted the monkey, Melvin looked up. "Nice roof," he said. "So if you don't want him, I'll take him with me. Do you want him?"

"Yes," Sarah and I said at the same time.

"OK," he said. "Maybe you can give me ten dollars." We didn't really want to encourage monkey trafficking, but as far as Melvin was concerned, he'd either get ten dollars now or ten dollars later. We rummaged around and handed him two five-dollar bills. Noting the rain had stopped, he said he needed to get back to the store. As he left, he said, "Do you want the bag?"

"No," Sarah said. After Melvin had walked back down the path,

Sarah set the monkey softly on the floor. He screamed, leapt on my calf, and began sucking his thumb rapidly. Cabot, Steve, Darren, and Butch stood nearby, looking baffled. (Zephyr had returned to Koror to greet some arriving friends.) In less than a minute, our lives had been turned upside down. Darren still even had the drill in his hand.

"We can't keep him," Sarah said.

"I know," I said. "Of course not."

"We need to put him back. Take him back to his mother. Or at least his troop."

"Will the other monkeys take him back? Will he be killed?"

"I don't know," she said. "But we need to make a plan. The longer we wait, the harder it will be—for him and for us. We may only have an hour or two."

We decided to regroup at the guesthouse and go online to find out what we could about monkey reintroduction. But how to get him there? We first put him in a cardboard box with a towel, but he leapt out, scrambled up my legs, and wrapped his arms around my neck.

"Maybe we should just carry him," Sarah said.

"Like this?" I could feel tiny finger- and toenails digging in to my skin.

"I have an idea," Sarah said. She rummaged around in a toolbox, then in a box of miscellaneous things, and eventually produced a safety pin. Without saying a word, she folded up the bottom third of my white T-shirt and pinned it about halfway, forming a soft cotton pouch.

"See if he'll go in here," she said.

I gently peeled him from my neck and placed him inside. He squirmed around a bit before lying down and sucking his thumb. I started walking. About the weight of a cell phone, he rocked quite a bit with each step, so I slowed down. At this pace, however, it would take us hours to walk the two miles or so back to the guesthouse.

"Do you think he'd be OK on a bicycle?" Sarah said.

"Not sure," I said. "Let's try."

I carefully climbed on a bike and started peddling. A few hundred yards later, I stopped to check inside. He was asleep. In ten minutes, we were back at the guesthouse.

When I sat down and opened up my computer, he must have noticed we were no longer moving. He popped his head out and chirped, "Ee-oo," before crawling out and wrapping his legs, arms, and tail around my forearm. Sarah asked what we should feed him.

"We have some fruit," I said.

"He seems too young for fruit. He should have his mother's milk. Maybe we could find formula."

"Can you give a monkey formula?"

"I have no idea. But the better solution is for him to be back with his mother."

"His mother was *shot*," I said angrily.

"Same team," Sarah reminded me. "Same team." She walked over to the kitchen. "What about cow's milk?"

"Seems bad," I said. "OK. I'm online."

"See if you can find some monkey sites," Sarah said. "What is he doing now?"

"He's asleep again."

"We could cook and mush up a potato. Think he'd eat that?"

"Not sure. Do we have a banana?" I said.

"Do monkeys eat those? Seems kinda clichéd. I think Angie, that woman who lives by the school, has a baby. Maybe she has some formula?"

"OK," I said, "here at least is a photo of someone feeding a baby monkey infant formula."

Sarah asked Steve and Butch to split up and try to find Angie. They slid their flip-flops on and headed for the door.

"I'm not finding anything about how to reintroduce an orphaned baby monkey. . . ."

"Just email someone and ask," said Sarah.

That seemed a good idea, so I started searching for professional-looking monkey-research sites. Whenever I found a contact email address, I sent this message:

> Subject: Urgent Monkey Inquiry
>
> Hello,
> My name is Alex Sheshunoff. I'm currently living on an outer island of Palau in Micronesia called Angaur. There is a resident population of introduced long-tailed macaques. Someone recently gave us a baby monkey after killing its mother. It is about six inches high and was found with the umbilical cord still on. My question is regarding reintroduction. We're worried about simply putting it back into the jungle as there are a lot of different troops and we fear it may be killed. It is not possible to find out the exact location where it was found but we could get a general idea (the island is only eight miles around). Do you have any advice? Perhaps you can tell us the odds it will be killed or adopted if found?
>
> Thank you in advance for your help,
>
> Alex & Sarah

Just as I sent the last of a dozen emails, Butch walked in the door. "Angie had some formula," he said. "She said a few years ago her cousin had a baby monkey and fed it formula."

"Great," I said.

"She also gave me an extra baby bottle."

Sarah sterilized the bottle and mixed up the formula. Just then, the monkey woke up, screaming a high-pitched screech. He arched his back angrily. Sarah held him in one hand and the bottle in the other. He sniffed it and screamed again. She softly brushed the bottle's nipple against his mouth but the nipple, about the size of his face, was way too big.

"Let's soak the tip of a paper towel," Sarah suggested. "Maybe he can suck it."

That worked—within ten minutes, he'd drunk an ounce or two of formula and was asleep again in his shirt pouch.

Back online, we already had a few responses. Two people suggested the kindest thing was to euthanize him. Another said we should just put him back in the jungle. "Worst case," a woman wrote, "he'd be killed but who knows, maybe not?"

Thankfully, the emails kept coming in. It seemed our inquiry was being forwarded broadly because zoologists, pet owners, and monkey experts from Italy to Indonesia were writing us. We even got an email from the director of the Dian Fossey Gorilla Fund in Rwanda. Of all the responses, hers seemed the most considered:

> Alex,
>
> I worked with many species of macaques for many years (including *M. fascicularis*). My colleagues sent me your email. The bottom line is that the chance the baby will be killed or die from exposure is great. If you knew what group the baby came from the chances for survival would be greater, obviously. However, there are several things to consider if and only if you could find the original group. If there is a super-mom (a female that is really into babies) who would be willing to adopt, or a sub-adult male (who sometimes adopt), the problem would be that they would not have any milk (unless the female already has an infant).
>
> If you put the baby macaque near a group that is not the original group, it will either be ignored or treated as an intruder and killed. Macaques by nature are very territorial

and not accepting of new members from outside their group. Males do immigrate, but only when they are older (subadults), and very cautiously, after having learned appropriate social skills. An infant is not capable of doing this.

If you keep the baby and hand-rear it, it will be difficult to release it into the wild for one major reason: it will not have learned appropriate macaque social skills and macaques are intolerant of individuals who do not know how to respond to social cues or behavioral gestures appropriately. I have worked with thousands of them and know this to be true. Wild-born macaques are especially intolerant.

The best you can hope for, in my opinion, is to think about putting the baby eventually in a captive group. If that is a possibility, I will be glad to explain ways to do that, but it cannot be done until the baby is older and healthy. A lot depends on the group composition.

I wish I could be more encouraging, but those are the facts from my experience. Please feel free to email me if I can do more to help.

Best wishes,
Alecia

Alecia A. Lilly, Ph.D.
Director Conservation Action Program
Dian Fossey Gorilla Fund International

Just as we finished reading her email, the monkey woke up, squawked, and pooped. Though a bit smeary, the poop was also tiny and, thankfully, almost odorless.

"Did you see any monkey diapers at the store?" I said.

"Last I heard, they were out of beer," Sarah said. "But I have an idea." She went into our bedroom and returned with one of my white T-shirts. She then grabbed a pair of scissors and started cutting.

"Umm," I said. "It's not nice to cut people's clothes."

"Like you don't have enough of them," she replied.

It was not an unreasonable point. Since leaving New York I had worn only white T-shirts—I liked not thinking about what I was going to wear every day.

"This looks about the right size," she said, holding up a swath of cotton about the size of dollar bill. "With some safety pins, we'll have cloth diapers."

"And they take up less landfill space than disposables," Steve offered from the kitchen.

"Let's wash him up and get him changed," Sarah said.

I held him in the palm of my hand as Sarah turned on the bathroom sink. His arms and legs clutched me tightly, but relaxed when I held him under the warm water. He closed his eyes as the water ran down his back. Because the end of the faucet was low relative to the sink—maybe six inches—there was just enough room for his body.

"Where's his tail?" Sarah said. I moved him slightly to see better. His foot-long tail had corkscrewed down the drain.

That afternoon, we biked until we saw a troop of monkeys and put the baby at the base of a tree, wanting to give an aunt or someone a chance to find him. Maybe, per Alecia's email, he'd be adopted. Immediately, however, he started screeching an almost indescribable terror-induced screech.

"We can't stay here," Sarah said, so we left him on the ground, biked around the corner, and, trying to remain hidden behind a tree, watched to see what would happen.

Typically, the monkeys of Angaur either ignored people or slowly moved deeper into the jungle when approached. But as soon as they heard the baby screaming, these monkeys went crazy. Some of them screeched wildly while bouncing on branches. Others started to surround him. A few threw sticks and rocks.

This was a bad scene—a lot of fierce evolution was at work. The baby screamed even louder. As we watched, a large adult monkey ran up to him and started hitting the ground. Sarah and I were both crying.

"They're going to kill him!" Sarah yelled. "Alex, get him! Get him!"

I ran back, waved the larger adult off as he hissed at me, and picked the baby up off the ground. He clutched my hand while breathing faster than I've ever seen any living creature breathe.

"Well, that didn't work," Sarah said. "Let's go."

Holding the monkey tightly against my chest with one hand and grasping the handlebar with the other, I started biking home, weaving, as always, around Angaur's ubiquitous tree roots.

CHAPTER 67

What You Can Expect to Learn in This Chapter:

► Do you skip baths if you have a baby monkey that happens to hate water?

► What if that monkey sleeps in your bed?

Normally, when a baby arrives, you have months to prepare a nursery, read books, and do whatever else expectant parents do. We'd, in effect, had a newborn dropped off by a stork. In our case, a gun-wielding Filipino stork carrying a grocery bag.

We quickly learned that newborn monkeys differ from newborn humans in one very important respect: monkeys climb. At least this particular monkey did. He climbed everywhere: up legs and arms, up window blinds, up pipes in the bathroom. And I'm almost certain no human parent, the day after getting home from the hospital, has ever found Junior stuck behind the refrigerator following a hearty midmorning climb up the Freon coils.

It didn't take us long, however, to monkey-proof the house. We wrapped up the blind cords, blocked off the back of the refrigerator, and put duct tape over the electrical outlets. We found that a large Hanes brand T-shirt can be cut up into about thirty-five tiny diapers—about nine cents apiece.

The monkey would nap in an open cardboard box, but at night he preferred the bed, between Sarah and me. Occasionally he'd wake up and squawk for formula, but within a week he was sleeping through the night.

During the day at the site, he'd either snuggle into the hammock of my safety-pinned T-shirt or climb to the top of my head, increasingly his favorite perch. He even started eating solids—mushed-up bits of banana. We didn't have much of a baseline for comparison, but beyond that first terrible day, he seemed pretty content for an orphaned baby monkey.

Sarah and I decided any creature that shared a bed with us should have a name, so we called a meeting to discuss it. Maria happened to be at the guesthouse too.

"We could call him Steve," Steve suggested.

"How about Chris?" Maria said casually. "That's my brother's name."

"That's a great name," Steve said. He said it so emphatically, it even seemed sincere, as though he had long admired the name Chris.

"Really?" Cabot said. "I have a very good friend with that name."

Perhaps sensing the trajectory of the conversation, Darren asked a practical question. "If you and Sarah have to leave the island, who is going to take care of him?"

"I dunno," I said, turning to Maria. "Would your host family take him?"

"Maybe," she said.

"If they'd had another boy," Sarah said, "do you know what they would have named it?" We'd long admired how the names of their three boys, Lopez, Valdez and Cortez, rhymed.

"I actually asked them once. They said Gomez."

"Gomez it is, then," said Sarah.

The monkey named, all we had to do now was finish the house. Fortunately, Zephyr returned from Koror with two friends, allowing three teams to work simultaneously. Some folks installed rain gutters and the water-catchment system, others the elevated path to the bathroom. Gomez and I worked on the shower platform.

For the first time, we were happy with our progress. The house was going up, the weather was perfect, and the ropes that held our little boat together seemed to be holding. Around this time, Darren recorded himself while walking from the site back to the guesthouse. "There wasn't a single thing about today that I could ask to be better," he said:

> We're working on this amazingly beautiful place. We swam with a hundred dolphins. The weather was sunny and beautiful. We're with an incredible group of people. Someone brought over ingredients for piña coladas. It was ideal. A lot of days here are like that.

On top of that, Sarah and I felt our presence on Angaur was becoming if not welcome, at least tolerated. Now, in addition to young men (though never Jamie), we also had middle-aged women dropping by. Following more or less the same pattern, they'd arrive in pairs and ask a few questions, most having to do with the cost of our materials. After just a few minutes, they'd tell us they needed to be somewhere and slip away down our little footpath. We'd usually run after them and offer a loaf of bread for their family and one of Cabot's wooden orbs. They'd accept, but only if we insisted.

About the time we installed our single solar panel—not much, just enough to power two car taillights dangled over the rafters— entire families began to visit. While kids climbed under the house or jumped off the deck, their parents or grandparents would walk slowly around the site, examining our progress. (Most children on the island were being raised by grandparents, their parents having left for jobs in Koror or beyond.) While we chatted politely about the house, they'd pick up something lying around, a bracket, say, then twirl it in their fingers before putting it back on the ground and finding a place to sit—usually the edge of the wooden deck—sometimes for hours, as their children played and we built.

Rarely did they say anything, though occasionally someone might point to a screw or something that had fallen on the ground. As the sun started to set, they'd stand and yell at their kids that it was time to leave. We'd thank them for stopping by and give the adults a gift and the kids a few lollipops. We often worried that our gifts had insulted them, but a week later, the kids always returned with a papaya or a fish or a platter of cooked crabs. One even showed up with a bag of ice. Given that our new propane-powered refrigerator struggled to stay below fifty degrees, it might as well have been a bag of money.

As the house neared completion, the competition for Maria's affections intensified, especially after Zephyr proposed a talent show. Maria was, of course, invited to attend. For his talent, Cabot did a hundred push-ups. Butch read a poem he'd written, with the lovely refrain, "Rain on a hot tin roof, reminding us of our youth." Sarah and I made turkey sandwiches (including sliced tomato) using only our feet, while Zephyr made an elaborate landscape drawing with her eyes closed. And in an impressive show of ingenuity, or at least flexibility, Steve applied sunscreen to his own back without help or, even, the use of a paintbrush, as had been his habit. Darren did six shots of maple syrup. Maria, however, was the clear winner. Butch, Steve, and Cabot sat captivated as she sang "I'm Gonna Wash That Man Right Outa My Hair" from *South Pacific* and swung her hips, wearing only a grass skirt and a top made of a piece of string and two coconut shells.

The morning after the talent show, Sarah's forty-eight-hour flirtation rotation—hitherto a success—collapsed. Cabot became a handicraft factory, producing a little box, a napkin holder, and an entire constellation of wooden orbs. Butch asked if Maria wanted to go camping on the secluded, far north of the island. Upon hearing that she'd accepted, Steve immediately ran to her house and asked Maria if he could come too. "Of course," she said.

For her part, Maria seemed charmed by all the attention. For each gift or entreaty, she simply expressed polite appreciation—always in the same sweet Southern drawl.

Sarah and I became obsessed by this little drama and spent hours speculating about who, if anyone, might win Maria's affections. Sarah predicted Butch would prevail. My bet was on Steve. Neither of us thought Cabot's handicrafts and push-ups, though impressive, would be sufficient. "But who knows?" I said as I made the evening's sun-downers. "I won your heart with rehydrated Pringles."

CHAPTER 68

What You Can Expect to Learn in This Chapter:

► What is possibly the world's scariest animal, and what do you do when one wanders into your living room?

► Why should you always double-check that your bed's mosquito net is tucked in tightly? (Hint: not to keep out mosquitoes.)

Palauan tradition says that all new houses need a housewarming party and that such gatherings can only occur at the full moon. Though the house wasn't quite finished, we started planning ours. (The next full moon wouldn't be until after Christmas, when our friends would all be gone.) We wanted the party to be great—almost everyone from Angaur would be there. Even Sarah's parents were coming all the way out to see what we'd done (or not done).

To free up space for our new arrivals, Sarah and I started sleeping at the new house. Almost immediately, we noticed a flaw in our design. We'd wanted a house that was as closely integrated with nature as possible, so we'd chosen simple canvas walls. But we didn't know the zippers would rust and break almost immediately, forcing us to keep the walls rolled up (down made the house too hot). Nor did we think through the fact that humans live in houses not to get closer to nature but to distance themselves from it. Especially from *Varanus indicus*.

You could see one every day for a hundred years and yet still nearly blow your cookies every time you happened upon one of these giant monitor lizards standing in the middle of your living room. With their long claws, slippery forked tongues, and sinister black scales, mangrove monitor lizards look exactly like dragons—not sleeping, treasure-guarding dragons but angry, drool-dangling dragons that set people on fire just for the fun of it. These five-foot-long lizards have the confidence of dragons too. Instead of, say, scampering away when seen, these brutes stand their ground. They just stare at you, waiting and watching and knowing you will soon scream in terror and throw valuable possessions at them, not so much to scare them away, but to placate them until, like scaly mobsters, they come around again.

If you're lucky, and you rarely are, something will have just died in the woods, and hoping for something to scavenge, they'll slowly saunter away. But even then, they may pause to look back and flick their long tongues at you a few times before moseying down the stairs, their tails whipping over a can of insect repellent on the way out. They're that kind of animal.

At least they're diurnal. We knew we should have spent more money on the walls when bats started flying through the living room area so often they didn't warrant a mention—not even a "Hey, honey, there's a bat"—as yet another one snatched up a moth attracted to the taillight dangling dimly overhead.

Not all wildlife, however, was such a casual presence.

The night before the big party, Sarah and I strung up a mosquito net over our inflatable sleeping pad. As we got ready for bed, I tucked in the mosquito net, but apparently I didn't tuck it in quite well enough. At about two a.m., I felt a set of claws burrowing into my chest hair. Gomez, I assumed. But after a few moments, I heard distinctly un-Gomez-like chirps. I opened my eyes—

"*Rat!*" I yelled, frantically swatting it off my chest. Sarah screamed. Then Gomez screamed. I fumbled around for a flashlight.

"Is it on the outside or the inside of the net?" Sarah said, scrambling out.

"I can't tell," I said. "Wait. . . . There it is. Inside, at the top of the net."

"Well, get it out," Sarah yelled, even more emphatically than she'd called for the removal of the chicken fetus. Gomez seemed to share the sentiment—he clutched my arm tightly.

"How?" I said as we watched the dark form of the rat, a high hump in the middle of its back, run in wild circles around the top of the net.

"Get a broom."

"Where am I going to bat it?"

"I don't know. Just get it out."

I went to the kitchen area—a utility sink without any water—and grabbed a broom.

"Hold the net out wide," I said to Sarah. "I'm going to knock it down. Can you hold Gomez?"

"This is terrible," she moaned as she took the monkey.

"You didn't have him on your chest," I said. "OK, hold the net up so it can get out." I swung a few times, before finally connecting. It fell on the sheets (on Sarah's side) and ran into the night.

"Whew," I said, climbing back in. "That was exciting." Sarah only grumbled and, with Gomez still lying between us, turned to her side.

While listening for the approaching patter of scampering little rat feet, I realized that I'd backed into Life Lesson nine: build houses with walls. Because houses, the physical spaces where we conduct the most important parts of our lives, shouldn't be shared with rats, wasps, monitor lizards, or even long-tailed macaques. Same with friends who, ideally, would just pop by instead of staying for months. A wall, after all, was just a handy metaphor for limits.

CHAPTER 69

What You Can Expect to Learn in This Chapter:

- ► In order to live long term in your house, what will you decide is missing? (Hint: pretty much everything.)

- ► Under what circumstances will it be necessary to toss a friend's bike into the bushes?

On the day of the party, we woke up especially early to get the house ready for our big lunch gathering by sweeping floors, picking up loose nails, and securing wobbly stairs with those loose nails. We then gathered our last three pieces of plywood and built one very long table, setting it up inside the house—a house only recently transformed from a deck to a deck with a roof.

Since our housewarming happened to fall near Thanksgiving, Sarah had called around Koror in search of a turkey and, amazingly, tracked one down at a grocery store, even talking whoever answered the phone into delivering it to the ferry for us (and accepting payment whenever we were next in town). Sarah's mother, almost as improbably, found an oven on the island to cook it in. When the turkey was done, she convinced someone with a pickup to bring her and the turkey—which she carried on her lap—back to the house.

By that time, almost every local on the island had already arrived, including a dozen members of the clan we leased the land from—and, in effect, had built a house for. Many were coming to the house for the first time, including one member, Carlos, who had to be pushed down the leaf-cluttered path in a wheelchair. Also in attendance: the governor, Lily from the Angaur State Office, the captain of the ferry and three deckhands, and the elderly chieftess who first gave us permission to look for land.

They came with folding plastic chairs and extravagant platters of food—sliced fruit, grilled lobster, and homemade bread baked over fires built in metal barrels. Even Jamie, the man who'd so tenderly expressed his affections for Sarah, showed up with a pineapple. Though just a low-key event to most, to me it felt momentous. We'd managed to become friends with, or at least not enemies of, the locals. We'd also kept our little group cohesive and fed—not a single one of us had died from starvation or a gnarly construction accident. And, of course, we'd built a house. Sure, it didn't have walls, but it did have a roof we'd built with our own hands.

While everyone gathered around the table or filled paper plates with food, Sarah and I noticed that there was good mixing happening. Steve sat next to Leon, who owned the store and the guesthouse; they were talking about fishing. Cabot was talking to a girl about his age who'd come back to the island for the holidays. Darren was pointing to the roof while talking to the guys who'd helped raise the trusses. Sarah's dad seemed to be discussing libertarianism with Zephyr.

"This is great," I said to Sarah, but she wasn't listening. She gave me a little nudge with her foot under the table. At the opposite end, Butch was helping Maria into her chair. We couldn't hear their conversation, but, as he sat down next to her, there was a lot of laughing. Followed by some intense talking. Then more laughing.

In a way, the two of them made perfect sense as a couple. They were both from the South. They had both been raised as Catholics. They both went to small single-sex colleges. And, somehow, both had ended up on a remote island in the South Pacific. But most of all, they seemed to enjoy each other's company greatly. Darren noticed how well things seemed to be going and made eye contact with Sarah and me. We all nodded.

Just before dessert of the Palauans' fresh fruit and our lukewarm chocolate pudding, Darren slipped away down the path toward the road. As we'd later learn, he'd noticed that Maria had walked to the house alone, and wanting to give Butch an excuse to walk back with her, he tossed Butch's bike into the bushes.

Like most events in Palau, ours ended with little fanfare. The Palauans simply waved good-bye and went home. While most of our crew stretched out to take a nap, Sarah and I went for a walk along the island's coastal path. Gomez, as usual, slept in a fold of my shirt, secured by a safety pin. Giant, almost spooky banyan trees filtered the late-afternoon light into patchy splotches along the path.

"So," I said, "what do you think we would need to stay here for a long time?"

"What do you mean?"

"I mean, assuming the house is done. What would we need to stay here for, I dunno, years?"

"Well, first of all, friends," she said. "I'm crazy about you, but I think we'd need someone else to talk to after a while." A hundred yards in front of us, a monkey ran across the path and leapt into a tree before disappearing into the forest.

"Given the lack of people here our age, we might have to import them again."

"I'd want a freezer too. Ideally, a walk-in freezer."

"Ice would be nice," I said.

"A guest room for family would be good so we don't all have to share a room together."

"Longer term," I said, "we'd want to arrange to get electricity from the village somehow. It's two miles away, so it would be expensive but possible."

"Broadband Internet access would be nice. A hospital might come in handy too."

"Well, at least a satellite phone so we could call someone in an emergency."

"Wait," she said. "You're being serious?"

"Well, kind of." We paused in front of a break in the foliage to watch the sea. It was rougher on this part of the coast. Driftwood spun around in frothy whitecaps sloshing against the rocks.

"You know," I continued, "I don't have to be on the world's most beautiful island. Or surrounded with every possible friend. Those don't feel as important as they once did."

"Being really choosy, it doesn't always end well. Wasn't Goldilocks eaten by the bears?"

"Maybe in the original telling. I think they changed it so she just runs away in the end."

"But here," she said, as we started walking again, "you're not even running away."

"What do you mean?"

"You're just re-creating your old life somewhere else. You said to live here longer term, you'd need all this stuff, right? Electricity, friends, a hospital—"

"And a walk-in freezer?"

"I was joking. But you're talking about digging a two-mile-long trench through the jungle for electricity and Internet access. And importing friends. All just to re-create home."

"I get your point," I said. "If you're working that hard to re-create home—"

"You might as well be home," she said.

"Or at least closer."

"Otherwise it's a lot of trouble for a complicated cultural experience . . ."

"And a view."

Without discussion, we turned around to begin walking back to the house. Just off the path, a large crab disappeared into a hole, carrying something heavy.

"Remember when I went fishing with Gibson?" I said, switching subjects.

"Yeah, I think so."

"Well, I asked him if he ever wanted a bigger boat engine, and he looked at me like I was crazy. I've been thinking about that a lot. He's not an idiot. He knows there are better boat engines out there—"

"And that he could work harder and buy one of those engines."

"But then there'd be more parts to corrode, more pieces to break," I said. "So he doesn't. And instead he buys the smaller engine and has time to fish—even on Tuesdays."

"I bet he doesn't think about those bigger engines a lot, either."

"No, he doesn't second-guess himself. He decides and moves on. So he's really present—"

"I think that's what was missing for you in New York . . . present-ness."

"And for that matter, Yap and Guam, even Koror," I said. "But out here, with this house, I just didn't think about whether I was happy or if the house was perfect or if that other peninsula would have been a better location."

"Why not?" Sarah said.

"I dunno. Maybe I was focused on the next nail or the next board."

"Or getting Cabot to stop making orbs."

I laughed. "Yeah, I think I just liked what I was doing. I was all in."

"Is Gomez OK?" she said. I stopped walking and glanced inside my shirt. His eyes were closed and his thumb was in his mouth.

"He's asleep," I said as we began walking again.

"Good. But we still have to make choices beyond the present," she said. "Surely there's some middle ground between all that New York City–ness and playing *Survivor*?"

"Having done both," I said, "I sure hope there is."

"I've loved this adventure," she said.

"Me too."

"But I want a new challenge."

"So what do we do next?" I said. "Where do we go?"

A few hundred yards ahead we could see our bikes, parked just off the side path leading to the house.

"I think I'm ready to go back to the States, but not all the way back. And it'd be good to be closer to family without being—"

"Too close."

"Exactly."

"So," I said, "Hawaii? People fish there on Tuesdays too."

"I'm thinking Alaska. I lived there before moving to Palau. I think you'd like it."

"I guess people fish there on Tuesdays—at least part of the year. But isn't it, you know, cold and dark?"

"I thought you liked adventure!"

"Warm adventure," I said, but noticing I was drenched with sweat, I added, "Maybe not this warm."

"We don't have to decide now," she said as we arrived back at the house. "It's late. I should check on my parents."

We got on our bicycles and, with Gomez still asleep in my shirt, biked quickly back to the guesthouse. There, we found out that Sarah's parents were asleep and, amazingly, Darren's plan had worked: After lunch, Butch couldn't find his bike, and assuming someone had taken it by mistake, he joined Maria and started the long, slow walk across the island—together and, for the first time, alone. At their wedding two years later in Knoxville, Butch made what was probably the first wedding toast ever thanking a friend for chucking his bike into the jungle.

STEP 9

LIVE PRETTY MUCH HAPPILY EVER AFTER

CHAPTER 70

What You Can Expect to Learn in This Chapter:

➤ When does neighborly advice become neighborly extortion?

➤ What, if anything, will you actually learn out there?

After our friends left, Sarah and I had a few days to take care of loose ends, including paying a man not to burn down our house. As we returned wheelbarrows and ladders and everything else we'd borrowed from different people on the island, a lot of people asked us who was going to look after the house. We'd never felt unsafe, but squatters, we were told, could be a problem—those and a guy named Jonathan. Apparently, Jonathan liked to burn down houses. He didn't do it often, but every once in a while, the urge struck him. We were, therefore, concerned when he stopped by our new house early one evening. He was young—maybe late twenties—and heavyset. And there was something not right about him. After some initial chitchat, he asked us, "Do you have someone to look after your house?"

"Not yet," we said. He then said he'd be happy to look after it. Since we wouldn't be here to exchange goods for his not-setting-our-house-on-fire service, we asked how much it would cost.

"Fifty dollars a month," he said. And we agreed. All things considered, it was a pretty good value.

And then there was Gomez. Now that we were living full-time in the house, we borrowed the Internet connection from Maria's host family to look into bringing Gomez back to the United States. It didn't look good. Import and quarantine rules were strict and inflexible for dogs—it seemed a wild macaque would need its own team of lobbyists.

"We could smuggle him in," I suggested.

"As long as we went through quickly, customs wouldn't be a problem.'

"I could probably keep him in my pants," I said.

"But then there's the seventeen-hour flight."

Because Gomez was in constant motion, this gave us some pause. As my grandmother used to say, "Anytime you find yourself seriously considering putting a monkey in your pants for seventeen hours, it's worth considering an alternate plan."

Fortunately, Maria's host family said they'd be happy to take him under their care.

The evening before we were scheduled to take the ferry away from Angaur and, ultimately, the Pacific, Sarah and I sat on the wooden platform of the outdoor shower—an outdoor shower that now worked. Or it did when all the planets aligned—when the batteries charged properly, when wasps hadn't built nests in the inverter, when the propane heater ignited, when the filters didn't clog. We could take hot-water showers while watching the western Pacific pound the rocks just a few feet below.

Gomez climbed around my legs for a minute before getting distracted by a small seedpod. We looked back at the house. The maroon metal roof was lost in the dark green of the ironwood pines, but the freshly cut wood of the house's beams glowed in the light of the setting sun.

"This might be the best the house ever looks," I said.

"I'm proud of the work we did," she said. I agreed. It certainly was rewarding to be able to look at every wood cut and every nail and know we'd had a part in each one. Mostly, though, it felt satisfying to have finally finished, in the same way that finishing anything you never want to do again—like the SAT for example—is satisfying.

"Are you glad we built it?"

"Yes," she said without pause. "Because if we hadn't, we always would have wondered what it would be like to build a house on a remote island with our friends." I loved that Sarah had wondered that too.

"Guess we can check that one off the list," I said.

"Yup," she said, nodding. As the wind died down, as it often does in Angaur around sunset, we watched a school of fish pass slowly by, their mouths agape, sucking in water, filtering out food. A fruit bat, black and silhouetted against the setting sun, flew down the coast.

"You know, I don't want my life to be a list," Sarah said. "Like someone checking off each species of bird they've ever seen. Golden-cheeked warbler—check. Move to a small island—check. Niagara Falls—check. "

"For me," I said, "the question is how to lead as rich a life as possible. As fully as possible. Because who knows how many more spins around the sun we have. So you got to have a plan."

"I also think that plans can be limiting, kind of entrapping. More important are the questions you ask yourself along the way."

"Right," I said. "Those matter more than following any particular route or plan."

"Because the choices are all kind of arbitrary, right? Like Hawaii or Alaska. Or your books. You could have chosen any combination, just like you could have chosen any island when you came out here."

"Exactly. But when you're picking the books, the islands, the site for building a house, they all seem really important," I said.

"They do," she said. "But, ideally, they're just a way of focusing the questions, right? In our case, about what's important to us, not what's important to anyone else."

"It seems so simple," I said.

"But is pretty hard in practice."

I looked up at the showerhead.

"Really amazing, isn't it?" I said. "To have hot water here."

"We did it," she said. "And you know, it doesn't really matter that we may never use it."

We sat, for a moment, in silence. Nearly dark, the entire house now blended into the trees. The line between sky and sea too was lost, the fish mouthing for food now hidden by darkness and the metallic blue of the ocean's surface.

"Did you know I've been making a list of life rules I've learned out here? I've been writing it on my ticket sleeve."

"Like, *You can lead a horse to water . . .* , that kind of thing?"

"Sort of. Mostly they come down to concentrating on what's important—not the city where you live or the house you live in. You know, focusing on what you really care about, not what anyone else thinks you should care about."

"That's it?"

"Well, it's a lot harder than it sounds."

She wrapped her hand tightly around my pinkie. As I put my head on her shoulder, a fruit bat swooped across the sea directly in front of us, and, after flapping awkwardly for a long moment above a forest of choices, landed in the absolute center of an ironwood tree.

EPILOGUE

What You Can Expect to Learn in This Epilogue:

➤ Where do you move if you suddenly find yourself in possession of $50 million?

➤ Why, looking back, should you have dug holes three feet deep instead of two and a half?

After Angaur, Sarah and I moved to Anchorage, Alaska, but after two winters decided to try to become safari guides, so we went to Safari School in South Africa. We didn't end up becoming safari guides, but we did get engaged while swimming in Lake Tanganyika as the sun set over the eastern shore of the Democratic Republic of the Congo. We moved back to Anchorage not so much for the wide-open spaces, but because we needed work and they pay people just to live there—about $1,200 a year per resident, even children. Which helps explain why we now have two of them: Ian Shenanigan Sheshunoff and Andrew Commissioner Sheshunoff.

In the winter of 2012, just as Sarah and I were deciding whether to spend three thousand dollars on a new roof, Super Typhoon Bopha hit Angaur. We'd been told that Angaur was below the belt where typhoons form, so we built the house to withstand not much more than a steady rain. Bopha, however, slammed the eastern shore of Angaur with 175 mph winds and fifty-foot waves. No one on the island was hurt, but our little house was swept out to sea. In the end, that was just as well: the house had served its purpose. And we were happy not to maintain a leaky roof twelve time zones away. Now when we go back to visit Gomez, we stay, like most sensible people, in the guesthouse.

These days, we live in Ojai, California, and take turns watching the kids while Sarah works as a criminal defense attorney for the indigent representing (usually guilty but always overcharged) criminals, and I write (usually fantastic but always underappreciated) articles and books. Or at least one book. This one, which I thank you for reading.

Bruce, by the way, settled his paternity suit against the founder of DHL on behalf of his client, Junior Larry. At the age of sixteen, Junior Larry received $50 million in cash and immediately moved to Guam.

To see photos of Chief Paul, Gomez, and the house or just to contact me, please visit my web site at www.nottthesharpesttool.com.

Appendix A
Recipe for Reconstituted Hash Browns

INGREDIENTS:

3 ounces of Original Pringles (about half a large can)
1 cup of water

DIRECTIONS:

In a bowl, mush Pringles into little bits. Pour in water, then heat mixture in a skillet until crispy. Enjoy!

Appendix B
Recipe for the Perfect Sundowner

INGREDIENTS:

1 part pineapple juice
1 part Malibu rum
1 banana
ice (if available)

DIRECTIONS:

Bend fork in middle and attach to power drill. On medium torque, blend all ingredients to taste.

Appendix C

14 Things to Know Before Building a House on a Remote Pacific Island

We get a surprising number of emails from people who think it's a good idea to build a house on a remote Pacific island. Here are fourteen things to know, as they say, before you go—no one told us these beforehand, but we wish they had.

1) Ship a container first. Go to Home Depot in Long Beach, California, and buy everything you may need for your house—every nail, screw, and bracket. Have it all delivered to the port in Long Beach and shipped, in its entirety, to wherever you intend to build. Also, throw in some furniture. You can send a container to just about any island in the Pacific in about three months—plenty of time to find the land and/or change your mind and have it shipped back.

2) Build on land you actually own. Just before we finished construction, we were told that the member of the clan who hadn't signed the lease wouldn't sign—he thought our payments should be at least twice the hundred dollars a month we'd agreed to. In response, Sarah and I told anyone who would listen that we were arranging for a contractor in Koror to move the entire house for us. It was, of course, a bluff. There is no way that house could have been moved. But it worked. He eventually signed the lease at the originally agreed-upon rate. Better, of course, to simply own the land before you build.

3) Choose an island between 750 and 1,500 miles from the equator. Closer than that and it's too damn hot. Farther than that, too cold.

4) Pick a country with the rule of law . . . but not too much. Keep in mind what Oscar Wilde said about socialism: "The problem with socialism is that it takes too many evenings." Accordingly, look for a country where a) no one will bonk you over the head, and b) you won't get stuck in endless meetings to discuss zoning requirements.

5) Reduce costs by bringing friends. At least 60 percent of the cost of new home building is the labor. The materials are actually pretty inexpensive. A two-by-eight stud might cost $1.85. A sheet of metal roof, $11.00. We relied on friends, which worked out well enough, though in retrospect we should have followed tip six.

6) Bring friends who are contractors. Just because you've lived in a lot of houses doesn't make you qualified to build one (any more than going to a lot of symphonies makes you qualified to write one). Building is, in fact, technical, confusing stuff—there's a reason contractors get paid so much—so bring along someone who knows what he's doing. Ideally, a team of people who know what they're doing.

7) Build small. Our house in Angaur was about nine hundred square feet, plus another five hundred square feet once you add the bathroom and outdoor space like walkways and the shower. That's at least twice as large as it should have been. So start small and end small. And use the extra time to go snorkeling.

8) Choose solar. During construction, you'll need a generator for power tools, but transporting fuel is an expensive headache. Solar works fine for almost all household applications, except air-conditioning, which won't be a problem if you followed tip three. Also, skip wind power—it's noisy and has mechanical parts that rust and break.

9) Rethink your relationship with rats. Toaster-sized rats will be part of your life on just about any island. You can trap them or poison them, but in the end, you're better off just declaring a truce.

10) Choose your life partner carefully. And make sure you have a good relationship going into it because, at least according to the marriage books, months of manual labor in the jungle rarely improves a relationship.

11) Buy a SteriPEN for water purification. Despite being protected by screens and grates, the interior of our water-catchment tank became lined with snails. When the snails died, as almost all snails eventually do, our water took on the musty, poopy smell you might expect of a big tank of dead snails. We considered emptying the tank and cleaning out the snails, but we could have been without water for weeks as we waited for the rain to fill it back up. Instead, we poured some Clorox in. The result: the water smelled like musty poop soaked in Clorox. About halfway through construction, a friend shipped us a SteriPEN, which, instead of traditional tablets or filters, purifies water with LED lights and magic. For us, at least, it worked. No one ever got sick.

12) Plan days off. You may not be working at a nine-to-five job, but you still need occasional breaks. We underestimated how much work (and didn't follow tip six), so we spent four months mostly carrying heavy stuff. The morning we left, Sarah and I were still screwing in the gutters.

13) Understand going into it where this fits into the four types of fun:
    a) easy fun that's also fun while you do it
        Example: sex.
    b) easy fun that's fun mostly in retrospect
        Example: fifth grade.
    c) difficult fun that's also fun while you do it
        Example: day hiking.
    d) difficult fun that's fun mostly in retrospect
        Example: building a house on a remote Pacific island.

14) Go as soon as possible. Don't plan to build a house in the Pacific ten years from now. In the interim, you'll be deluged by questions,

details, and, eventually, doubts—almost all of which will be reasonable. So for ten, maybe fifteen minutes, think really seriously about whether this is something you want to do and then start making arrangements. You won't regret it. I'm almost certain.

Acknowledgments

Often, when I'm reading the part of a book where the writer acknowledges a long list of people whom I don't know they start with something like . . . For their encouragement and steady support, I'd like to thank Robin Hemley, Patricia Foster, Susan Lohafer, Christopher Merrill, Paul Collins, Jenny Lewis, Katherine Jamieson, Colleen Kinder, Michael Murphy, Vik Patel, Marika Athens, David Paape, Liz Perry, Eula Biss, and, of course, Bonnie Rough.

Then they say something like . . . I'm forever grateful to New American Library's gifted (and patient) Executive Editor, Tracy Bernstein, who deftly guided this from proposal to book, along the way removing heaps of navel-gazing and wince-inducing jokes (yes, there was once even more of both). At New American Library, I'm also indebted to Craig Burke, Director of Publicity, and Associate Director of Publicity Heather Conner, who somehow still convinces people to buy books in an age when three hundred thousand videos are uploaded each day to YouTube; Emily Osborne, who created this beautiful jacket and had the good judgment to ignore all of my suggestions, and the talented copy editor who found literally thousands of mistakes (most of which I gave up trying to fix on my own after I Googled "How to use the colon?" Tip: Never do this).

This book never would have happened—and many probably wish it hadn't—without the efforts of my brilliant (and impatient) agent, Jeff Kleinman, who, as far as I can tell, backed this project only because he thought he'd get a free stay at our place in Palau, yet stayed involved after he found out the house had been destroyed in a typhoon.

Jeff works harder than anyone else I've ever met. He's one of the funniest too. Jeff, thank you. Really.

For not reporting my loitering and electricity theft, I'd also like to thank all the friendly folks at O'Henry's, Ojai Roasters, Middleway Café, La Taberra, the Westmark Hotel, and the Anchorage Barnes & Noble Café with the view of the Xpress Lube. John at the Coffee Connection was especially tolerant of my presence.

I'm also deeply indebted to all the poor dopes (i.e., friends) who thought it would actually be a good idea to build someone else a house on an almost-impossible-to-reach island. Those include the long termers: Steve Henry, Butch Allen, and Cabot Teachout. Not to rank our friends, but among the long termers, I'm most appreciative of Darren Sabom, who took on the serious bits of construction, waking up early and staying up late to figure out work-arounds resulting from the lack of supplies, crappy weather, and a work crew more keen on making margaritas than actually building. Had he not come, the project would have fallen apart three crowbar whacks into that limestone.

Thank you to the medium termers who made life on the island better too: Kumiko Tomazawa and Zephyr Teachout. And, for showing up and occasionally watching the rest of us hammer nails into wood, I'd like to thank short termers: Justin Roberts, Marjorie Allard, Matt Findley, Josh Bearman, Steven Elliot, and, especially, Kelly McCann, who, due to circumstances I'll never fully understand, ended up on a three-day blind date with Steve. That date didn't make it into this story, but I suspect it could fill a book, if not an entire trilogy.

I'm deeply grateful to the good people of Angaur, who no doubt were confused by the group of foreigners who arrived unannounced and uninvited. I'll always appreciate the kindness and generosity they showed us as we blundered our way through their beautifully complex culture. Among them, I'd especially like to thank Carlos and the Kedidai clan for their trust; Margarette and her late husband,

Emiliano, for their seemingly endless supply of crabs and papaya; the fellow in the canoe who gave me my favorite story in the book and who had the courage to come by our house afterward; Governor Horace Rafael for making the garbage truck available on occasion and for not kicking us off the island; and all the folks in the Angaur state office, who not only answered all of our many questions but also signed for and forwarded boxes of screws, brackets, bagels, and who knows what else to the ferry; Mario Gulibert for helping us navigate the more complicated legal and political aspects of the project; and Leon Gulibert for providing running hot water at his charming guesthouse and for allowing his tenants to have a primate as a pet.

For their cultural translations, I'm tremendously grateful to Abby Rdialul in Koror and Maria Perry—now Maria Allen—in Angaur. Abby took me in when I was at my most lost. Maria guided us through the complexities of Angaur's birth ceremonies, weddings, and funerals—and its barter system, which I still don't understand, despite many long talkings-to.

Thank you to Geoff Cook and Josh Bearman for allowing me to use their stunning photographs. And thank you to the friends, new and old, who bothered to respond to my little cover survey:

Sylvia Busby, Zebrina Petrie, Todd Miller, Justin Kring, Ron Stokes, Roger Hansrote, Allison Hailey, Mark Robert Yarry, Breeze, Rob Stull, Nisah Rehuher, Cheesy Ale, Amanda C. Kalish, Captain Vik, Chuck Moore, Katie, Shana A. Bagley, Laura Roberts, Nathalie M. Harris, Chantel Nel, Marianne Steele, Onepiecepants, Floris Evers, Mike Thornton, Kate Ladd, Celia Concepcion, Rockne Locey, Michael Abshire, Martin Hadley, Betsy June, Karen Sherwood, Alexandre Sazonov, Zdenek Lund, Marika "Alex owes me 1/8 of his profits" Athens, Kristan Curtis, Ryan Harrison, Butch Allen, Daven Forrest, Sally Franklin Cottingham, Myra Lepp, Ingrid,

Kennedy Cosgrove, Francine Paston, Laken Danielle, Dawn Bailey, Tex, Brillo Pants, Lee Wally, Ames Hutton, Maria Allen, Jameson Mah, Mark Crockett, Margie New, Kiki, T-Wolf, Terry Donohue, Erica, Tim Poole, Paul Thompson, Martina Migenes, Jack McKenna, Christopher Morabito, Austin Quinn-Davidson, Faye Durough, Trang Nguyen, Billie D., Simone Herskind, and Jenna McCarthy (not Jenny McCarthy).

My life would have been very different without Rosemary James and Joe Desalvo of Faulkner Books in New Orleans. Their efforts on behalf of writers and the arts in general have made the world a better place. (Not that this book has made the world a better place, but that's not their fault.) May you two never, ever retire!

I'm deeply grateful to my mother, who, despite the snippets of conversation included here, came to embrace this project—not just the book but the whole move-to-a-deserted-island thing, even if it's not the way she would have done either. I'm also grateful to her charming and kind husband, Rudolph, who came onto the scene just in time to distract her from insisting on seeing earlier drafts of this. And I owe much gratitude to my father, who I'm pretty sure has spent more time thinking about this book than I have. His daily (hourly?) words of encouragement will stay with me well beyond when this sells for $.01 plus shipping. I could not have asked for more loving parents. At heart, they are not just wonderful parents, but also wonderful people.

Finally, to Sarah: Thank you for deciding to go on a full-moon kayak ride despite having a cold . . . for being confident and open-hearted enough to share that kayak with a stranger . . . for making me laugh that night and every night since.

This book is, of course, yours as much as mine. An uncomprehensive list of the crazy sacrifices you made for this would include . . . moving to southeastern Iowa, allowing me to share our story with strangers, creating the time and space for me to write that story, and, if I was in the room while you read, smirking at jokes that weren't funny. Thank you for managing my publication expectations while also doing your damnedest to midwife every one of these 119,257 words into life beyond a Word file on my computer. As such, any faults herein are yours, any strengths mine alone.

But beyond this book, I want to thank you for making my life and the lives of our two boys immeasurably more full of wonder and possibility and humor and plain old-fashioned love than I ever knew was possible. Every day is better because of you. For that and so much more, I feel profoundly grateful. Darlin', it is, and always will be, an adventure.

And thank you to Ian and Andrew for enduring countless monkey stories and tales of the west Pacific: May all of your dreams come true—just as they have for your father.

. . . and so it is, when I reach this point in the acknowledgments that I find myself wishing the writer would have just thanked all these people in an email instead—which is why I'd never bore you with such a thing.

Alex
Ojai, CA

P.S. A *psst* to the fellas . . . Sarah is very spoken for, but her lovely sister, Amanda C. Kalish, is available! She's even on the Facebook.